THE ARCHITECTURE
OF LOS ANGELES

THE ARCHITECTURE OF LOS ANGELES

BY PAUL GLEYE
IN COLLABORATION WITH
THE LOS ANGELES CONSERVANCY,
JULIUS SHULMAN,
AND BRUCE BOEHNER

Rosebud Books
Los Angeles

First published in 1981 by Rosebud Books, a division of
The Knapp Press, 5455 Wilshire Boulevard, Los Angeles,
California 90036.

Design by Laura LiPuma

Library of Congress Cataloging in Publication Data

Gleye, Paul.
    The architecture of Los Angeles.

    Bibliography: p.
    1. Architecture – United States – Los Angeles.
I. Shulman, Julius.   II. Boehner, Bruce.
III. Los Angeles Conservancy.   IV. Title.
NA735.L55G53   720'.9794-94   80-28988
ISBN 0-6558-004-9   AACR1

Printed in the United States of America

ACKNOWLEDGEMENTS

For their contribution during many phases of the project, I wish to express my sincere appreciation to Martin Weil, Ruthannn Lehrer, David Cameron, and Margaret Bach. Each reviewed the manuscript, and their ideas greatly influenced my own. Richard Rowe, Tom Owen, John Miller, Bill Mason, Lee Draper and Carol Goldstein also reviewed portions of the manuscript and offered important insights. Tom Owen, Bill Mason, and Alan Jutzi gave generously of their time in searching for historical photographs. Julius Shulman, Carlos Von Frankenberg, and Bruce Boehner provided their own photographs and their knowledge of Los Angeles architecture. Hynda Rudd was most helpful in my search through the City of Los Angeles archives and Hildegard Ober kindly provided access to the photo collection of Julius Shulman. In the end, the final decision as to what to say and illustrate rested with me, and the views herein are not necessarily those of the Los Angeles Conservancy's membership.

The book would not have been possible without the vision of its publisher, Donald D. Ackland, who believed that the time was right for a thorough look at Los Angeles architecture. I wish to acknowledge as well the wisdom and unflagging support of our editor, Helen Abbott. The difficult task of designing a complex book was handled gracefully by Laura LiPuma. The maps were designed by Sheila Wallen, and the index was prepared by Anita Keys.

Paul Gleye

Santa Monica, June 1981

CONTENTS

INTRODUCTION

Until about a hundred years ago, the Los Angeles River Basin had passed through eternity in a fairly natural state, at least from our urban point of view. There were settlers here, of course; by 1880 Los Angeles had a population of 11,000 people, who had turned much of the chapparral lands into fields and orchards. It was still a rural environment then, not a smoky metropolis like the great eastern cities of the day. A century before that, all of Southern California had been touched by only a relative handful of semi-nomadic Shoshonean peoples – about 30,000 of them, in fact, living in small villages that clung to the main watercourses, the valleys, and the open canyons of this dry land.

Today, Los Angeles is legend: the county had a population of 7,477,000 in 1980; it encompassed over 4,000 square miles with 495 miles of freeways and approximately 5,650 miles of surface streets. Where Los Angeles County ends begin the suburban counties of Orange, San Bernardino, Riverside, and Ventura. Los Angeles is the second largest metropolitan area in the United States, a center for the entertainment, armaments, and agricultural industries. And probably to the surprise of Phelipe de Neve, who founded the city in 1781, Los Angeles today has one of the largest Spanish-speaking populations in the world.

If one trend represents the historical development of Los Angeles, it is certainly that of rapid growth. Like many American cities, Los Angeles is a product of mechanized transport – the railroad, the trolley car, the automobile – which allowed it to expand far beyond the limits of settlement imposed by horse and human foot. Yet Los Angeles is very different from other American cities. From the time the first crude palisades were driven into the ground to define and protect the settlement, visionary designers of this city have been engaged in a search for not merely a prosperous life free of the shackles of the past, but also for an architecture and urban form that would make Los Angeles something special.

The Franciscan missionaries trekked through the vast expanses of the southwestern deserts to establish Roman Catholic missions among the native Californians, and they created a unique architecture of adobe and brick which has exerted an influence on California – and the United States – ever since. When the railroads came, they touched off a land boom in the mid-1880s that not only brought thousands of settlers to sunny Southern California from their cold midwestern farms, it brought the latest East Coast architecture – the Queen Anne, which was built here with exuberance.

When the city became too picturesque from the bay-windowed Queen Anne homes and stores, people turned back to the missions for inspiration, recreating a whole California architecture from the style of an original handful of buildings. They also invented a new style, the California Craftsman— low bungalows with exposed rafters and decorated with burlap and Indian pottery—establishing an American house type still with us in new forms.

Los Angeles was similar in climate and possibilities for human development to the fount of civilization around the Mediterranean Sea, according to early boosters. Not similar, actually; it was *better*, and it demanded a better architecture than had ever been known before, where the best forms and the best ideas could be united to create a paradise of a city to match the paradise of its climate. Thus in the teens architects reached beyond the California missions to the great architecture of Spain and Mexico, bringing forth a whole generation of Spanish Revival architecture which was Spanish in detail, but Californian in spirit, an expression of the easy lifestyle offered in Southern California.

Los Angeles is endowed with an incomparable array of historical revival styles from the early years of this century: from the formal Beaux Arts of the old downtown, to the colorful Egyptian Revival apartment buildings having battered walls and lotus-flower capitals. The climax of historical revivalism in the 1920s was accompanied by an outpouring of Art Deco architecture in zigzag forms and dazzling

Los Angeles County Museum of History, Science and Art (now Museum of Natural History), Exposition Park, 1912. Hudson and Munsell, architects.

Case Study House #22, 1959. Pierre Koenig, architect.

colors. During the depression, fantasies of a better life led to streamlined forms in architecture that saw buildings styled in windswept lines and porthole windows.

Los Angeles is also a great source of the Modern Movement in the United States. A small coterie of architects in the 1920s and 30s showed the potential of Modern forms to a still conservative country. This Modern Movement continued into the 1950s with the development of post-and-beam architecture whose glass walls left the home entirely open to gardens, patios, and the mountain vistas beyond.

In the 1980s, a new generation of Los Angeles architects is looking beyond Modern forms to create unique, personal statements in architecture, once again posing the basic questions of architectural design and keeping Los Angeles in the forefront of international architectural practice.

At the same time, there is a new realization that Los Angeles and its surrounding cities have a rich architectural heritage worth preserving. The increasing membership rolls of the Los Angeles Conservancy, an organization founded by a group of concerned citizens in 1978, and the enthusiasm shown for the conservancy's events – when over 2,500 people have shown up on a Sunday to tour an unrestored Victorian neighborhood, for example – suggest that people are beginning to notice Los Angeles as a historical place.

It is true that Los Angeles is primarily a twentieth-century city, even though it is now celebrating its bicentennial anniversary. Yet Los Angeles came of age in the *early* twentieth century, so that the great architecture of the 1920s, now more than fifty years old, emerged in a period quite different from our own.

The Architecture of Los Angeles has been written in an effort to discuss important trends and styles in Los Angeles architectural history. Since no previous book has attempted this task in a comprehensive fashion, it often ventures into uncharted territory, trying to highlight things that have been neglected – which includes almost everything except the Modern Movement and the offbeat stucco apartment houses that some people see as the whole city. If this book encourages further discussion of the points it raises and further study of topics not adaquately covered, it will have served its purpose well.

Three dates can often be given for a building: the year it was designed, the year construction was started, and the year it was completed. Since this book treats architecture as part of the streetscape, the date of the building's completion is used where possible.

I present *The Architecture of Los Angeles* with the hope that this book may inspire you to enjoy the architecture of the city as much as I have enjoyed writing about it.

ARCHITECTURE IN THE SPANISH AND MEXICAN PERIODS

I n the period of the great sixteenth-century explorations, hardly a non-European people escaped the sight of European explorers. No more than half a century elapsed from the time Columbus brought a whole new continent into European consciousness until Juan Rodríguez Cabrillo sailed up its far western coast, entering what is now Santa Monica Bay in 1542. The first European settlement in California, however, was established only in the eighteenth century, in the dying days of the Spanish empire, fully two and a half centuries after the Spanish had founded Mexico City as the capital of New Spain on the ruins of the Aztec city of Tenochtitlán. During that period California had remained *una tierra incógnita*, an unknown land of desert and mountains, whose potential bounties were not even dreamed of by the crews of the Manila galleons that bypassed it year after year on their return voyages to Mexico.

The reasons for the colonization of California are of some historical complexity, but clearly this new land could serve several interests. There was a lingering hope to find the same wealth that the *conquistadores* had stumbled upon in Mexico and South America. Spain feared encroachments into Mexico from the north by the Russians, the French, or the English unless the northern frontier were safely under Spanish domination. The legend of the Straits of Anían held that beyond California lay a sea passage providing a short route to the riches of Cathay; were the straits ever to be found, California would become strategically crucial. Finally, the Spanish needed an intermediate base between Mexico and the Philippines to service their trading ships.[1]

To hold this vast country in North America for her own, Spain would have to colonize its northern reaches. Who would serve as colonists, however, posed a problem. Mexico had insufficient population to spare able-bodied colonists for the task, and the Spanish did not allow foreigners to settle in her colonies. The Pope had assigned all of America except Brazil to Spain on conditions that the inhabitants be Christianized, however, and pagan peoples had been discovered all along the California coast.[2]

So a scheme for the occupation and colonization of Alta California was devised between the church and the state: the church would convert the natives, train them in habits of industry, teach them to be self-supporting, and prepare them for citizenship; the state would send its soldiers to protect the missionaries while they engaged in the work of conversion, and to punish recalcitrant natives.

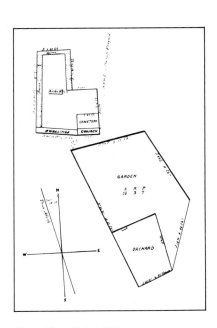

Plan of San Gabriel Mission, as drawn by the United States Land Office, 1904. The missions were usually built surrounding an interior courtyard. Beyond the mission compound were the open fields and orchards.

OPPOSITE:
San Gabriel Mission

The indigenous house type discovered by the Spanish in the Los Angeles River Basin was the domed, circular wickiup thatched with fern, tule or carrizo. Easily constructed, the wickiup was burned and built anew elsewhere if it became infested with vermin. This wickiup has been reconstructed at the Los Angeles State and County Arboretum in Arcadia.

OPPOSITE:
San Fernando Mission, the restored arcade of the convento, *1980.*

The Franciscan Missions

During the brief half-century when Spain held its California colony, from 1769, when Misión San Diego de Alcalá was founded on the site of the present city of San Diego, to 1822, when the region passed into the hands of Mexico,[3] the Spanish Franciscan missionaries established twenty-one missions stretching northward to Sonoma. In addition, *presidios*, or military garrisons, were located in San Diego, Santa Barbara, Monterey, and San Francisco to guard the missions under their respective jurisdictions.[4]

These institutions were imposed on an indigenous culture very different from the societies the Spanish had encountered in Mexico and the Rio Grande Valley. The Indians of the Los Angeles basin, members of the Shoshonean language group (later given the tribal name of Gabrielino, from their association with the mission of that name),[5] lacked the large-scale, hierarchial structure of the Aztec and Mayan peoples, and the salubrious Southern California climate precluded the need for insulated shelters. Thus the Gabrielino did not build monumental structures of stone or adobe, but developed an efficient and minimal architecture of domed, circular huts thatched with fern, tule (a large bulrush that grew in the marshes), or carrizo (a reedlike grass). Some of these structures were quite small, while others were apparently large enough to hold fifty people. In huts located near the sea, doorways opened seaward, to avoid the cool north wind.[6]

At the time of first contact with Europeans, the Gabrielino lived in about 50 to 100 mainland villages, plus settlements on the offshore islands; each village was inhabited by 50 to 200 persons. In addition to the circular dwellings, a typical village had a number of sweathouses (small, semicircular, earth-covered structures used for cleansing and as a meeting place for adult males), and menstrual huts. Each village also had a *yuvar*, an oval, open-air enclosure made with willows inserted wicker-fashion among willow stakes, decorated with eagle and raven feathers, skins, and flowers. Inside the enclosure were painted and decorated poles. The *yuvar* was the center for activities relating to the Chingichngish cult.[7] Another building, similar in structure and design to the *yuvar*, was sometimes used for ceremonial instruction and practice.

The introduction of the Spanish missions into this civilization had several effects on Gabrielino culture that were instrumental in its eventual annihilation. The Christianizing of the native peoples required crop cultivation to supply sufficient food for the new population centers, so the Spanish brought to California their own familiar plants, including citrus fruits, olives, figs, grapes, cereals, and garden vegetables. They were to be grown by the neophytes, as the mission Indians were called, under the supervision of the Franciscans. Also introduced were domestic cattle and horses.[8]

In this way began a gradual transformation of the California landscape from its original semi-arid ecology to an eventual landscape of lush greenery and exotic species that by the twentieth century would make Southern California one of the most completely altered natural landscapes on earth. The necessary ingredient was water, and the Spanish brought with them a knowledge of irrigation, enabling them to harness the intermittent streams of this dry land to support large permanent human communities.

Along with their crops and technology, the Spanish brought the settlement patterns they had established for crop cultivation in Spain and Mexico, replacing the small Gabrielino villages with huge farmsteads surrounding the missions. They taught the natives the skills necessary to maintain such a community: tanning, shoe making, weaving, harness making, hat making, blacksmithing, carpentry, cattle and crop raising, and they taught as well the Spanish language and Christian doctrine.[9]

Another principal effect of the missions on native culture was the eventual obliteration of indigenous architectural forms and their replacement by crude versions of the European buildings the missionaries knew, using the meager resources available in California. If the buildings were crude, it was partly because the architects were the missionaries themselves, assisted after 1790 at San Gabriel and a few other locations by the master mason José Antonia Ramírez.[10]

Kurt Baer, in his study of California mission architecture, traced the sources of the forms we associate with the missions to the architecture of classical Rome as it was reformulated in the buildings of the Renaissance. Toward the end of the eighteenth century, just at the time California was being colonized, Classical forms in European building had evolved into "a revival of purity and simplicity of proportion and restraint in decoration."[11] It was the architecture of the monumental column, arch, and pediment that has pervaded much of Western architecture during the past seven centuries.

The decorative elements of the mission buildings, suggests Baer, were also heavily influenced by the Moors, through their 700-year occupation of Spain. "Theirs was a luxurious ornament, filled with complex geometrical patterns often of carved stone and alabaster and wood, more commonly of stucco, varicolored tile work; graceful and often intricately conceived arches; bulbous or onion-shaped domes."[12]

In Mexico the Spanish could build upon the rich masonry architecture of the indigenous peoples, creating fine monuments. In California, however, because of the lack of resources and architectural skills on the part of both Indian and Hispanic residents, even a modest attempt to emulate high architecture demanded perseverance and ingenuity. A few graceful details in window arches or the curve of a wall parapet or *espadaña* were the major stylistic embellishments, and thus became rich symbols in themselves. The rest was plain and homely.

The history of mission architecture can be viewed as a series of stages in coming to terms with the limitations and potential of local materials. At first, the missionaries had to grapple with the structural weaknesses of the resources at hand. Thus the very first mission buildings in California were not even as elegant as the ones we know. They were constructed of *palisada*, wooden posts of pine or cypress set close together, plastered inside and out with clay, and further roofed with earth. Sometimes, walls were made of adobe, but roofs were supported by forked wooden poles, so that the friable adobe was spared from having to serve as a structural element.[13] The second stage of mission construction saw the more extensive use of adobe as structural walls, holding up a roof of poles and rushes. Stone was used where possible, as in the 1791 mission church at San Gabriel.[14]

San Fernando Valley from the northwest, ca. 1882, showing the San Fernando Mission surrounded by orchards and planting fields. Each mission was a frontier outpost and the center of a large farming, ranching, and industrial community. Since the native vegetation was a chaparral of little nutritive value, the Spanish introduced nearly everything grown; thus beginning the transformation of Southern California landscape into a lush garden where today almost none of the trees, flowers, and grass is native to this region.

If cared for and protected from the weather, adobe could last indefinitely, but in rain it melted rapidly into the mud from which it came. The colonists quickly discovered that the earthen roof offered insufficient protection to the soft adobe walls. Roofs made of reeds in the Gabrielino style were vulnerable to fire. Thus by 1790 the missions had replaced older roofs in all major buildings with fired brick roof tiles. Floors were usually of tamped earth covered with square brick tiles.[15]

Iron was not a local material in California, and consequently most structural members of any size had to be held together with rawhide thongs; rawhide was also used in the construction of ceilings to be plastered.[16] The laths holding the plaster were the stems of the cattail, which grew abundantly in the marshes. They were bound together into a fabric by means of interlacing rawhide strings and were laid on top of the ceiling joists to which they were secured by rawhide ties. The lower side was then plastered with a mixture of lime and sand, a crude form of stucco. Iron was used sparingly for such things as rails, hinges, locks, nails, bolts, ties, and window bars. Few of these accessories remain today, although a fine set of old window bars can be seen on the *convento* at San Fernando.[17]

The most striking formal elements of mission architecture, judging by what was borrowed by architects who revived the style in the late nineteenth century,[18] were the tower, the *espadaña*, and the *campanario*. The tower, which "reached toward heaven" and held aloft the bells that regulated each day's activities,[19] tended to be massively designed in a series of setbacks and was capped by a small dome. This form allowed the missionaries to construct a tall tower that looked much like a proper tower should, using the materials they had available.[20] The mission tower was an adaptation, although again very plain, of the more ornate Baroque church towers of Spain and Mexico.

The *espadaña*, the raised and often ornately scrolled gable at the end of a church building, provided a structural termination for rafters and tiling, while protecting the wall from the rain. The device of extending the gabled or pedimented facade of a church upward was employed as a very effective visual element to give height and impressiveness to an otherwise low elevation.[21] Although this high, ornamented gable was a common feature of European architecture of the Middle Ages and Renaissance, the simple, curvaceous forms developed in the California missions were quite different from their antecedents, and thus contributed a new form to architectural history.

The *campanario* was essentially an *espadaña* that served as a bell tower; it was a single wall capped by a scrolled parapet, pierced with niches to hold the mission bells.

The unique visual quality of the mission churches is due in part to the missionaries' limited knowledge of truss building and roof construction, along with the scarcity of large timber. When compared to the best Classical proportions, for example, the missions are quite narrow for their length.[22] Rather than

attempting complex vaulting techniques as had been the case in Mexican churches, the missionaries in California generally limited the width of the nave to the longest available *viga* or roof beam.

By simplifying Classical details that had become extremely ornate in Spain and Mexico (where the Churrigueresque had been at its height as the Spanish prepared to colonize California), the missionaries created a folk art derivative of European high architecture. Through the judicious use of available materials and the understatement of style and decoration largely resulting from the scarcity of stone, wood, and iron, as well as from the limited skills of the Indian labor force, they developed a unique and beautiful architecture which is still admired, even though the remaining or rebuilt mission churches themselves have all but been engulfed by modern California.

The Los Angeles Area Missions: San Gabriel and San Fernando

San Gabriel Arcángel, the fourth mission to be founded in California (1771), was the northernmost of the missions under the protection of the San Diego *presidio*. Its original site was about five miles southeast of its present location, near the intersection of present-day San Gabriel Boulevard and Lincoln Avenue, along the Rio Hondo. The mission was moved in 1775, apparently because the present site offered higher ground safe from flooding, an oak grove from which timber and firewood could be obtained, and access to irrigation.[23]

As with other missions, the first church at San Gabriel was made of logs, tule, and adobe. It was replaced in 1783 by an all-adobe church, and by 1789 the roofs had been covered with tile. After 1800, new rooms were constructed to serve as granary, weavery, carpenter shop, pantry, storeroom, and missionaries' dwelling, and were roofed with tile over pine timber. In 1807, tile-roofed houses for the Indians were built of adobe, with pine doors and window frames.

The long, narrow, stone and brick church standing today was completed in 1805, and once had a tower on its northeast corner. The tower was destroyed in the earthquake of 1812 which also leveled the church at San Juan Capistrano. Buttresses on the sides of the church are testimony to the original vaulted roof, which threatened to collapse and was replaced in 1808 by a flat roof of brick and mortar (since the 1880s replaced by a modern timber and tile roof).[24] The absence of a tower and *espadaña* leaves the end of the church severely plain, with only a simple arched entrance and square opening above. Much more interesting is the facade toward the street, with its massive buttresses surmounted with pyramidal

San Gabriel Mission Church, interior, 1980. The interior of San Gabriel reflects the changing tastes of nearly two centuries the church has been in use. Behind the altar, the retablo *remains little changed from the 1790s. A wooden ceiling supported by scroll-sawn wooden arches was built in 1886, when the church was remodeled in the Victorian style. By the 1930s these arches were seen as inappropriate for a Spanish church and were removed. The wooden ceiling itself still remains, along with WPA stencilwork around its borders, painted in the 1930s.*

merlons. Near the front an exterior stone stairway leads up to a doorway opening into the choir loft.

The picturesque *campanario* at the rear of the church is similar to several built earlier in Mexico, most notably to that of the Santuario de Guadalupe in Guadalajara, which might have served as its inspiration.[25] The *campanario* is irregular in form, the left side marked by three stages near the top and the right side attached to the church buttress. Brick moldings form bands along the edges of the steps and carry the architectural line to the adjacent church. Six arched openings in the *campanario* correspond in size to the bell hung in each.

Because of its masonry construction and its continued use as a parish church after secularization, San Gabriel did not fall into ruins as did many of the California missions during the late nineteenth century. It stands today much as it did in its early years, though with some modernization and restoration.

Misión San Fernando Rey de España, founded in 1797 as the fourteenth California mission, was situated north of the Los Angeles pueblo in the valley that now bears its name, on a site chosen for its abundant water supply, humid soil, and plentiful limestone for mortar.[26] Although fairly close to the San Gabriel mission, it was under the protection of the Santa Barbara *presidio*.

The first church built at San Fernando was completed in 1797, but a permanent church of adobe was not constructed until 1804. This church was rectangular in form, with its baptistry on the left side and bell tower on the right. The walls appeared to be leaning outward, since they were constructed at a

San Fernando Mission today. Currently the mission is a restored architectural monument and museum open to visitors. The church was stabilized and rehabilitated beginning in the 1890s by the Landmarks Club, under the leadership of Charles F. Lummis, but it was irreparably damaged in the 1971 earthquake; a replica (below left) now stands in its place.

tapering angle with the south wall having greater pitch than the north wall. The leaning effect also stemmed from the difference in the thickness of the wall at its base, where it was five feet deep, to its top, where it was three, and served to reduce the tremendous weight of the thick adobe walls.

San Fernando Mission church in ruins. Photograph ca. 1890.

Architecturally the church itself was overshadowed by the *convento*, actually several small buildings unified by a long arcade, or *corredor*, 243 feet in length, supporting a sloping tile roof. The *corredor* was a common feature of the missions, for underneath it was cool in summer and dry during the winter rains.[27] At San Fernando the arches arose from piers, rather than from columns as was the practice in Europe, probably because of the scarcity of building materials and trained craftspersons.[28] Begun in 1810 and completed in 1822, the *convento* contained over twenty rooms, including quarters for the two resident priests, guest accommodations, a chapel, reception room, kitchen, storehouse, winery, and refectory. Today it houses a museum of mission artifacts.

After secularization, the San Fernando mission fell into ruins; its restoration was one of the primary programs of the Landmarks Club (see Chapter 4) at the turn of the century, and was finally completed in 1941. In the 1971 earthquake, however, all seven buildings of the mission were severely damaged. The *convento* required the replacement of one exterior and several interior walls, and the addition of steel reinforcement. The church of 1806 was damaged beyond repair and was razed in 1973. In its place an exact replica was built the following year.[29]

Today the two missions are dwarfed by the scale of Los Angeles, but in the early nineteenth century they certainly appeared stupendous compared with the Gabrielino wickiups which had been the only previous structures on this land. Given the isolation of California, these churches must have served as the embodiment of monumentality for the Californios themselves, since by 1810 the second generation of inhabitants had seen nothing else.[30]

It should be noted that the buildings from the mission settlements that remain today are not representative of the settlement as a whole; as often happens, only the most impressive structures have survived. The missions were large industrial complexes, not just churches, and many of the surrounding workshops and the dwellings of the Indians had neither a formal style nor were built with lasting materials. These have disappeared from memory.

The Founding of the Pueblos

The missions and the *presidios* were two separate institutions, often in conflict over basic issues such as the provision of food. Although the missions were self-sufficient, the *presidios* were provisioned largely

San Gabriel Mission church with date palm, looking northwest from the residence of Mr. Hubbard. Completed in 1805, the mission church at San Gabriel, like most California mission churches, is long and narrow, similar to the original Christian basilica form. Until the earthquake of 1812, a tower stood at the northeast corner. Today the end facade is quite plain. During most of the church's existence, the main entrance has been from the side wall.

by ship from Mexico and the supply lines were too long to be dependable. The need was acute in California for additional agricultural production sufficient to provision the garrisons.

In 1777, the Spanish governor of California, Phelipe de Neve, toured the region and recommended sites for two *pueblos* or agricultural villages.[31] The first to be organized was San José de Guadalupe, settled in 1777 in the Santa Clara Valley about midway between the *presidios* of Monterey and San Francisco; this pueblo has survived as the city of San Jose.[32] The second pueblo, founded in 1781 along the Río Porciúncula about three leagues from Misión San Gabriel, marked the beginning of Los Angeles. A third pueblo, Branciforte, was founded in 1797 and is today part of the city of Santa Cruz.[33]

Even though California was on the edge of the empire, and the new pueblos were small and utilitarian, the Spanish were inclined neither toward insignificant names ("El Pueblo de la Reina de los Angeles" or "The Village of the Queen of the Angels") nor insignificant plans. The founding of an agricultural village in the semiarid climate of the Los Angeles basin was predicated on a constant supply of surface or ground water that could be used for irrigation. Neve's crew found a place where a small river, the Porciúncula,[34] discharged a meager but constant supply of clear water from an underground reservoir in the San Fernando Valley.[35] During the winter rains, however, the river could become a torrent which would fill its wide arroyo from bank to bank.

To escape winter flooding and to facilitate the distribution of irrigation water, the pueblo was laid out on a broad terrace about half a mile from the arroyo's edge. A simple dam was constructed two miles upstream, where the river rounded the steep bluff of the present Elysian Park hills, and from this point the water was diverted into *zanjas* (irrigation ditches) to water the fields below; the settlement itself was situated on nearby high ground within sight of the fields.[36]

Not only were the agricultural lands carefully laid out, but the Spanish had also developed a grand and detailed city planning tradition for their colonial cities in the New World, embodied in a 1573 document promulgated by Phillip II of Spain, called Laws of the Indies. This set of 148 ordinances set forth standards for site selection, street patterns, facades, and the appropriate distribution of land uses. Although largely forgotten today, particularly in Los Angeles, the Laws were probably the most complete set of instructions ever issued for the founding and building of new towns, and in their widespread application and longevity they were certainly one of the most effective planning documents in the history of urban settlement.

The ordinances drew their provisions from European city-building and from the earliest Spanish colonial cities in the New World, like Cuzco and Mexico City in the early sixteenth century.[37] While each location would differ according to climate and topography, the Laws ensured that each settlement would be consistent with the guiding Christian ideology of Spain, and would provide the Spaniard in the colonies a recognizable urban environment.[38]

For the colonists of Los Angeles, therefore, the town plan was largely predetermined. Central in location and importance was the *plaza*—the open square which was the focus of social, economic, and religious life, and was surrounded according to specific instructions by the necessary secular and religious structures. An excerpt from The Laws of the Indies describing the requisite plan for the plaza is shown on page 26.

According to Neve's instructions for the pueblo's founding, the original Los Angeles Plaza was a rectangle measuring 200 by 300 feet. It was laid out with its corners facing the four winds, and its streets running at right angles to each of its four sides, so that no street would be swept by the wind. Fronting on three sides of the Plaza were the house lots, each about 55 feet wide and 110 feet deep; half of the

San Gabriel Mission church, ca. 1882. The principal facade of the church is the south side of the nave. Its ten capped buttresses once supported a vaulted roof. Only the curves of the espadaña above the bells suggests the "Mission Style" of architecture. In 1886 the windows were enlarged to admit more light.

Our Lady of the Angels Church (Plaza Church); constructed 1822. The original facade of the Plaza Church had a gently curved espadaña with a small pediment at its apex above the arched entrance-way. The campanario is to the left. Like the mission churches, the Plaza Church was long and narrow in plan with a flat roof. In 1869 the church was modernized with a pitched roof and a wooden cupola in the Victorian style, perhaps adopted from English Gothic models of the period. By 1910 (above) the Plaza had become a grassy park with large trees and was the center of the Chinese community in Los Angeles.

remaining side was reserved for public buildings—including a guard house, a granary, and a church—and the other half was an open space. Unfortunately, visual records in the form of paintings or sketches of the earliest years of Los Angeles have not come down to us, and our knowledge of the pueblo's first architectural forms is very limited.[39]

The original assignment of land was provisional, and five years later, in 1786, the governor commissioned José Argüello to make a final disposition. For this purpose Argüello drew the earliest known plan of the pueblo, which shows the lots surrounding the Plaza and, at a much smaller scale, the planting fields distributed to the settlers. These fields lay between the Zanja Madre (the main irrigation canal) and the Río Porciúncula, south of the road to San Gabriel.

The plaza shown in the Argüello plan is actually a different one from the Plaza we know today. Its location is not exactly known—it may have been several blocks south of today's location—and may also have been moved more than once.[40] At any rate, about thirty years after its foundation, the pueblo suffered a disaster that required a move to near its present location.

The Pueblo Church and the New Plaza

Of primary importance to a Spanish colonial pueblo, and one of the first and finest buildings to be erected in a new settlement, was of course the church. In Los Angeles the first religious building was a small chapel (twenty-five by thirty feet) on the south side of the Plaza, begun in 1784 and finished five years later.[41] There are no extant illustrations of it, but the church was apparently of whitewashed adobe. Its roof was thatched with tule, over which were laid coarse grasses and mud, and perhaps *brea*, the tar that oozed to the surface of the ground a few miles to the west, for waterproofing.[42]

Despite the Laws of the Indies and experience with settlements along intermittent streams, however, the Spanish did not plan the pueblo carefully enough. A large church was under construction in 1815, when a flood diverted the river channel from the east side of the valley to the west and washed away its foundations. The church's location was too vulnerable and would have to be moved to higher ground.

Plaza Church, 1980.

The relocation of the church posed certain city planning problems under the Laws of the Indies. Since the principal church had to face the plaza, and since the plaza had to be the center of the settlement, the relocation of the church required the relocation of the entire pueblo center and the abandonment of houses existing on that site.[43] The scheme was carried out, however, and a new church, Nuestra Señora de los Angeles (Our Lady of the Angels) was completed in 1822. Although altered several times, it still remains as the Plaza Church. For a brief period a plaza may have fronted its north wall, but the Plaza we know today appears to have been dedicated in 1835.[44]

Ruins of an older church stood until the late nineteenth century near the present intersection of Broadway and Sunset Boulevard, but today they have entirely vanished.[45]

In 1861 severe rains washed away much of the new church's adobe facade, and it was replaced with a more modern, red brick facade, still seen today, having a triangular pediment flanked by two pointed buttresses. These elements may have been adopted from English Gothic models of the period, since the city was by then well under Anglo influence. Tom Owen has suggested that the Plaza Church, despite having become one of the great symbols of Spanish Los Angeles, has a facade that was intended precisely *not* to appear Spanish when it was built.[46]

A steeply pitched roof was added in 1869, replacing the *brea* roof and the interior ceiling, along with a wooden cupola that served as a bell tower. Since then the cupola has been replaced by a Mission style *campanario*, and the church separated from its old Plaza by the major traffic artery of North Main Street. Now, church and Plaza are almost totally unrelated to each other, although the original design under Spanish colonial city planning placed them in harmony.

The Laws of the Indies were not so clear with respect to the parts of town beyond the Plaza. Especially given the state of the Spanish empire by the late eighteenth century and the location of California far from established colonial governments, the pueblo of Los Angeles was allowed to develop in an irregular pattern as it spread outward from the Plaza; even the Plaza itself was not safe from the encroachment of buildings in the later years of Spanish and Mexican rule.[47] Although moderate deviation in the Plaza

Mission San Luis Rey de Francia, San Diego County, completed in 1829; photograph ca. 1882. One of the later California mission churches to be constructed, San Luis Rey was "the most beautiful and most regular in architecture" of all the missions, according to French diplomat Duflot de Mofras in 1840. Much of the imagery for the Mission Revival style at the turn of the twentieth century was taken from its stepped tower and curved espandaña.

boundaries was apparently not noticed, the *ayuntamiento* (municipal government) was known to pull down houses that crept too far into the Plaza.[48]

Elsewhere in the pueblo, when a house was to be constructed, the builder selected a site convenient to his material, and the relationship between houses and streets became a rather fluid one. The Ord map of 1849 (see p. 31) shows well-defined streets, but certainly not straight ones, in much of the old pueblo. Not only were the irregular streets the result of rather haphazard development patterns, but also the settlement was built on a slope, and straight streets are not sensitive to the horse or person who must climb a hill. In addition, residents had few wheeled vehicles other than *brea* wagons, and it is a general observation of human settlements that horse and foot paths meander rather than proceed in straight lines. Only with the Anglo influx in the nineteenth century, and the need for careful surveying for real estate purposes, did regular street patterns begin to appear.

The Architecture of the Pueblo

The building forms of some cities in the North American Spanish colonies were adapted from pre-Columbian native cultures. The Spanish architecture of northern New Mexico retained many visual qualities of indigenous Pueblo Indian architecture of the Río Grande Basin, for example, though some structural elements had been supplanted.[49] To the Los Angeles Basin, however, the Spanish imported a set of urban forms from more established colonies to the south and east. They saw nothing in the Gabrielino villages that they could—or wished to—use, for the wickiup of twigs and branches was hardly an architecture for a colony of the Spanish Crown.

San Buenaventura Mission, photo 1880s. The last mission founded personally by Junípero Serra, in 1782, San Buenaventura was situated about seventy miles northwest of the Los Angeles pueblo. The present stone church was completed in 1809. It was damaged in the earthquake of 1812, after which the large buttresses on the front and west side were added for support. After secularization it was retained as a parish church and the other mission buildings were destroyed. Like the church at San Gabriel, the interior of San Buenaventura was remodeled in the late nineteenth century.

El Molino Viejo (The Old Mill), 1120 Old Mill Road, San Marino, constructed ca. 1816. In order to grind and store grain for the San Gabriel Mission, this mill with a horizontal water wheel was built by neophyte Indians about two miles northwest of the mission, at the confluence of two small streams. Its lower walls are five feet thick, composed of oven-baked brick and volcanic tuff; the upper walls are of adobe. Rafters, ceilings and beams are of local pine and sycamore. Seashells were burned to yield the lime for the plaster covering the structure. El Molino Viejo now serves as an office of the California Historical Society and is listed on the National Register of Historic Places.

The first buildings in Los Angeles were *jacales*, huts of chinked *palisada*, but within a year they had apparently been replaced by more comfortable adobe homes.[50] Mary Mooney has provided a description of the interior of an early adobe dwelling, whose thick walls were pierced with small openings to let in light:[51]

> The small window had neither sash nor glass. The door often consisted of a dried hide hung over the opening. Oftener it was made of willow or elder branches laced together with thongs of leather or rabbit hide, and a leather string was used to fasten it on the inside. The table was a rude board, supported by notched stakes, stuck into the earth floor. *Bancos*, or benches, made in a similar way, served as seats.
>
> The cooking utensils were of soapstone and were brought from the coast islands. They also had clay *ollas* (pots) and baskets brought from Mexico.
>
> The bed consisted of a sort of rude stretcher, made of willow or elder saplings, set down in a corner of the room, resting a couple of inches above the earth floor. This was heaped with dry grasses, and covered over with a dry hide. In some houses there were a few coarse blankets. Others boasted of a seat, called a *pretil*, which was of adobe, built around the walls of the corridor or dining room.

Houses generally had flat roofs of *brea* applied over a layer of matted tule placed directly on the *vigas* that formed the ceiling and then covered with a thin layer of earth. The *brea* offered better protection than earth and tule; but natural, unprocessed asphalt is proof against neither sun nor rain. It melted and dripped off the eaves in summer, and the thin places leaked when it rained in winter.[52] Pitched roofs of red tile were known but were probably less common than modern restorations would suggest. Tile floors

Los Angeles Plaza, in 1867. This earliest known view of the Plaza was taken after Los Angeles became part of the United States, but it probably retained many features from the Spanish and Mexican periods. The fenced enclosure and water reservoir in the center were later additions. On the far side of the Plaza, the two-storied Vicente Lugo house, built in 1830, later received a pitched roof and stood until 1951. It was the last of the early buildings to remain on the Plaza. The Carrillo house with its red tile, pitched roof—to the right of the Plaza—was an exception to the one-story adobe dwellings in long rows, their flat roofs covered with brea, that composed the streetscape of the early pueblo. To the right of the Carrillo house is the two-story brick Masonic Temple (1856), with its three arched windows, which today stands as part of El Pueblo de Los Angeles State Historic Park.

Avila Adobe, Olvera Street, constructed ca. 1818, photo of the street facade, ca. 1928. The oldest existing house in Los Angeles, the Avila Adobe consists of two contiguous rows of high-ceilinged, spacious rooms. The inner series opens by means of numerous doors and windows upon a corredor facing the interior courtyard and upon another corredor facing the street. Although extensively damaged during the 1971 earthquake, the house has been rebuilt and stands today as a museum and part of El Pueblo de Los Angeles State Historic Park.

BOTTOM RIGHT:

City Planning Ordinances of the Laws of the Indies, excerpt. In 1573 Philip II of Spain issued a series of 148 ordinances regulating the planning and design of colonial cities in the Spanish Empire, which included Los Angeles. The design of the central plaza was specified in ordinances 112–117 (translated by Dora P. Crouch and Alex Mundigo).

BOTTOM LEFT:

Plan of the Pueblo of Los Angeles, 1786. This schematic plan of the pueblo was drawn by Jose Argüello five years after its founding, to confirm the distribution of lots and planting fields that had been made in 1781. Fronting the Plaza (P) are the house lots and spaces reserved for municipal buildings. El Camino Real, connecting the pueblo with the San Gabriel mission, enters the Plaza at (O). Below the Plaza are listed the names of the nine heads of families to whom lands were granted, and to the right, beyond the Zanja Madre, is the distribution of planting fields, drawn to one-fourth the scale of the Plaza. The Río Porciúncula, now the Los Angeles River, flows to the east of the fields. The exact location of this original plaza is not known.

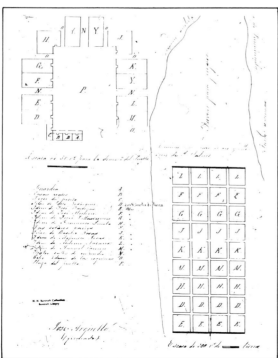

112

The main plaza is to be the starting point for the town; if the town is situated on the sea coast it should be placed at the landing place of the port, but inland it should be at the centre of the town. The plaza should be square or rectangular, in which case it should have at least one and a half its width for length inasmuch as this shape is best for fiestas in which horses are used and for any other fiestas that should be held.

113

The size of the plaza shall be proportioned to the number of inhabitants taking into consideration the fact that in Indian towns, inasmuch as they are new, the intention is that they will increase, and thus the plaza should be decided upon taking into consideration the growth the town may experience. [The plaza] shall be not less than two hundred feet wide and three hundred feet long, nor larger than eight hundred feet long and five hundred and thirty-two feet wide. A good proportion is six hundred feet long and four hundred wide.*

114

From the plaza shall begin four principal streets: One from the middle of each side and two streets from each corner of the plaza; the four corners of the plaza shall face the four principal winds, because in this manner, the streets running from the plaza will not be exposed to the four principal winds which would cause much inconvenience.

115

Around the plaza as well as along the four principal streets which begin there, there shall be arcades, for these are of considerable convenience to the merchants who generally gather there; the eight streets running from the plaza at the four corners shall open on the plaza without encountering these arcades, which shall be kept back in order that there may be sidewalks even with the streets and plaza.*

116

In cold places the streets shall be wide and in hot places narrow; but for purposes of defence in areas where there are horses it would be better if they are wide.

117

The streets shall run from the main plaza in such manner that even if the town increases considerably in size, it will not result in some inconvenience that will make ugly what needed to be rebuilt, or endanger its defence or comfort.

were particularly rare, and clean-swept, hard-packed earth floors were the norm. The large fireplace for heating was also rare. Some houses did have a fireplace in the kitchen, but most cooking was carried on outdoors.

Wood for home construction was scarce in the pueblo, but as early as 1800 ships from Boston found their way to California, even though they were legally prohibited from trading until 1822. The Mexican government allowed trading but imposed heavy duties. Along with silks and fans and combs, traders brought finished lumber from New England sawmills. Not until 1851, however, when a sawmill was opened by Mormons who had settled in San Bernardino, were wagonloads of lumber available for sale in Los Angeles. As wood became generally more plentiful, pitched roofs covered with shakes began to replace the old flat roofs.[53] Customarily walls were finished inside and out with a fine white plaster, of lime made in kilns in the San Fernando Valley.[54]

Ceilings in the better houses were of wood, with beams exposed, and often decorated with grooves; they were sometimes painted a shade of green-blue, using a kind of lime wash. In houses with a pitched roof there was often no interior ceiling, but a thin canvas was stretched from wall to wall in lieu of one.[55]

Architectural records of the earliest buildings in Los Angeles are scanty, and particularly little is known about ordinary dwellings. Since the more elegant homes of the wealthy tend to be illustrated and described in the historical record and less interesting structures omitted, there is a tendency to associate an entire past period or past culture with its highest achievements. Although homes such as the Stearns mansion above represent part of the history of Los Angeles, they should not be taken as its entire history. We have no illustrations of a house like Mary Mooney described above, but it probably represents a good deal of early Los Angeles.

"El Palacio," home of Arcadia Bandini Stearns, ca. 1875; constructed 1838, demolished 1878. The Stearns home, at the corner of Main and Arcadia streets, was one of the finer adobe homes of the Mexican period in Los Angeles. Like most houses of the period, it had one story with a flat roof covered with brea, and a simple corredor running along the street facade. A wooden sidewalk fronts the dirt street in this photograph. Today the Hollywood Freeway passes through this site.

Hugo Reid Adobe, Los Angeles Arboretum. This three-room dwelling was built in 1839 as the ranch house for the Reid family to oversee their orchards and vineyards. They also maintained a home in San Gabriel. The Reid adobe was extensively restored in 1961 and furnished with artifacts of the period. It is a reminder of the very plain architecture of early Los Angeles, though today it is probably more precisely plastered, and its lines are more exact than when it was originally built. Surrounding the house are an outdoor cooking oven and stone stove, a well, and a group of rebuilt Gabrielino wickiups.

OPPOSITE:

Sketches of Los Angeles by William R. Hutton, 1847. Hutton accompanied E.O.C. Ord in the preparation of the 1849 plan of Los Angeles and drew pencil sketches of the pueblo. The top view shows the Plaza as a rectangular field devoid of landscaping, surrounded by low buildings. The Plaza Church is seen in the foreground. From the same vantage point Hutton sketched the southern part of the pueblo (bottom). On the left is the Bell Block, the first two-story building in the pueblo. In front of it is the Stearns home, and the street in the foreground is Main Street. Most roofs are flat and covered with brea, *and some houses do not have chimneys since most cooking was done outdoors.*

The Passing of the Missions

The Spanish colonization of New Mexico, Texas, Arizona, and California followed architectural and historical paths distinct from one another, but they did share one common trait. Rather than the conquerers building a great civilization on the ruins of conquered cities, as in Mexico, they were overwhelmed by the great southwestern deserts of the future United States. In California, though the Spanish largely obliterated the culture of the native peoples, they were unable to replace it with more than a subsistence economy, and could share neither the wealth nor the new technology developing in Europe in the late eighteenth century.

John Gilroy, one of the first English speaking residents of California, said that when he arrived in 1814 there was not a sawmill, whip saw, or spoked wheel in the entire region. Money was a rarity, and there were no stores nor merchandise to sell. Even such things as dinner plates were rare unless one counted the brick tiles from which people ate.[56]

By that time, of course, the United States was developing a pragmatic and technologically more advanced civilization to the east, and California would soon feel its influence. To the south, centuries of Spanish oppression drove the Mexicans to revolt, and they brought California with them into the Mexican Republic after their victory in 1821.

Many of the California mission priests remained loyal to the Spanish crown, however, and the success of the Mexican Republican cause would spell doom for the Royalist priests' stronghold in California.[57] In the meantime the Indian population of the missions was steadily declining. The birth rate at the missions never equaled the death rate, and the mission population could only be maintained through importing Indians still living in their native habitat. Not only were their numbers dwindling, but their intricate web of traditions and survival skills, which had allowed them to prosper before European contact, was torn asunder and replaced, as it turned out, by little real education in the Spanish mold; within the missions, the succeeding generations of Indians remained ignorant of all but rudimentary civilized ways.[58]

By the time of the Mexican Revolution, then, the mission had become a political anachronism and a failure as a socializing agent. The Mexican government had in store for the missions their own day of reckoning, called "secularization," which was carried out from 1834 to 1844.[59] All the missions were systematically closed, and the management of their temporal affairs turned over to civil administrators. Lands, other than those that were supposed to be distributed to heads of Indian families, were to remain at the disposal of the government.[60]

By this time the missions had become exceedingly successful in agricultural production and animal husbandry; the San Gabriel mission alone was operating 17 extensive ranches with 105,000 head of cattle, 20,000 horses, and 40,000 sheep. The pressure to plunder these estates soon became much stronger than the capacity of the Mexican government to enforce its secularization decrees. Large blocks of land, carved from mission holdings, were granted to the politically favored rather than to the Indians, and by 1845 all Southern California missions had been sold or their properties leased. About 500 large ranches, with vast herds of cattle and horses, operated by thousands of former Indian neophytes, had replaced the mission establishments. And most of the mission buildings themselves, abandoned architectural monuments of early California, began to fall into ruin.

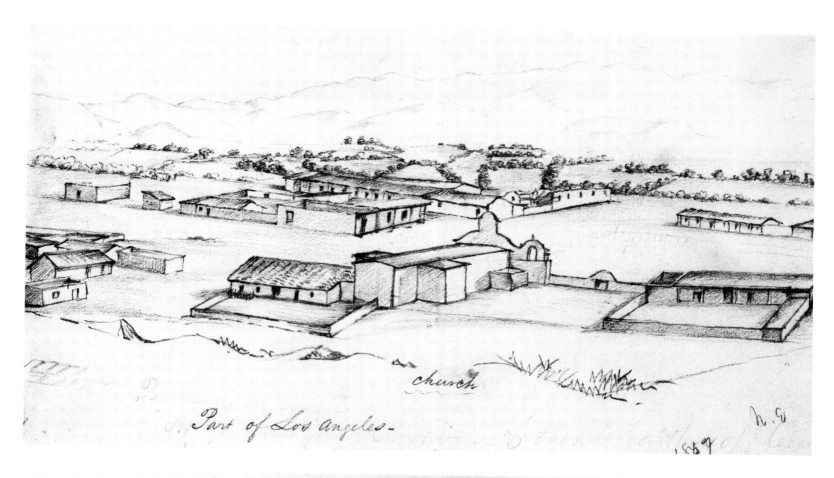

church

M. Part of Los Angeles.

1847

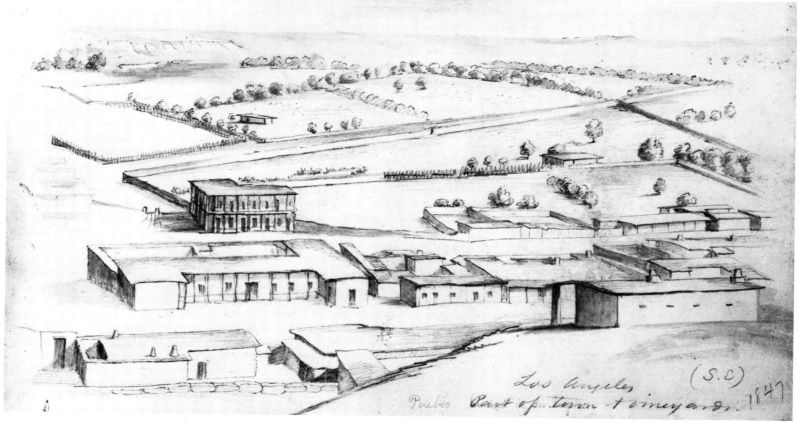

Los Angeles (S.C.)
Pueblo Part of town & vineyards. 1847

2

FROM MEXICAN PUEBLO TO AMERICAN TOWN

In 1822 California became part of Mexico, but other than in the replacement of a few administrative personnel, it made little difference.[1] A new population and difficult pressures for change, however, would soon appear. Traders and trappers began to reach Los Angeles from the United States via Santa Fe,[2] and foreigners began to arrive in American and English ships despite the continuing policy of the Mexican government to control them.[3] Through their pursuit of commercial expansion, the newcomers increasingly upset the precarious social and economic life of the pueblo, which to that time had been based on subsistence agriculture and ranching.

In the Mexican period the pueblo had no plat or plan to our knowledge, no map, and no official survey of its boundaries. The streets were irregular as were the house lots, and the houses stood at different angles to the streets. The well-defined individual lots and neighborhood districts we are accustomed to in Los Angeles today were little needed, since land was plentiful and the community small. The user of a parcel of land was its owner as long as he was a citizen of the pueblo and a Roman Catholic, provided that he registered his tract with the authorities.[4] When one ceased to use a piece of land for three consecutive years, it reverted back to the public domain. Agreements transferring title to land were written, but lot boundaries were often vaguely defined; they were usually given a precise width, but their depth was undefined, since behind them lay vast, unused land.

Within the settlement, houses of the local gentry were built fronting on the new Plaza, which, in the haste of relocating it after the flood of 1815, the authorities never managed to lay out according to the Laws of the Indies. It was smaller and more irregular than the stated requirements, arcaded shop fronts were not built around it, and residents of the pueblo occasionally tried to build on it. A municipal commission on streets, alleys, and plazas was founded in 1836, but it was unable to restore the order of the Laws.[5]

The natural tendencies of human settlement patterns run counter to the logical and self-conscious order imposed by central planning documents such as the Laws of the Indies which would create an arcaded plaza, straight streets that ran diagonally to the four winds, and a city plan immediately recognizable to a stranger. As the Spanish dominion waned, so did the influence of the Laws; individual

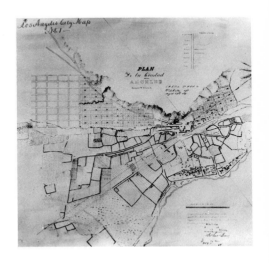

The first plan of Los Angeles. As illustrated in this drawing by Ord in 1849, Los Angeles was still huddled around the Plaza, from which the village extended south (to the left in this illustration) about four blocks. The settled area was sharply delineated on the west by a row of hills, and on the east by the Los Angeles River.

OPPOSITE:
Commercial Street; looking southeast from Main Street, stereoscope photograph ca. 1870.

Lopez de Lowther home, 330 North Santa Anita Street, San Gabriel; constructed ca. 1806, photograph ca. 1928. Originally one of the structures along the west wall of the San Gabriel Mission, this building was converted into a residence in 1849 and today serves as a historical museum operated by the San Gabriel Historical Society.

First Palomares Adobe, 1569 South Park Avenue, Pomona. The first home constructed by Ygnacio Palomares, perhaps as early as 1837, has five rooms arranged in a row, with a corredor supported by slender posts of roughly sawn timber along the front and one side. Today the building is owned by the Historical Society of the Pomona Valley.

builders in Los Angeles attempted to construct their own sense of order, and to accommodate their designs to their specific needs. This deference of overall plan to the social and physical peculiarities of each location creates a social order if not a comprehensive visual one. What appears unfathomable or chaotic to an outsider can be well understood by one who knows the reasoning behind its unique form. The problem with such an organization is that it is not efficient when land is a commodity, subject to frequent exchange and rapid development.

With the annexation of California into the United States by the Treaty of Guadalupe Hidalgo in 1848, Los Angeles came under a legal system where property was defined as a commodity, an instrument of personal possession to be exploited. In addition, the new city government found itself owning the four square leagues of land (about 17,000 acres) that had been granted to the original pueblo. Most of this land was vacant, and the city had no financial resources with which to support its administration. The solution, given the American belief in private property holdings, was to sell off the vacant land to private buyers who would encourage the growth of the city's population and economy.[6]

To this end the existing land and buildings had to be exactly delineated, and their organization made comprehensible to strangers and newcomers—this time American, not Spanish—as well as to longtime residents. In 1849, as one of the first major administrative actions of the American authorities, Lt. E.O.C. Ord, United States Army, was hired to survey the city and prepare a map of the lots and planting fields. His document (see p. 31), drawn sixty-eight years after the founding of the pueblo, remains the earliest verified map of the city. It shows that the Los Angeles of 1849, like the pueblo of 1781, nestled around the Plaza. To the west, the town was sharply defined by a row of hills, while to the east the settled area stopped abruptly at the Río Porciúncula, now called the Los Angeles River. The residential section occupied the higher ground west of the Zanja Madre, and the cultivated fields the lower ground to the east.

The sharp difference between the Mexican pueblo and the American plan for it is apparent in the map. The irregular layout of buildings and streets that characterized Mexican Los Angeles is evident near the Plaza, while in the newly platted sections to the north and south there is a conventional grid pattern. By the 1860s in the old Mexican section, house placards emblazoned with "Sonora," "Chihuahua," or

"Zacatecas" came to serve as beacons for Mexican travelers looking for others of their homeland, and the area was soon dubbed "Sonoratown" by the Anglos.[7]

Los Angeles held its first auction of lots in November, 1849, with purchasers favoring the newly platted lands to the south. The auctions continued over the years until only Block 15 was left in the public domain; in 1866 this block was dedicated as a city park and is now known as Pershing Square (see p. 109).[8]

The Americanization of Los Angeles

Until the 1870s, when Anglo commercial interests began to play a dominant role in the city, Los Angeles remained a rural agricultural community. But agriculture made fewer advances in Southern California than in the north, where disappointed gold miners turned to farming after the gold rush of 1849. Wheat became the big crop in the Sacramento Valley and fruit in the Santa Clara Valley, while the southern counties generally remained a landscape of vast, open cattle ranches. The only major effect of the San Francisco gold rush on the Los Angeles area was to increase the demand for beef.

The flourishing cattle ranches, according to Robert Cleland, were a symptom of the region's slow economic development.[9] Few lands could be farmed successfully without irrigation, and there was insufficient investment interest for the widespread development of irrigated lands. Without irrigated lands, the region could support only a limited population, and without a population the attraction of capital to develop the ranches more intensely remained unavailable.

Cleland has suggested that two events helped to dismantle the large ranches into ever smaller parcels, eventually culminating in the great scramble for house lots that would radically alter the Southern California landscape by 1890. In 1861–64 torrential rains and great floods, followed by a severe drought, decimated the California cattle population and largely destroyed the fragile economic structure of the cattle industry; sufficient replacement cattle and the funds to procure them were unavailable to the ranchers.

The aftermath of the American Civil War unexpectedly provided a supply of willing buyers. In the late 1860s hundreds of families from the former Confederate States sought economic opportunity in the Far

Central (now Pershing) Square, view from Fifth and Olive streets. By the 1860s, this parcel of land was the only remaining vacant public land in the city; in 1866 it was declared a public park. In 1870 it was fenced in and planted with fruit and forest trees, as shown in this photo from about 1880. At this time the park was on the southern edge of the city, bounded by neat Italianate homes amid citrus orchards.

Andres Pico residence, 10940 Sepulveda Boulevard, Mission Hills. Constructed in the middle of the Mission San Fernando orchards in 1834, a second story was added in 1873 with a corredor of post-and-beam construction. It was restored in 1930–32 and today serves as the headquarters of the San Fernando Valley Historical Society.

The Round House, bounded by Main, Spring, Third and Fourth streets; constructed in the late 1840s, demolished ca. 1887. Photograph ca. 1885. Monuments to an eccentric vision have a long history in Los Angeles. In the late 1840s Raimond Alexander, a French sailor, built a copy of a cylindrical house he had seen on the coast of Africa. His two-story house had a conical roof which looked like an umbrella. In 1856 the German baker George Lehman, who came to be known as "Round House George," bought the property, planted it with fruit and ornamental trees, and opened it as a resort called the "Garden of Paradise." He nailed boards over the adobe walls, changing the cylinder form to an octagon, and placed heroic statues of Adam and Eve and other Biblical curiosities in the garden.

Don Juan Temple residence, Rancho Los Cerritos, Long Beach, constructed 1844, photograph 1910. In 1830, Jonathan Temple married into a wealthy California ranch family and built this large home on a bluff overlooking the Los Angeles River. It is the largest adobe house from the early period remaining today in the Los Angeles area.

West.[10] They began to purchase portions of the old ranches, but took up the occupation they knew—farming, not ranching. The influx of population into Los Angeles itself brought rise to the precursor of a great Los Angeles tradition—a land boom.[11]

The town could not boom too much, however, because it was still very hard to reach Southern California. A telegraph connected the city's 4,400 people with the east in 1860, but there was no railroad. Steamships arrived twice a month at the port of San Pedro, bringing mail and news. The Butterfield overland stage route between San Francisco and St. Louis via Los Angeles had been established in 1858;

although the stages traveled night and day, it took nineteen days to cover the 1900 miles between Los Angeles and St. Louis.[12]

In general, Los Angeles was transformed rather slowly from a Mexican pueblo to an American frontier town, but in its details the Americans brought rapid change. In 1852 Mrs. Benjamin Hayes, a new Anglo resident, noted from her Eastern perspective that the "site of Los Angeles is lovely but the city is very ugly. Most of the houses are built of mud, some are plastered on the outside and have a porch around them looking neat and pretty as any house but these are few." She also described her own house:[13]

> It is a mud house with a mud floor. The walls are whitewashed but the ceiling looks like an old smoke house and leaks finely when it rains. There is a little fireplace in one corner where I do my cooking. We have no andirons. The dirt floor we have covered up with matting. In a long narrow box nailed to the wall in a corner we keep our dishes. On one side of the room we have a wash stand on which I am now writing and where I keep the few books I have and over this stands the Madonna which the priest gave Mr. Hayes for me. On the same side but in the corner stands a cricket [wooden footstool] where the bucket of water sits and the wash bowl. Opposite this is the bed. Around the bed we have a calico curtain; this forms a dressing room. We have five cane-bottom chairs and a great table.

LEFT:
Vicente Lugo home, 6360 East Gage Avenue, Bell Gardens, built 1850, photograph ca. 1892. The Lugo residence represents the Monterey Style at its height, with its two-story veranda of wood posts and railings on an adobe house. The Greek Revival influence is seen in the shallow pediments over the first floor windows and doors.

Ygnacio Palomares adobe, 491 East Arrow Highway, Pomona. Built in 1854 during the prosperity that the San Francisco gold rush brought to the Southern California cattle industry, this one-story building has adobe walls, cloth ceilings, and a shake roof. The home was restored in 1939 and is now a museum listed on the National Register of Historic Places.

Comparing this description with that of the Los Angeles house in the pre-Anglo period, what is apparent are the furnishings and fabrics imported from the eastern United States that would not have been available earlier. These appointments served to Anglicize an otherwise Mexican dwelling. Cooking was also moved from outdoors to an indoor fireplace, something Mrs. Hayes certainly took for granted in the East but which had been unusual in Los Angeles. In short, new residents quickly began to adapt the indigenous forms and materials to their own use and to introduce their own styles, objects, and social forms into this new environment. Architecturally, this hybridization resulted in the house type we call the Monterey style.

Don Juan Temple residence, courtyard, 1981. The house has been restored and is now a California research library maintained by the City of Long Beach. It is on the National Register of Historic Places.

The Monterey Style in Los Angeles

The adobe home we generally associate with the Mexican period is long and low, and covered with a flat or shallow pitched roof. Its most salient feature is the *corredor*, now more commonly called the veranda, extending the entire length of one or more facades, formed by extending the roof outwards from the exterior wall to form a canopy. Its outer edge is normally supported by wooden posts. Two-story buildings usually have a two-story veranda, and later homes beginning in the 1860s often had ornate spindlework balustrades and wooden decorative elements.[14]

It is certainly true that Monterey style buildings existed in Los Angeles during the Mexican period; William Rich Hutton drew several in his 1847 sketches of the pueblo (see p. 29). But most of the Monterey style homes existing in the Los Angeles area today were either built or extensively remodeled after 1850. (For example, the Vicente Lugo, Leonis, and other adobe residences illustrated in this chapter.) In a sense, then, the early secular architecture of Los Angeles that we know today was influenced by Anglo traditions as well as by Mexican, even though many of these homes were built by Hispanic Californios.

The name "Monterey Style" is taken from the California city where the archetype of these homes was built, in 1835, by the Boston merchant Thomas Larkin. As Trent Sanford has written,[15] up to that time the Spanish and Mexican adobe dwellings had been long and rectangular, of one story, covered with a saddle roof of thatch or tile. Larkin, remembering his native New England, applied Cape Cod architecture to adobe and built a two-story house with a hip roof and a two-storied veranda at the front and sides. Neighbors who could afford it immediately began building two-story houses with balconies and verandas.

Officers' quarters in the Drum Barracks, 1053 Cary Avenue, Wilmington, 1859. Drum Barracks, the only major Civil War landmark in California, was established in 1862 as the U.S. military headquarters for Southern California, Arizona, and New Mexico. Most of the barracks are no longer extant, but the Greek Revival officers' quarters is being restored. It was prefabricated in the Navy Yard at Portsmouth, New Hampshire, and all lumber, hardware, marble, and bricks were shipped around Cape Horn. The front section is large and rectangular with two smaller wings at the rear. Inside are sixteen rooms, including a high-ceilinged, central hall and a stairway with a polished mahogany balustrade. The four marble fireplaces with U.S. eagles on the mantels and andirons have disappeared. The building is listed on the National Register of Historic Places.

RIGHT:

General Phineas T. Banning residence, 401 East "M" Street, Wilmington, constructed 1864. In the 1860s, wealthy residents could build large homes in American architectural styles, rather than in the more common Monterey style. In doing so, however, one had to cope with limitations in skilled builders and materials. Banning, the developer of the ocean port at Wilmington, hired ships' carpenters to build this rather crude Greek Revival home with some Italianate elements—a generation after Greek Revival had passed from favor in other parts of the country. Simple posts replace the stately columns of Greek Revival mansions in the East. Today the building is owned by the City of Los Angeles and has been restored as a historical museum. It is on the list of the National Register of Historic Places.

The hip roof was not part of the California tradition, so many built houses with saddleback roofs, often with a cantilevered, second-floor balcony along the front, supporting an overhanging roof.

The Larkin house and its offspring throughout California have been seen by Harold Kirker[16] as an attempt to build in the Greek Revival style which was popular in the eastern United States when Larkin came to California,[17] but the notion that the Monterey style is but a crude pastiche of this style denies the breadth of influences that operated on California architecture in that period.

First, the wooden veranda served much the same function as the adobe arcade that was an important architectural element in many of the California missions. But post-and-beam construction out of wood was much easier than making arches of adobe or stone, provided that lumber and tools were available. The arcaded plaza was of central importance to Spanish Colonial cities as promulgated in the Laws of the Indies (see p. 26), although Los Angeles never fully developed such a sophisticated urban design. Finally, in sixteenth-century Mexico, verandas very similar to those in Los Angeles, though perhaps more massive, were common.[18]

The full veranda was known to Americans outside of New England as well. Many early Anglo immigrants to Los Angeles, as well as those from the Confederate States after the Civil War, must have known the ornate grillwork of New Orleans, for example,[19] or the verandas of Savannah or Charleston. Don Juan Temple, who came to Los Angeles in the 1820s from the Hawaiian Islands, certainly had seen broad verandas there.

Casa Adobe de San Rafael (Tomas and Maria Sanchez home), 1330 Dorothy Drive, Glendale, constructed ca. 1870, photograph ca. 1936. This adobe building represents a more simple but probably commoner type of house than the "L" or "U" plan often associated with the period. It is essentially a rectangular, one-story form with four interior rooms and an exterior corredor and kitchen. The Californios seldom excavated for their buildings, and the four rooms here are all at different levels, following the contours of the ground. The house has been restored by the City of Glendale is presently furnished with nineteenth-century antiques. It is open to the public.

Ossa and Garnier residence, 16756 Moorpark Street, Encino. Don Vicente de la Ossa acquired this land from San Fernando Indians who had been granted the land under secularization, and in 1849 he built a long, narrow adobe house with a corredor along the front and back. In 1869 the Frenchman Eugene Garnier bought the ranch. Since the Californios generally cooked outdoors, the Ossa home had no kitchen. Garnier thus constructed a two-story building as a kitchen and bunkhouse. It is built of limestone quarried from the ranch, in the style of a French provincial farmhouse that Garnier would have known in his native land. The buildings have been restored since this 1970 photograph and are part of Los Encinos State Historic Park, listed on the National Register of Historic Places.

Catalina Verdugo residence, 2211 Bonita Drive, Glendale, probably constructed in the 1870s. The romance of California living during the Mexican period has had an enduring effect on the region's architecture, even though the reality of that life was not always so inspiring. In this serene photograph from 1905, vines grow in front of the veranda, keeping the home cool even in the bright California sunshine. One could sit on a rustic bench and enjoy the sun even when invalid (note the crutches behind the bench), or could lounge in Craftsman furniture in the shade of the porch. The residence is listed on the National Register of Historic Places.

Leonis home, 23537 Calabasas Road, Calabasas, originally constructed 1845. One of the most beautifully restored and maintained adobe homes in the Los Angeles area is this late Monterey style remodeling from 1879, when Miguel Leonis walled in the upstairs and downstairs porches to add on more rooms, paneled the living room walls, and added the Queen Anne veranda on the front. The house was narrowly saved from destruction in 1962 and has been restored to its 1879 condition by the Leonis Adobe Association. The house is now a museum with furniture and other items dating from the 1870s, and is surrounded by a barn, windmill, blacksmith shop, and ranch buildings. It is listed on the National Register of Historic Places.

Whatever the actual sources of the ideas that came together in the Monterey style, the result was an architecture unique to California. Here it served as a bridge between the old Spanish and the new Anglo building, and it spread to other parts of the United States in later years as part of revival trends. After the missions, the Monterey style is the second major contribution of California to the history of American architecture.

Several graceful Monterey style homes are still to be seen in the Los Angeles area, some restored and open to the public as museums. In what is now Long Beach, Don Juan Temple built the house known as La Casa del Rancho de los Cerritos in 1844. Using adobe and redwood on a foundation of brick, Temple combined the Monterey style with a traditional Mexican plan enclosing a central courtyard. It is today a museum housing artifacts from nearby Indian archaeological sites and historical artifacts including furniture and costumes from the period 1866–81.

La Casa de la Centinela, which served as the main house for the Rancho Aguaje de Centinela, is a beautifully restored one-story adobe with furniture from the Victorian period. It serves as the headquarters of the Historical Society of the Centinela Valley and is open for tours.

In the San Fernando Valley, the very-Monterey style Leonis adobe in Calabasas dates from about 1879 in its present remodeling. The two-story veranda is decorated with ornate wood spindlework and capitals on the supporting posts in the Queen Anne style, which was the very latest trend in 1870s Los Angeles. The home has been restored to its 1879 condition by the Leonis Adobe Association. The grounds, which are open to the public, include the adobe house with furniture and other items dating to the 1870s, a barn, windmill, blacksmith shop, and other ranch buildings.

The Los Angeles Streetscape

For a decade or more after the American occupation, the Plaza remained unchanged from its old Spanish version of a treeless common, "its surface pawed into ridges or trodden into dust by the hoofs of the numerous mustangs tethered on it or ridden over it."[20] The notion of a landscaped plaza, with trees and grass, was strictly an Anglo one, but the Americans did not have the same tradition as the Mexicans of evening promenades at the Plaza, nor of centralizing town life there. In fact, the American attitude was fairly ambivalent, judging by their treatment of the space.

On the one hand the Plaza was treated like any other piece of real estate; something to be put to practical use. In 1857 the city council granted to Judge William G. Dryden the franchise to distribute public water in the city. He built a reservoir on the Plaza, holding water raised by a pump in the Zanja Madre and distributed to houses in the neighborhoods by hollow-log pipes.[21]

On the other hand the Plaza was viewed as a public park, a midwestern Courthouse Square. An attempt was made to beautify it in 1859, when it was enclosed by a fence, laid out with walks, and planted with shrubbery. The landscaping was apparently not maintained, however. Tethered mustangs gnawed the fence and wandering goats nibbled the shrubbery, until by 1870 the Plaza had lapsed into its former state of dilapidation (see p. 41). In that year the City Water Company, successor to Dryden, relandscaped

Geronimo Lopez home, 1100 Pico Street, San Fernando, constructed in 1882. The Lopez home is a vestige of late nineteenth century adobe architecture in rural areas surrounding Los Angeles. Its adobe walls are two feet thick, but the veranda is Queen Anne spindlework, and the original roof was shake rather than tile. Thus, the home was an attempt to build in the latest architectural style using locally available materials. In 1973 the house was purchased from the Lopez heirs and restored to its original floor plan; it is now a museum run by the City of San Fernando and is listed on the National Register of Historic Places.

Sketch of Los Angeles by Kuchel and Dreisel; looking north from First Street, east of Main Street, 1857. While wealthy residents built spacious two-story Monterey style homes with pitched roofs and tall verandas, the ordinary residents of Los Angeles lived in low, flat-roofed, attached dwellings. The homes had relatively few windows and were square and simple in plan; this drawing, however, shows spacious, landscaped courtyards. Smoke is coming from chimneys, but the outdoor oven in the lower left corner suggests that some cooking took place outdoors.

Los Angeles, Thursday, May 13, 1869; looking east from Bunker Hill. Los Angeles had been an American town for two decades when this photograph was taken. The Temple Market Block stands as the most imposing monument in the city, to the north of which (left in the photo) is one of the other Temple Blocks that would surround this original market. The pitched roof building in the foreground is the First Episcopal Church, the city's first Protestant church; Temple Street runs along its north side. By 1869 the northern part of the city, in the vicinity of the Plaza, was an irregular mixture of wood and adobe buildings, pitched and flat roofs, and Italianate and old Mexican architecture. To the south one sees neat rows of Italianate houses behind white picket fences. The city's shopping district was to the north of the Temple Market Block. In those days there were only limited goods for sale and the town was quite small—about 5,700 people—so that the conspicuous advertising taken for granted in today's city is largely absent.

the Plaza and built an ornamental fountain in place of the reservoir, which was removed. The form of the Plaza was changed from a square to a circle at that time.[22]

In 1870 the Plaza was still the center of the city, but it would not be for long. A year earlier the Los Angeles and San Pedro Railroad built its station on what is now Alameda and Commercial streets. Passengers from San Pedro now disembarked well south of the Plaza. A year later a horsecar line was franchised from the Plaza south along Main, Spring, and Sixth streets to Figueroa, linking the finer residential districts to the commercial center of the city by public transportation for the first time. Although the northern terminus was the Plaza, this local line provided the impetus to extend commercial establishments along its route, away from the Plaza itself.

The city quickly began to move south toward today's downtown. The immediate new center was First Street, only four blocks from the Plaza but far enough away to isolate it, given the scale of the city in the 1870s. By the time one traveled beyond Sixth Street, one saw only farmhouses amid orchards and gardens. Eventually the Plaza, the old heart of the city, began to be viewed as merely a vestige of a former culture, largely forgotten and irrelevant to Anglo Los Angeles. In 1879 a newspaper article would complain of the "repulsive aspect of the disgraceful Plaza, a filthy, neglected, tumbled down eyesore."[23]

In the 1870s, Los Angeles Street south of the Plaza, in the area called "Nigger Alley," served as a terminus for livestock drovers and freighters. Shipments were loaded and unloaded to and from the mines and overland points as far away as Salt Lake City. The adjacent street frontage was occupied by wholesale houses, cattle and hide dealers, blacksmith shops, and wagon, harness, and saddle makers. As high architecture these buildings were hardly a visual delight, and the heart of the city became purely a commercial proposition struggling for survival. There appears to have been little concern for the aesthetics of public spaces, though individual buildings such as the Pico House (see p. 58) represented substantial architectural achievements for isolated Los Angeles.

The salient qualities of the place were those of a frontier town. In summer the streets were layered in deep, puffy dust, while in winter, when it rained, the mud was ankle-deep. There were few sidewalks upon which pedestrians could take refuge, and few shade trees. The *Los Angeles Star* reported on June 18, 1870 that city hall prisoners cleaning the streets in one day found five hundred old boots and shoes, a half ton of straw, seven dead cats, and five cart loads of orange peelings. So much we know about the diet of 1870 Angelinos.

Los Angeles in 1873; view from Ninth Street, at the convergence of Main and Spring streets. From the southern part of the city in 1873, residents of the neat white houses on spacious lots could look up the broad streets of the city (such as Broadway on the left) to see the San Gabriel Mountains.

Plaza and Plaza Church, 1869. In 1859, the Plaza had been enclosed by a fence; ten years later, however, as this photo shows, it had become an eyesore. In the center of the Plaza, to the far right in this photo, is the reservoir for the city's water system, beyond which is Olvera Street. To the left is the dusty expanse of North Main Street.

Los Angeles Plaza, 1883; view from the east. In 1870 the Plaza was re-land-scaped with grass, formal plantings, and sidewalks; its shape was changed from a square to a circle. The water reservoir was removed and replaced with an or-namental fountain, and an ironwork gate was placed around the perimeter. Plaza Church, with its wooden cupola, is be-yond the Plaza on the right, and on the left is the Pico House. In the center, the two-story building with five arched win-dows is the Garnier Block of 1883, still standing, although stripped of its orna-mentation. In the background is Fort Moore Hill, where today stand the offices of the Los Angeles Board of Education.

Los Angeles Plaza, 1895; view from the west. In 1895 the Plaza was metic-ulously landscaped, and its vegetation was maturing; the four Moreton Bay fig trees still stand today. Streets surround-ing the Plaza were still unpaved. Behind the Plaza is the two-story Vicente Lugo residence, seen with its original flat roof in the 1860s panorama on page 25. The siding and the pitched roof were added in the 1880s. The last secular building from the Mexican period to stand on the Plaza, it was demolished in 1951. When this photograph was taken, the Plaza was the center of the Chinese community in Los Angeles. Union Station now stands in the area behind the Lugo residence.

The Los Angeles Plaza, 1980.

By 1875 the principal streets of the city were being macadamized, helping to alleviate the dust and mud problem, though there were continued reports of impassable streets into the 1880s.[24] Some streets existed only in plats; in reality they were completely blocked by squatter settlements or by owners of adjacent property who fenced in segments of the street for use as kitchen or garden, such as Figueroa from Seventh to Pico.[25]

Other than the handful of buildings designed with some architectural pretension, most business was carried out in old adobe buildings along Main and Spring streets. Most of the shop fronts were open to the street, and "in the fruiters' stalls hung great bunches of oranges with the leaves on, as if just plucked," reported Mrs. Frank Leslie in 1877.[26] In front of other stalls were "rows of great red jars for water coolers" and "gay stuffs for dresses, mantles, and scarves."

Amidst the simple adobes and the Monterey style homes of those who could afford them, by the 1870s Los Angeles boasted a new American architecture replete with Italian Renaissance designs—the same forms that were, and still are, hallmarks of the nineteenth-century American midwestern small town.

The Italianate Period, 1860–1880

In the early 1850s, some Americans in Los Angeles broke quickly away from the constraints of adobe. The first all-wooden building was constructed in 1851 on the site of the present Merced Theater; it was framed in Boston, and the material, shaped and ready for assembly, was shipped around Cape Horn—

LEFT:

Nigger Alley, 1882; looking northeast. Los Angeles's early version of a heavy industrial zone was Nigger Alley, the northern end of Los Angeles Street where it met the Plaza. Here was the shipping and trading center, as well as the center of gambling and prostitution. The building on the far left with the small tower is the Plaza firehouse from the rear. Some elements in the streetscape, such as utility poles, have changed little in the last century.

a distance of 18,000 miles. This dwelling may be seen in the panorama on page 25, to the left of the Masonic Hall. It is quite different from the usual flat-roofed house of the pueblo.

Also in 1851 the Mormon sawmill in San Bernardino was opened, supplying plentiful wood for construction. An iron house was built in 1852, erected with wrenches and sledgehammers, its material shipped from England via the Cape Horn route. Red brick was first fired in the city in 1852, and the first brick house was built the following year. It stood until the turn of the century on the west side of Main Street, north of Fourth.[27] In 1854 a firm specializing in brickmaking was established and by 1858 was turning out two million bricks per year.[28]

Adobe as a building material quickly fell into disfavor within the city itself, though in rural areas it would continue to be used more frequently. In the 1860s adobe houses in Los Angeles were dismissed as "relics of a former and more incomplete age of civilization."[29]

Much of the new Americanized architecture was introduced by Anglo merchants, who generally did not begin to acquire importance in the city until the 1850s. A few early non-Mexican immigrants had already established themselves, however, being required to marry into Mexican families and take Spanish names. In 1827 Jonathan "Don Juan" Temple founded the first general merchandise business in Los Angeles, at what is now the corner of Main and Temple Streets, and in 1845 he had become successful enough to retire from merchandising and acquired the old Dominguez Rancho, on which the city of Long Beach would later be built.

Masonic Hall, 1856, and the Merced Theater, 1870, 416–418 North Main Street. The two-story Masonic Hall is one of the earliest remaining commercial buildings in Southern California. It has a relatively simple Italianate facade. An early view of this building may be seen in the 1865 panorama of the Plaza on page 25. Shortly after the Pico House was constructed, furniture dealer William Abbott and his wife Merced Garcia decided to build a three-story brick building with the lower story for the business, the second for a 400-seat theater and the third for living quarters. The theater, designed by Ezra F. Kysor, closed in 1878, as the neighborhood around the Plaza ceased to attract the type of people who would support a fine theater. In 1954 the California Historical Society purchased the building and has restored the exterior as part of the Pueblo de Los Angeles State Historic Park.

Bella Union Hotel, North Main Street at Arcadia. The Bella Union began as a single-story adobe residence in 1835. Sometime later the second story and Monterey style facade were added, and the house was turned into a hotel. In 1858, when the Butterfield Stage route was opened to Los Angeles, the facade was redesigned in the Italianate style. Ten years later, in order to compete with the new Pico House, the third story and the two-story wing were added and the facade brought to completion with a large bracketed cornice. By the 1870s, parts of downtown Los Angeles resembled a small midwestern American town. In the twentieth century, the Bella Union suffered the same decline as much of downtown. The first floor was remodeled, large show windows replaced the arched windows of the old hotel, and the building was used as a boarding house during the years before its demolition in 1940.

In the center of the city he constructed the Temple Market Block in 1859, Los Angeles's first secular building of monumental aspirations; it was on land now covered by City Hall. His building was somewhat crudely fashioned after the first Faneuil Hall in Boston, although much smaller, with its lower story divided into market stalls and its upper story into judicial offices. It later served as the Los Angeles County Courthouse until the completion of the Red Sandstone Courthouse in 1888 (see p. 47).

Architecturally the primary feature of the Temple Market Block was its outlandish rectangular tower in a loosely American Colonial style, fully as high as the building underneath it, with a large finial jutting another story above the roof of the tower. Angelinos told the time from the apparently noisy tower clock, which had one face on each side.[30]

At the time that Temple was building his market house, there was approaching from the east a new and distinctive architectural ethic. More sophisticated than the provincial interpretation of eastern styles that characterized Temple's market, it would come to dominate the Los Angeles streetscape until the Boom of the Eighties. The new architecture was the Italianate,[31] a style that found its first American application not in the Mediterranean climate of California but in the eastern United States, where the Greek and Gothic revivals had run their course.[32]

The Italianate used Renaissance forms such as quoins, balustrades, and bracketed eaves, but the great characteristic of the style was its window treatments: round or segmental arched windows capped by close-fitting, ornamental window heads. The style became quite popular in domestic architecture, but it became *de rigeur* in commercial architecture, where row upon row of closely-set, arched windows came to dominate the facades of Main Streets in American towns all across the country. The style received its inspiration from masonry construction, but it found widespread application in the castiron fronts of commercial structures that began to be built in the 1860s, with castiron pilaster moldings marching along entire facades.[33] Where castiron was not used, as in most Los Angeles buildings of the period, the masonry facade would often take on visual aspects of the more up-to-date castiron facades. The masonry Pico House in Los Angeles has such a rigidly repetitive facade.

The progression of style in Los Angeles from Monterey to Italianate is illustrated by a brief look at two hotels from this period. One of them, the Bella Union, no longer stands, but the Pico House remains as one of the great monuments of early Anglo Los Angeles.

The Bella Union Hotel stood on North Main Street at Arcadia (through which the Hollywood Freeway now passes) from 1835, when it was built as an adobe residence and mercantile store, until it was razed in 1940 for a parking lot.[34] As were most Los Angeles buildings of the 1830s, it was at first a plain, one-story building with a flat roof. Its lot was enclosed by an adobe wall, with a corral to the rear. After several different uses it was outfitted as a hotel in 1849, and a second story was added in 1851. Its facade stood behind a two-story veranda typical of Monterey style buildings of the period.

The Bella Union as a hotel was crude, to say the least. On the north side of the corral were several small rooms, about six by nine feet, and seven feet high. When the winter rains came, the adobe walls would disintegrate, covering the unhappy lodgers in a sea of mud. In the new second story, the walls were so thin that noises easily penetrated them, so that the most honored guests were not given a room at all but rather slept on the billiard table in peace and quiet.

In 1858, when the Butterfield stage route was opened to Los Angeles, the Bella Union's architecture was Americanized with a stucco facade, the veranda removed, and a small balcony in the Italian style built across the front of the second story. The windows were made stylish with round arches, each capped with an ornamental window head. Ten years later an even more pronounced Italianate third story was added, with segmental, arched windows and window heads, plus a small iron balcony fronting the center window. The walls of this addition were of red brick. A bracketed cornice brought the 1868 facade of the Bella Union to completion.[35]

In the early twentieth century the Bella Union, under the name of the St. Charles Hotel, suffered the general decline of central Los Angeles and was finally used as a boarding house until its demolition.

In order to compete with the Bella Union and a handful of other, lesser hotels, Pio Pico, the last of California's Mexican governors, built an even finer hotel on the Plaza in 1869–70, and it remains today in beautifully restored condition, as mute testimony to the architectural aspirations of early Los Angeles.

Los Angeles in 1869 was still a small town of 5,700 persons, and given the scale of the city the Pico House was a project of great importance. The city was still accessible only by Butterfield stage or ship via Wilmington. The Plaza itself was a chaos of commercial activity, but the economic aftermath of the Civil War, soon to culminate in the Panic of 1873, was rapidly spreading to the Pacific Coast. It was hardly an auspicious time or place to build an elegant hotel, but Pio Pico mortgaged part of his land holdings

in the San Fernando Valley and purchased the hotel site from his former brother-in-law, José Antonio Carrillo. Since the 1820s Carrillo's own house had stood on that site. Its high, gabled roof of red tiles and shakes and its white walls must have contrasted sharply with the flat roofs and clay-colored walls of the houses of less wealthy Angelinos (see p. 25).

Today we often think that the rediscovery of interest in our historical buildings is a new trend, and in earlier years Los Angeles showed only disregard for its past. This attitude did prevail in recent years when the Modern Movement in architecture dominated our thinking about the city, but in earlier Los Angeles there seems to have been a concern about the little city's still meager traditions. The Carrillo house was apparently considered to be a significant historical building, for on September 7, 1869, the Los Angeles News reported:[36]

> The old tile-covered house on the corner of Main and the Plaza is being torn down and removed, and a first-class hotel is to be erected on the lot by the owner thereof, Pio Pico. Thus one by one, the old landmarks are disappearing, and Los Angeles will soon have few things to remind the visitor that she is one of the oldest cities on the Pacific Coast.

The architectural plans for the Pico House were drawn up by the early Los Angeles architect Ezra F. Kysor, who designed a brick facade to be plastered and painted in imitation of light blue granite.[37] The facade was, and is, a splendid Italianate creation, its large shop windows along the ground floor resembling the arcade called for in the Laws of the Indies. Surrounding the windows are pilasters and round arches, with a broader arch fronting the main entrance. The second and third floor windows are set in slightly recessed panels separated by stylized pilasters with capitals, and all facade windows are arched and surmounted by decorative window heads. The window arches are differentiated by floor: segmental arched windows on the second story and round arches, symmetrically placed above the first floor arches but not as large, on the third story. Capping the building is a formal bracketed cornice, each corner accented with a merlon, and surmounting the center of each principal facade is a panel bearing the hotel's name, in the form of an *espadaña* reminiscent of the California missions—long before any formal thought was given to the revival of their style. For many years a wooden canopy, succeeded by a more formal portico with balustrade, covered the sidewalk above the first floor.

Downey Block, Main and Temple streets, 1871. One of several two-story Italianate store and office blocks constructed in downtown Los Angeles in the 1870s, the Downey Block—built by T.J. Baker—had four stores downstairs (grocery, jewelry, furniture, and dry goods), plus thirty-two office rooms upstairs for attorneys, real estate agents, surveyors, and a saloon called "The Office." The facade was of castiron made in Los Angeles, and the style was described as "enriched Corinthian" when the building was new. It was demolished in 1905.

LEFT:
Foy House, 633 South Witmer Street, ca. 1873. One of the few Italianate houses left in Los Angeles, the Foy House was originally built on the site of the Hilton Hotel on Wilshire Boulevard and later moved to its present location. Today, the front porch has been enclosed.

TOP RIGHT:
Among the earliest intact buildings remaining in Los Angeles are these workers' dwellings on Albion Street at Avenue 18, Lincoln Heights. They date probably from the 1870s, and are of board and batten construction in a simplified version of the Italianate style.

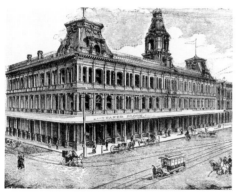

Street of Italianate homes, 1870s. The typical home of well-to-do Angelinos in the 1870s was a simple white Italianate house surrounded by a white picket fence and a small orange grove. These homes lined streets such as Broadway south to about Seventh Street.

BOTTOM:

Baker Block, 345 Main Street; by Buchanan and Herbert. The city's most magnificent early building was constructed in 1879 by R.S. Baker. He married the widow of Don Abel Stearns, demolished the Stearns mansion which occupied the site, and built the Baker Block, modeled after the Hotel de Ville in Paris, as a monument to the eternal faith in a prosperous future that characterized much of early Los Angeles. It stood until 1942, when it was demolished for the Hollywood Freeway.

Brick sidewalks were installed on the Main Street and Plaza sides. These were quite elegant for their day, when the few sidewalks in the city tended to be of wood and poorly maintained, so that one might unexpectedly step through a rotting board at any time.[38]

The Pico House proved to be the economic downfall of Pio Pico. The proceeds from his San Fernando Valley property and additional holdings were insufficient to keep the hotel open, and Pico retained ownership for only ten years. It passed to a series of owners and was used for cheap accommodations until about 1930, when the city authorities condemned the upper floors as unsafe. For the next three decades only the first floor was used. The building escaped demolition, however, and at this writing is undergoing restoration as part of El Pueblo de Los Angeles State Historic Park.

House forms of the 1870s

As the Anglos came to predominate the population of Los Angeles, their Italianate and other European revival house styles became a major part of the Los Angeles streetscape. The Californios, on the other hand, apparently irrespective of class, tended to keep their architectural traditions. In his 1878 account of Los Angeles, Ludwig Salvator noted the sharp delineation in style between the houses of the two groups. The houses of the Mexicans were of adobe, and retained many of the structural features of a generation earlier, while the houses of the Anglos were of wood frame, usually redwood, with white pine flooring. "From the outside these houses present a fairly good appearance; those of the more prosperous families are ornamented with verandas covered with masses of flowers. Usually the paint is gray or grayish-yellow in color; many of the houses were left in an unfinished state."[39]

In any settlement in any age there are people with substantially different class and wealth. Most of the discussion in this chapter, this book, and most architectural history, describes the forms and styles of the wealthier classes. Few records of the "other half," pass down through history, since we have a tendency to look upward rather than downward for the images of our past we choose to remember.

The great symbols of old California are the handful of missions rather than the thousands of hovels where the Indians lived, and similarly in early Anglo Los Angeles we know much more about the courthouses, hotels, and mansions than about the more typical dwellings of the period. Mrs. Frank Leslie, however, has left us the following description of a Mexican hut of the 1870s:[40]

> The huts were compounded of mud thatch and sailcloth and are hardly larger than a rabbit hutch. At the door of one of the huts a stately woman with a black shawl round her head invited us, with an air of condescension to come in and sit down. We accepted so far as to step inside and look around. In one corner of the mud floor some hens were peacefully burrowing. A small fire burned in a hole at the center, the stars peeped through the ragged thatch; and in a dark corner was a dim horror that may have been a bed. The whole house was no larger than one small chamber, and the roof was too low to allow a tall man to stand upright; but it was the home of a large family.

These buildings too are an important part of an architectural heritage, for they give perspective to the level of achievement of an entire society, not merely the elite.

Los Angeles by the end of the 1870s was still a struggling outpost at the end of a long trail, and its two architectural traditions were rather belated reflections of earlier American and Mexican forms. But in 1876 the Southern Pacific Railroad entered Los Angeles from the north, linking Southern California for the first time by rail to San Francisco and Chicago. Los Angeles was no longer isolated, and in another ten years the city's booming growth would tear asunder these fragile architectural traditions and leave precious little of this period as a living heritage today. By now nearly every structure in the old business district has been replaced, some sites having seen two or three generations of buildings since then. Other than the few monuments around the Plaza such as the Pico House, relics of this period are limited primarily to ranch houses, and many of these have been extensively altered. The "Old Los Angeles" existing today is generally not the city of the 1870s, but the city of the Boom of the Eighties and its aftermath as we shall next see.

St. Vibiana's Cathedral, bell tower.

TOP LEFT:

St. Vibiana's Cathedral, 114 East Second Street, by Kysor and Matthews. Until 1876, the Plaza Church was the only Roman Catholic church in Los Angeles, but in that year it was superceded by St. Vibiana's. St. Vibiana's is an enlarged version of Puerto de San Miguel in Barcelona. In 1922 the Main Street facade was replaced with a copy of its former self—but in Indiana limestone rather than red brick. Photograph ca. 1890.

MIDDLE:

House, Castelar Street. The Mexican section of Los Angeles in the late nineteenth century, called "Sonoratown," stood in contrast to the Monterey style homes of the wealthy Hispanic landowners and the Italianate dwellings of the Anglos. The left portion of this house is of adobe, while the center is of red brick and was probably a later addition. The far end, with its brick chimney, was probably the newest part of the house. It was demolished in 1925.

BOTTOM:

Temple Market Block, site of the present Los Angeles City Hall. In 1859 Jonathan Temple, who had come to Los Angeles after having made a fortune in the Hawaiian Islands, constructed this building as a market house and theater. The design was inspired by the first Faneuil Hall in Boston. Two years later it also became the county courthouse. The clock tower made this building the most monumental structure in the city. It was used until 1891.

THE QUEEN ANNE
AND CRAFTSMAN CITY

In 1880 Los Angeles was an American small town, but vestiges of its Mexican heritage could still be seen around the Plaza, which was then inhabited by the Chinese community, and in Sonoratown, which was beginning to suffer from severe neglect. The business quarter had expanded south from the Plaza down to First Street, in the area now largely taken over by the Hollywood Freeway and the Civic Center.

Although most businesses were housed in unpretentious, two-story buildings fronting cluttered streets, Los Angeles had begun to develop an architectural identity of relative style. A handful of well-designed business buildings, such as the Downey Block, Pico House, and the imposing Baker Block, expressed confidence in a prosperous future. This optimism was reflected as well in the neat rows of white Italianate houses surrounded by white picket fences and orange trees that lined the wide, dusty streets platted by Lt. Ord. Angelinos did not yet realize that within a decade the small town of 11,000 residents would be transformed into a booming city of 50,000, caught up in one of the great speculative land developments in American history.

The Boom of the Eighties, as it is called, was largely the product of that great American enterprise, the railroad. In this case two railroads, with competing lines to Los Angeles, who waged a prolonged and bitter rate war that could be won only by the line attracting the greatest number of travelers to Southern California.[1] The companies deluged the East and particularly the Midwest with advertising that beckoned the masses away from their harsh winters and rocky farmlands to the balmy and healthful climate, lush agricultural potential, and economic opportunity of Southern California.[2] To further encourage westward-bound travelers, the railroads lowered their fares in a price-cutting spiral that saw a one-way ticket from the Mississippi Valley to Southern California drop from $125 in 1885 to under $25 during 1886; in March of 1887 the fare from Kansas City to Los Angeles briefly plummeted to one dollar.[3]

By that time one could hardly afford *not* to come to Southern California, and indeed trainloads of newcomers streamed into Los Angeles. As the price of the train ticket dropped, the cost of property increased accordingly. "Prices of real estate rose with a rapidity that caused the old-timers to open their eyes and mouths in astonishment," wrote one observer. "They thought these newcomers crazy, and

E. F. KYSOR.   O. MORGAN.   J. A. WALLS.

Kysor, Morgan & Walls,

❉

Architects,

❉

No. 36½ South Spring Street,

LOS ✦ ANGELES, ✦ CAL.

❉ Architect

Kysor, Morgan and Walls advertisement in the Illustrated Los Angeles Herald, *June 1889.*

OPPOSITE:

Stimson house, 2421 Figueroa Street; by Carroll H. Brown, 1891. It is on the National Register of Historic Places.

hastened to sell them property at prices which gave the conscience of the more susceptible among them a twinge to accept. Yet not a few of these same old-timers, later in the Boom—when prices were two or three hundred percent higher still—became intoxicated with the general excitement and bought back some of this very same property."[4]

Everybody, it seemed, was suddenly in the real estate business. "What many of them did not know of Southern California was astonishing; but this did not prevent them from giving an intending purchaser the most positive and definite information upon every subject connected with the land which they had for sale." It mattered not; the land sold, in a frenzy of futures trading where some purchasers never saw or handled what they bought. "You could buy lots from $50 up, and payable in monthly installments of $5; which looked very reasonable, except when a person happened to reflect that these lots, a dozen miles from anywhere, were not worth over $25 an acre, and that an acre made 8 or 10 of them. But then, in those days, nobody ever thought of thinking."[5]

Advertisement in the Illustrated Los Angeles Herald, *September 1887.*

The Boom was by no means confined to Los Angeles proper. Paper towns rose like magic amidst the cactus and chaparral, and prospective buyers were wooed with the bandwagon, free lunch, and musicians; developers hired shills to work up enthusiasm for the "few remaining choice lots" in a town that often consisted of several thousand surveyor's stakes and a salesman's shack a mile and a half from the nearest house, some thirty miles via horse and buggy from Los Angeles. More than a hundred towns were platted in Los Angeles County between 1884 and 1888, of which only about thirty-eight became permanent parts of the Southern California landscape. Many of the others disappeared without a trace.[6]

By the spring of 1888 the Boom was faltering. Land prices had risen beyond anything imaginable five years earlier. Each wave of buyers had counted on a new wave of immigrants to purchase at a profit from them. However, the influx suddenly dwindled in 1888, apparently frightened off by the intensity of the Boom itself, and the anticipated new buyers were not to be found.[7]

Unlike some booms, this one did not suddenly collapse into chaos. The land market gradually shriveled up over a period of months as interest rates rose, loans were extended, and assessments reduced. In the long run, the overpriced property did not prove a poor investment. Many of the newcomers

First house in Ontario, California, 1880s. Many settlers who came to Southern California during the Boom of the Eighties built simple homes, but rather than borrowing the styles and materials of California, they brought their own architecture with them. The white clapboards and front porch on this small home would have been built on a Midwestern farm house.

Moving a palm tree, ca. 1888. During the Boom of the Eighties, real estate sales offices were located conveniently for persons newly arriving in Los Angeles. In this photograph of Fifth and Central streets, the Southern Pacific depot is the large building on the left. The palm tree was in fact being moved to a new site in front of the depot so that the first sight to greet newcomers would be the lush tropical vegetation of Los Angeles. They did not realize that almost all of the area's beautiful flora was introduced from elsewhere.

Ontario, San Bernardino County, looking north on Euclid Avenue, ca. 1900. The town of Ontario was established in 1882 as a model agricultural community with a mutually owned irrigation and hydro-electric power program. Chief crops were oranges, lemons, peaches, and grapes. Its founder, George B. Chaffee, who named the town for his home province in Canada, laid out the town along the axis of Euclid Avenue, a seven-mile-long divided boulevard with a streetcar track running along the median. It was planted with eucalyptus, pepper, and grevilleas. The land office (lower left in the photo) was conveniently located next to the Southern Pacific Railroad tracks, so that one needed only step off the train to buy land.

stayed; and by the mid-1890s, streets and services had finally been extended to many of the developments, making them comfortable and attractive neighborhoods.[8] Land prices in many places rose again to a level as high as during the Boom.[9]

Although many had come to Southern California to invest, far more had come to settle, and they found in the climate and land the realization of the advertisers' images. People who came to Los Angeles were not enamored by and large with Mexican traditions, and few built adobe houses. The typical newcomer was characterized by Charles F. Lummis as a "hardhearted man who values one edible slice of bread and butter over a year in a library."[10] More than 100,000 people had migrated to Southern California within ten years, many from the Midwest,[11] bringing many of their architectural traditions with them even though "physical geography, climate, and consequent habits and necessities of life were radically unlike those of whatsoever section they had previously inhabited."[12]

The new homes they built here were more up-to-date, grandiose, and adventuresome than those they had left behind. In the new land they quickly picked up a style already popular in San Francisco and the East: the American High Victorian architecture called Queen Anne, with its Eastlake variant.

Weller house, 824 Kensington, ca. 1880.

The Queen Anne in Los Angeles

From our vantage point we look back with a mixture of awe and incredulity on the towering, complex homes that were at first called "Jacobean," or "Elizabethan," or "Gothic Cottage," but which we call Victorian or, more precisely, Queen Anne. For two generations after these homes were built in the late nineteenth century, they were excoriated as exercises in architectural overindulgence. Time has been extremely unkind to this period, as rambling Victorian mansions have been partitioned, remodeled, and demolished.

In the 1980s we view the survivors with a new interest. Remnants of Victorian neighborhoods like Angeleno Heights and North University Park are being reborn as the amenity value of their homes increases. The visual quality of the home that was sought in Queen Anne designs—the architects of the day called it "picturesque"[13]—is once again coming into favor, in contrast to the veneered plainness of today's tract home.

We picture Victorian houses as fragments of a different, less complicated world. They serve as links to a beneficent heritage, when the materials and workmanship were part of the builder's art, when the home was a haven and the family a nurturing institution. But these buildings also reflect the self-conscious promotion of such values in the late nineteenth century. The United States in the 1870s and 1880s was caught up in an era when fundamental changes in the human condition were being wrought by technological innovation; machine technology was entering its period of triumph. Metals and textiles and crop harvesting had been removed from the realm of craftsman and cottage industry, and given to mechanized technology. Photography, the sewing machine, the electric light, and a thousand other inventions in rapid succession had transformed American life from dependence on the traditions of handwork to dependence on large-scale technology.[14] The transition from Butterfield stagecoach to railroad train as the principal access to Southern California brought forth a far more basic change in the social and economic system in Los Angeles than did the later transition from train to airplane, for example.

During the 1870s, writes Mark Girouard,[15] the desire to escape from the wicked, smoky city into the purity of the country was one motive behind the rush to the seashore. A boom in summer resorts sprang up along the northeast American coast and in California, whose healthful climate seemed to provide a haven from the chronic invalidism that was sweeping the United States.[16] Along with the surging population of Southern California, its landscape was changing from a handful of dusty villages and a few orange groves amidst scraggly chaparral into a resplendent garden of exotic fruits and plants, carefully cultivated by human hands.[17]

Progress in American architecture reflected the progress of technology. Widespread use of the balloon frame, indoor plumbing fixtures, central heating, and gas lighting had, in one generation, allowed

BOTTOM LEFT:
Upland, San Bernardino County, looking north, ca. 1900. Upland was subdivided in 1887 at the foot of the San Gabriel Mountains. With its architecture of wood and false fronts, it epitomized the small town of the American West, borrowing little from local traditions.

people of even modest means to live in greater style and to exercise greater control over their environment than ever before in history.[18] These changing notions of human potential were expressed in the multiplicity of forms used in the architecture of the period, as if greater abilities to create comfortable domestic environments stimulated higher levels of stylistic innovation among builders.

In the eastern United States, Queen Anne architecture, as the expression of this confidence in human potential, flowered in the 1870s and eventually developed into a grand American architectural movement called the Shingle Style.[19] In other areas of the country, however—and nowhere outdone by San Francisco and Los Angeles—homes built in the Queen Anne style did not become decoratively subdued; they became continually *more* picturesque, more complex, in an exuberant expression of freedom and prosperity.

The style gave particular emphasis to the silhouette and surface texture of the exterior. Houses were adorned with an array of gables, dormers, high chimneys, towers and turrets—sometimes hexagonal or square—with tall, conical roofs. Exterior walls, usually of wood but occasionally of masonry (such as Sespe stone in Los Angeles), were covered with rich patterns, from sunburst-shaped clapboards to fish-scale shingles, and a grandiose porch was often wrapped around the first floor. Chimney construction became an exceptional art form: the brickwork of a chimney was known to cover half an exterior wall and rise in complex forms high above the roof. The chimney was often decorated in brick tracery patterns, and sometimes the brickwork surrounded an entire window or even a door.

Exterior colors and decorations danced and played with the observer's eye. Spindlework was lavishly applied to porches, eaves, and turrets; even windows were not left a mere pane. Beveled crystal was

Baldwin "Queen Anne Cottage," Los Angeles State and County Arboretum, Arcadia; by A.A. Bennett, 1881. This ornate Queen Anne house, one of the earliest in Los Angeles, was built by entrepreneur E.J. "Lucky" Baldwin on this site as the guest house for his Rancho Santa Anita. Beneath a large belvedere, a veranda shaded by decorative slats runs along all four sides of the small wood-frame dwelling. Interior appointments include marble fireplaces and stained-glass windows. After a period of decay, the home was restored in the 1950s and today contains nineteenth century furnishings. Behind the house is a matching coach barn, also restored and painted the original white with red trim. The house is listed on the National Register of Historic Places.

de rigeur, along with leaded and sometimes stained transom windows. In round towers, windows were curved to fit the contour of the exterior wall. Adding to the articulation of the exterior was the ubiquitous bay window, which allowed designers even greater opportunities to design fanciful woodwork and window panes and complicated corner treatments.[20]

Particularly in Los Angeles, where there was room for large lots, the Queen Anne home was designed to be not only as visible as possible from the street, but also to impose itself on the street through its height, its huge porch, its dominance of the space surrounding it.

Inside, the Queen Anne home continued the exaggerated decorative motifs on the large newel posts, stamped woodwork, high ceilings often surrounded by friezes, and picture moldings around the walls. This decorative exuberance was, however, counterbalanced by a formal arrangement of the rooms. The front door opened into an entry hall, often containing an outsized staircase leading to the upstairs bedrooms. The first room off the hall was the parlor, where guests were received, and beyond these formal spaces were placed the family sitting room, the dining room, and the kitchen in the rear.

Some observers of architecture were not prepared for the decorative onslaught of Queen Anne, and they found it hard to take. One critic wrote in the *California Architect and Building News* in 1885 that, in the Queen Anne,[21]

> Shingles and roof tiles, used upon roofs from time immemorial, have crawled down upon the walls. The upper story and all dormers are covered with them. . . .The perversion of shingles has gone further. The walls of rooms are not seldom lined with them, giving a sort of rustic summer-house effect. The straining after novelty or oddity, with total disregard of beauty, is evident in the color that is lavished upon the outside of houses. Red, yellow, chocolate, orange, everything that is loud is in fashion;. . . .If the upper stories are not of red or buff shingles or tiles, they are parted up into uncouth panels of yellow and brown, while gables and dormers are adorned, not with tasteful and picturesque designs, but with monotonous sunbursts and flaming fans done in loud tints.

RIGHT:

Hale house, Heritage Square, ca. 1888. This ornate home with a redwood frame originally stood in the fashionable Mount Washington district of Highland Park and was moved to this site in 1970. Repainted in its original colors, it is a Queen Anne home with Eastlake decorative elements: clapboard siding with wood carvings and cast-plaster ornamentation, fish-scale shingles, wrought iron, stained glass, ornate brick chimneys, and a turret crowned with a copper fleur-de-lis. The Hale house is on the National Register of Historic Places.

Haskin house, 1344 Carroll Avenue, ca. 1895.

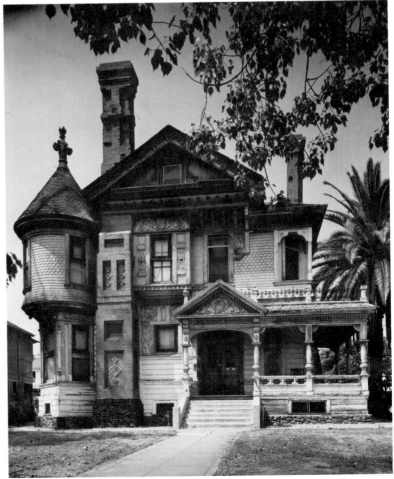

In all these decorative elements, the Queen Anne style was a statement of careful craftsmanship, but this craftsmanship was not the product of traditional handwork as much as it was an application of technology to building construction. Most of the architectural embellishments were turned out by machines—lathes, stamps, and molds. They were mass-produced items available to any builder from widely available catalogs. The definition of artistry in building was not to design new architectural elements, but to combine ready-made elements into flamboyant but pleasing patterns.[22]

The Eastlake Variant

The Eastlake architectural style that at first paralleled and then was subsumed in Queen Anne existed only briefly as an autonomous architecture in California. In fact, it was never intended as architecture at all, but as an "honest and straightforward" style of *interior* decoration developed by the English designer Charles L. Eastlake. His vision, based on the decorative forms of the Gothic Revival that had been popular in England during the early nineteenth century, was set forth as a book published in London in 1868 under the title *Hints on Household Taste in Furniture, Upholstery, and Other Details.*

An American version of the book appeared in 1872 and immediately found a receptive audience; it went through six American editions by 1881. Unfortunately for Eastlake, however, what the Americans liked about his style was not what he had in mind. Eastlake's designs were rather reserved for the period, but when American firms began to mass-produce so-called "Eastlake" products for their customers, "it was the irregular, eye-catching, picturesquely lavish character of Gothic decoration that appealed to the manufacturers, and they made it the bombastic expression of an untrammeled era."[23] The term "Eastlake" was soon applied to forms that Charles himself had never envisioned—and to products such as castiron sinks that had little to do with decoration at all.[24] Soon there were exterior "Eastlake" products such as ornamental metal shingles, and eventually an entire style of domestic architecture that had nothing at all to do with the designs in *Hints on Household Taste.*

Hale house, interior. The Eastlake was actually a style of interior decoration which had little relation to the English style whose name it borrowed. The interior has been restored to its original Eastlake decor. The wallpaper and fireplace tile have been reproduced, and the woodwork has been refinished as it was when the house was new. The Eastlake style was characterized by a rectangularity, stressing a vertical look to its objects and decor.

Pico House hotel, Los Angeles Plaza. Designed by Ezra F. Kysor in 1870, the Pico House was the city's first three-story structure. It remains as Los Angeles's finest example of the commercial Italianate style which was the look of the American main street during the mid- to late nineteenth century. It is constructed of brick, plastered and painted to look like light blue granite. The building has been restored as part of El Pueblo de Los Angeles State Historic Park.

OPPOSITE:

Morey house, 140 Terracina Boulevard, Redlands. Founded in 1887, today Redlands contains a rich legacy of its early architecture. Like many towns in the Los Angeles region, it was intended as a mecca for gentleman farmers who wished to grow oranges in the balmy Southern California climate rather than brave the harsh eastern winters. Sarah Morey tended the orange groves on her land and founded an orange tree nursery where she grew trees from seeds. Her husband David, cabinet maker, built this Victorian home for her in 1890.

It is uncertain where the "Eastlake" architectural designs came from,[25] but the "Eastlake" house was characterized primarily by wall surfaces divided into rectangular panels outlined by board moldings. Within the panels were pieces of wood jigsawed into complex patterns. Structural members such as roof beams, or things that looked like them, were carried out in delicate wood spindling, especially under eaves and at corners where they would be particularly visible. Eaves themselves tended to jut out at sharp angles, making the entire composition seem taut, as if breaking one of the spindles would make the entire house collapse. Whereas Queen Anne was curvilinear and angular, "Eastlake" was perpendicular and boxy. In scale and room arrangement, however, "Eastlake" was similar to Queen Anne.

By the early 1880s, the "Eastlake" style had come to California, where the *California Architect and Building News* immediately geared for the attack. "Eastlake" was subject to "excessive gaubery"; so unrestrained in its requirements that "the wildest conceits of the uneducated pretender may be imposed, and the most absurd and distorted features defended as in keeping with the style."[26]

The problem for us today in understanding the contemporary criticisms of a style such as "Eastlake," is that quotes such as the above could also have been applied to Queen Anne, which the *California Architect* eventually accepted as an appropriate style. In retrospect, it seems that the problem with "Eastlake" was not that it was unrestrained, but that its visual tautness made its buildings constrained rather than expressive. Its rules were precise, and it managed to grate against the very freedom that allowed Queen Anne to flourish.

The *California Architect* was not alone in deploring "Eastlake" architecture. Charles himself was not too pleased with what was being built in his name. The San Francisco magazine wrote Eastlake a letter asking his opinion of the "Eastlake" style, and he replied that it "may be said to burlesque such doctrines of art as I have ventured to maintain by criticism of modern works, or deduce from the study of ancient examples. . . .I regret that their author's name should be associated there with a phase of taste in architecture and industrial art with which I can have no real sympathy, and which by all accounts seems to be extravagant and bizarre."[27]

By the time the "Eastlake" style arrived in Los Angeles, it existed largely as a decorative treatment of Queen Anne buildings, although some full Eastlake designs such as the Abbotsford Inn (see p. 66)

were carried out. A typical example of its use is its application to flat surfaces and gables on the facade of the Hale house (see p. 56), now in Heritage Square. As an ancillary decorative element it provided additional picturesque motifs for Queen Anne buildings, while not imposing its constraining rules on an entire structure.

Samuel and Joseph Cather Newsom: the Picturesque Climax

One team of architects Charles Eastlake certainly would have excoriated, but who were probably the masters of California Queen Anne architecture, were the Newsom brothers, Samuel and Joseph Cather. Born in Montreal and immigrants to San Francisco, the Newsoms began to design homes and a few commercial buildings in California during the 1880s. By applying a decorative ethic that would strain the bounds of even the California imagination, they achieved a financial and critical success unmatched in Western domestic architecture of the period.[28] In an era when a fine house was one that caught the eye, they built homes one could not avoid looking at; they took already exaggerated Victorian elements and embellished them to make fantastic creations of unsurpassed architectural imagery.[29]

Their *chef d'oeuvre* was undisputedly the Carson house in Eureka, but their imprint on Los Angeles was felt as well. Today many of their best buildings are gone, victims of changing economic fortunes that often claimed the finest buildings first. The Melrose Hotel on Bunker Hill is gone, along with the Bradbury mansion and the gingerbread-Romanesque Bryson-Bonebrake Block downtown. Of their more than 650 executed commissions, however, enough remain to serve witness to their vision: the Sessions house on Carroll Avenue (see p. 209), with its expansive moon gate and Chinese spindlework; or the S.J. Lewis house on Miramar Street (see p. 186), with its massive gables and tower. Their finest remaining porch in the area is probably the sweeping broken pediment of the Pinney house in Sierra Madre.

The Newsoms did not work only in the Queen Anne idiom. Their desire to create a startlingly different facade encouraged them to incorporate stylistic elements from a variety of sources, never straying too far from the latest trends. In his later years, for example, Joseph Cather designed the "Italian Gothic" Fitzgerald house (1903) on West Adams Boulevard, and the Mission Revival Severence house (1904) on 23rd Street.

Miller and Herriott house, 1163 West 27th Street, ca. 1890. North University Park was subdivided in the 1890s as a conservative, well-to-do neighborhood. This lofty house, which originally had a moon gate (spindlework arch) around the front entrance, has a Chippendale Chinese balustrade and a mass of delicate spindlework, most of which is intact.

The End of Queen Anne

By the 1890s the appeal of the Queen Anne and its Eastlake adjuvant began to wane; despite its popularity it had always been hard for many to comprehend. When the Newsom brothers had finally finished with Queen Anne, there was no place for the style to go. On the one hand, one could hardly conceive of a more adventurously decorated exterior. Queen Anne forms had carried the decorative properties of wood to the extreme and could not be further elaborated in any meaningful way. On the other hand, the style overwhelmed some observers by the glut of its decorative forms. For persons with conservative or unpretentious tastes, the Queen Anne offered little, and it certainly never attempted to relate to its surroundings.

If the future of residential architecture did not lie in wooden jigsaw puzzles that jutted three stories above the ground, perhaps it could be found in the direct and earthy forms of the California bungalow.

Miller and Herriott house, interior. The present owners are restoring this home to its Victorian elegance after a long period of neglect. The house survived twenty-seven owners in ninety years, and by the early 1970s it had been divided into several dwelling units and the porches had been enclosed. The original stained-glass windows were sold to a restaurant near Disneyland. The home is on the National Register of Historic Places.

The Evolution of the Craftsman Bungalow in California

The Craftsman movement in American domestic arts and architecture that emerged at the turn of the century was an outgrowth of the English Arts and Crafts movement, which had blossomed under the leadership of William Morris (1834-1896). In America, the craft ethic was promulgated largely in the pages of Gustav Stickley's magazine *The Craftsman*, published in New York from 1901 to 1916. As a reaction to the fear of dehumanization by industrial society, the Arts and Crafts movement rejected the social and aesthetic forms determined by the machine and sought to create a new environment based on the ethic of "craft"—straightforward forms that expressed the unity of art and handwork.[30]

At the turn of the century there arose from the cross between the incipient Craftsman ethic and the California lifestyle a type of house that has continued to influence American domestic architecture long after the Craftsman movement itself has passed from the scene. This architecture was the first style since

the Monterey that was indigenous to California and was the third major contribution of the area to American architectural history. Craftsman house forms were partly a reaction against Victorian decorative excesses and the estrangement of the Queen Anne style from the builder and his materials, and partly an expression of a uniquely Western interaction of natural environment and cultural forces.

The Craftsman ethic was applied to the normal two-story American home that had derived from New England models (a row of such homes may be seen today on Menlo Avenue, south of Adams Boulevard), but the house form upon which the Craftsman creative spirit lavished its attention was the *bungalow*. The bungalow was an unpretentious single-story dwelling type whose roots extended back to British India,[31] and which was constructed in many styles according to what was in vogue.[32]

In California the Craftsman movement turned the bungalow into something special—the low house with shallow, pitched roof and broad, overhanging eaves that is still a common feature along older Los Angeles streets. The covered front porch of the Craftsman bungalow was usually large and deep, supported by massive piers of stone or clinker brick, sometimes designed so that the house seemed to grow right out of the ground on which it stood. Often structural members like roof rafters were exposed and even emphasized to give the feel of handcraftsmanship in the construction of the entire house.

Craftsman bungalows had simple, box-like shapes and informal floor plans. The front door usually opened directly into the living room rather than into the foyer as would have been typical for the Queen Anne home. Thus, the visitor was immediately thrust into the main areas of family life rather than these being cloistered by the formal entry hall and parlor. Earth colors predominated both on the exterior sheathing of clapboards, shingles, or board and batten, and on the interior, which was often built with exposed woodwork and built-in cabinetry.

The origins of the California bungalow remain shrouded in mystery, although some attempts have been made to explain the roots of its form. The most colorful theory holds that it evolved from the barn. Many newcomers to Southern California around the turn of the century were people of limited means, and they often built a simple barn to live in while they put all their money into their orchards. According to one writer in 1907,[33] the tenants would decorate their barn-homes with "Old Government Java" coffee bags and a few pieces of simple furniture until such time that a real house could be built. Clay Lancaster, in his book *The Japanese Influence in America*, combined the barn theory with the suggestion that the spindlework and Oriental details of the bungalow came from the influence of Japanese exhibits at the World's Columbian Exposition in Chicago in 1893 and the California Midwinter Exposition in San Francisco in 1894.[34]

The Japanese influence is apparent in the California bungalow, but the barn theory is difficult to trace because there seem to be no photographs of early bungalows in the Los Angeles area. Views of Los Angeles at the turn of the century show neat, ordinary houses surrounded by barren ground and wide streets—much like new subdivisions today. Moreover, homesteaders in rural areas apparently lived in simple cabins, not barns (see p. 68).

Another theory, promulgated by Henry "The Bungalow Man" Wilson in his bungalow pattern book of 1910[35] holds that the bungalow descended from the California mission. "It surely can trace its simple artistic lines directly back to the old Missions of the Spanish Padres, and its low overhanging eaves, large porches and general air of hospitality and coziness to the adobe houses of the pioneers." The lack of photographs of transitional forms between mission and bungalow leaves this theory open to question as well; it is another area of architectural history in need of further research. At any rate, as will be discussed in Chapter 4, the Mission Revival became extremely popular during the advent of the Craftsman bungalow. When Wilson wrote his book, the tendency to claim the affinity between the missions and the bungalows of his pattern books would certainly be strong—whether or not it was true.

Whatever its origins, the bungalow came to convey a lifestyle of "roughing it a bit, of living more or less in the open air for pleasure,"[36] as one had come to California to do in the first place. The bungalow hinted at "extemporized conveniences, with a suspicion of Bohemianism and laxity of conventional conduct," in contrast to the stuffy Victorian manners and conspicuous consumption associated with the Queen Anne. "The word stimulates the town dweller to let his imagination wander into the greenwood, where railways and streetcars cease to trouble, and where there is no such thing as an office or place of business."[37]

If California was the escape from the pressures of the East, the Craftsman bungalow was its palpable symbol, seeming to crouch cozily when the winds of sea or mountain howled about it.[38] If the Queen Anne home was a metaphorical marching band, outplaying all the others around it, the Craftsman bungalow was a piece of poetry amid the cacophony. As one of the praisers of the Craftsman ethic put it,

Gamble house, detail of interior woodwork with Tiffany glass lighting fixture.

OPPOSITE TOP:

Gamble house, 4 Westmoreland Place, Pasadena; by Charles and Henry Greene, 1908. The Craftsman bungalow began as an unpretentious Southern California architecture around the turn of the century. The Greenes combined these rustic forms with Japanese and Swiss influences to create Craftsman mansions as high architecture. Every exposed surface of this home is smoothed and rounded; a nail hole is not to be seen. The broad eaves, consciously exposed beams, and open sleeping porches on the second floor were common characteristics of Craftsman homes, both large and small.

OPPOSITE BOTTOM:

Gamble house, living room and foyer. While some wealthy clients invested in lavish decoration, the Gambles invested in the look of fine craftsmanship. The interior is lavish in its simplicity, with finely rubbed woods and Tiffany glass. Throughout the house—in woodwork, furniture, and accessories—runs a motif in shaped wood called the "flying cloud," making the entire home a unified art object. The Gamble house is now owned by the City of Pasadena and the University of Southern California and is open to the public. It is listed on the National Register of Historic Places.

Hollenbeck Hotel, northwest corner, Spring and Second streets; constructed 1884, demolished 1932, photograph ca. 1905. Queen Anne architecture was not confined to residential structures. Much of downtown Los Angeles by the 1890s was a Queen Anne streetscape of bay windows and dramatic turrets, especially at street corners. The Hollenbeck Hotel had aspirations to match its architecture. In March 1892, the Illustrated Los Angeles Herald wrote, "The rooms nearly all face to the east and south, so that in winter time, when tourists most abound in this section, the early sun lights and warms the rooms, so that they are pleasant, sunny and warm as in summer." The Hollenbeck served as a hotel until 1932, when it was demolished for a parking lot.

TOP RIGHT:

Abbotsford Inn, Eighth and Hope streets. The Eastlake style was composed of rectangular wood panels with scrolled decorations and tall, narrow vertical elements. The hooded bay windows seen here were a particular hallmark of the style in Los Angeles. Only briefly in vogue as a complete architectural style, it was frequently incorporated in Queen Anne buildings. The Abbotsford—named after Sir Walter Scott's residence in Scotland—was one of the finest pure Eastlake buildings in the city, built in 1887 as Hanna College for girls. The First Methodist Episcopal Church now stands on this site.

"The same hypersensitive intellectuality that it takes to write a beautiful poem or to paint a beautiful picture must be brought to bear in the making of a home if it is to be beautiful."

Despite the aura of roughness, of making do with simple things, the bungalow developed a set of precise rules. In 1906 the "correct" Craftsman bungalow was described by Una Nixson Hopkins in *The Architect and Engineer of California*:[39]

> Rough boards—the rougher the better—put on lengthwise, are rustic enough in appearance to pass muster in the ranks where surfaced materials are prohibited. Plaster is not tabooed entirely, though it must be rough, and used in connection with plenty of wood, but wall paper is not quite appropriate. Burlap, however, both natural and colored, is looked upon with favor, and rightly, for its rough surface makes a pleasing combination with rustic effects.

The house also required appropriate appointments: no overstuffed horsehair chairs, of course, but furnishings that were then called "Mission Style"—which we know as "Craftsman"—were "for the most part quite appropriate"[40] to set off the primitive American art that was called for:

> Collectors of Indian baskets, curios and rugs have found a fitting background for their collections in these houses. The bright baskets, which are too strong in color to suit the ordinary cut-and-dried house, are admirable on the floor of a rustic bungalow, and Indian baskets make a frieze that is not only interesting, but beautiful in color against a dark-beamed ceiling. These, along with the pottery used for wild flowers, will make a surprising good room.
>
> Even hardware and fixtures must have their own individuality and belong to this or that house, and can never be bought at random at the shop. They had better be congenial spirits with the light fixtures—made by the blacksmith or metal worker, as they frequently are, and in one house where handwrought things were not to be thought of, common japanned hardware was bought and soaked in lye, taking off the paint, and after weathering, as it were, they had the appearance of something hand made.

Like many Queen Anne and Eastlake houses, the typical bungalow was constructed by an anonymous builder, its design often taken from one of the pattern books that offered easily constructed house plans to anyone interested in building a house. Thus many streets came to be lined with homes having slight variations in decor and lot placement, but retaining unmistakably similar designs and floor plans. Few such streets remain intact, but Wilton Place in Los Angeles, near Beverly Boulevard, offers a glimpse into this bungalow past. Thousands of Craftsman bungalows still exist in the Los Angeles area and represent one of the finest legacies in the country of a regional architectural movement.

The Craftsman Homes of Charles and Henry Greene

In sharp contrast to the anonymity of most bungalow builders is the fame of a team of architect-brothers, Charles Sumner Greene (1868-1957) and Henry Mather Greene (1870-1954), who took the middle-class, Craftsman bungalow and transformed it into a magnificent art object and a true masterwork of architecture.[41]

The Greenes had been designing houses in the Pasadena area since 1893, their first commissions resulting in fairly uninspired boxy Victorian cottages and Mission Revival residences. Although their clients

Point Fermin Lighthouse, 805 Paseo del Mar, San Pedro. The Point Fermin Lighthouse was constructed in 1874 with lumber and bricks brought around Cape Horn by sailing ships. One of the earliest buildings in the Eastlake style in Southern California, it remains as the sole example of the several wooden lighthouses established in the 1870s between San Francisco and San Diego. The original cupola has been rebuilt and the light removed since these photographs were taken about 1910. The building is on the National Register of Historic Places.

Garnier Block, at Los Angeles and Arcadia streets, El Pueblo de Los Angeles State Historic Park. In 1890 when Phillipe Garnier built this business block, the area surrounding the Plaza was occupied by the city's Chinese community, and the building, during its early years, was occupied by the importing firm of Sun Wing Wo. The two-story brick building with sandstone trim lost its original south wing to the Santa Ana Freeway in 1952.

Pasadena, 1893. Much of the land around Los Angeles was developed as citrus orchards in the late nineteenth century. The small houses of the farmers were grouped around schools and drying sheds.

Homesteader's shack with cow, undated. During the Boom of the Eighties, thousands of people without means, as well as the wealthy, gave up their Midwestern farms and began new lives in Southern California. Many of them built simple board and batten shacks raised from the ground on short stilts to protect them from moisture. This style of shack used American materials and building techniques, borrowing nothing from local traditions. In this photograph, the shack is surrounded by newly planted citrus trees.

Urban shack with palm and citrus trees, undated. Before the turn of the century, cities in Southern California were dotted with the tents and shacks of newcomers, but even these were soon surrounded by the lush vegetation that made the region a semi-tropical paradise.

Bungalow, 837 Olive Street, Burbank, ca. 1910. The Craftsman bungalow looked firmly attached to the ground as seen here in the massive stone foundation. The large eaves are supported by only one small post rising from the huge piers, giving the stonework more relation to the ground than to the house. The Oriental influence is combined with the practical engineering look of the Howe truss that supports the roof.

seemed to like their work, the Greenes found these styles frustrating and not particularly appropriate for Southern California. Apparently they had been influenced by the Japanese exhibit at the World's Columbian Exposition of 1893 in Chicago, and it began for them a long interest in Oriental art forms. They had also traveled in Europe and had seen the half-timbered dwellings of the English countryside and the heavy-eaved houses of the Alps.[42] These forms, when combined with inspiration from the first issues of Gustav Stickley's *Craftsman* magazine in 1901, set them on an independent architectural course that would repudiate much of their earlier work and create an original and highly artistic version of the Craftsman bungalow for a more affluent clientele. In turn, their innovations fed back into the Craftsman movement by the 1910s, stamping untold bungalows with flying eaves, Japanese architectural proportions, and the uncertain boundary between landscaping and house.

The Greene and Greene masterpiece, and an incomparable creation of domestic architecture, is the Gamble house of 1908, on Westmoreland Place in Pasadena. While the builders of many mansions gravitated to Classical monumentality and ponderous decoration to express their achievements, the Gambles invested in the subtle aura of craftsmanship. Fine woods and Tiffany glass are the norm here, but equally striking is the painstaking concern for the assembly and finishing of every visible architectural detail. Each protruding edge, be it door panel, window sash or roof rafter, is rounded to a lustrous smoothness that links all elements of the house into one harmonious entity and expresses a reverence for the qualities of wood.

Culbertson house, detail. Greene and Greene, architects.

Van Rossem-Neill house, 400 Arroyo Terrace, Pasadena. This house is one of Charles and Henry Greene's early Craftsman works, constructed in 1906, and is notable for its clinker brick wall with insets of Chinese tile. The Craftsman house blurred the distinction between house and ground by a gradual transition of materials from natural to man-made. Natural stone foundations blended into fired brick, which yielded in turn to the wooden house.

Several of the Greene's finer houses were detailed with a design motif that ran through doors, moldings, and furnishings; in the Gamble house it is the Flying Cloud, a graceful dip in horizontal lines running throughout the house. The theme is carried to the exterior as well, in exposed woodwork and beams. The shingled siding of the house rests on a foundation of smoothed arroyo stones, which merge the building gently into the undulating landscape that surrounds it.

The Gamble house is perhaps the supreme bungalow, for it takes natural materials and carries their assembly to a level of superb craftsmanship. At the same time, however, it is the supreme anti-bungalow, for it smoothed the intendedly rough elements of the prototypical bungalow into a pristine finish of fine woods, and it turned simplicity into formality—complete with formal entrance hall, servants' quarters, and the preemption by the architects of even the most minute interior decoration on the part of the residents.

The Late Bungalow

Craftsman apartment building, 1040–1042 West 42nd Street, ca. 1915.

In its original conception, the Craftsman bungalow was the architectural expression of a lifestyle defined by simplicity, rusticity, and the handicraft ethic. As long as the bungalow remained simple, as long as it fostered the values of making a comfortable home using one's own creativity and a few readily available materials, it could flourish. But as soon as its rusticity became self-conscious, as soon as it came to be celebrated and rules for its proper design established, the bungalow took on a preciousness that destroyed the very spontaneity that made it work.

While the Greenes and other architects were bringing the Craftsman home to its fullest development, critics began to attack its overblown pretentiousness. In 1918, for example, Ernest Freese presented a "Bungle-Ode" to the readers of *The Architect and Engineer of California*, in which he defined the bungalow as a "composite of Swiss chalet, Japanese teahouse, Frank-Lloyd-Wright leaded glass, Spanish hacienda, Chinese influence, Mission furniture, monstrous originality, disappearing beds, and disillusioning appearance."

By the 1920s, the Craftsman architectural ethic had passed its prime. From about the turn of the century to 1906 was the period of experimentation, when its forms were being developed apparently with little formal guidance. By 1906 the style had come to the attention of critics who publicized it in magazines such as *Indoors and Out* and *Country Life in America*, as well as the architectural journals and *The Craftsman*. They established a formal vocabulary for the bungalow, eliminating the need for invention, and pattern books like that by Henry Wilson standardized building plans.

The vocabulary by the 1920s was being applied to vast numbers of Craftsman bungalows throughout Southern California and elsewhere, without discovering fresh elements or further developing an aesthetic. By the 1930s the style had disappeared completely, but it left its legacy in the California "ranch house" built all over the United States in the 1940s and 50s.

Today, when the vestiges of this architecture are rapidly disappearing, the Craftsman bungalow takes on a new importance and exuberance. A drive through Eagle Rock or down Wilton Place in Los Angeles or Griffin Avenue in Highland Park brings back a vision of pre-Depression Los Angeles, when the booming city of the 1920s was accompanied by the appeals of many residents for a home that represented the enduring values of handwork and unpretentious living.

The Bungalow and House Court

Craftsman bungalow court, 336 West 61st Street.

The popularity of the early bungalow with the winter tourists in Southern California towns, according to Charles Francis Saunders,[43] led to the establishment of the bungalow court, a group of perhaps a dozen small bungalows on two or three city lots, arranged about a central open space devoted to lawn, flower beds, and a common walk. The idea was similar to that of a Spanish house around a patio, except that in this case entire, unattached dwellings rather than the rooms of one house were arranged around this central space. The early bungalow courts were rented, usually furnished, for the season, with the grounds cared for by the landlord. Many, though not all, were built in the Craftsman style. Later, attached apartment units were built in the same configuration and took the name "bungalow court," even though the dwelling units were no longer bungalows.

The bungalow court had another link, as well as to the Craftsman bungalow itself. Contemporary observers saw it as the upper range of a housing type that had been developing in the late nineteenth century to house the poorest class of workers in Los Angeles. The general word for the type was the "house court."

Some newcomers from the East who arrived destitute but with hopes of realizing the American dream built tent cities in areas such as Watts which eventually became established communities.[44] Other im-

Duncan-Irwin house, 240 North Grand Avenue, Pasadena. Originally built in 1901 as a small cottage, this house was expanded in 1906 by Charles and Henry Greene into a two-story Craftsman masterpiece. Its openwork beams and its unpainted, shingled walls are hallmarks of the Craftsman style, and the Greenes lent their personal touch of juxtaposing closed and open forms and consciously revealing immaculate joinery.

Craftsman bungalows, 4000 block, Griffin Avenue, Highland Park.

E.J. Blacker house, 675 South Madison Street, Pasadena; by Charles and Henry Greene, 1912. The Greenes produced masterworks of the Craftsman style only during a brief period. Already by 1912, their Blacker house is considered "late." In their subsequent work they would return to boxy forms and heavy houses.

migrants, however, particularly Mexicans, who were not so assured of rising on the economic ladder, tended to live in a kind of slum fairly unique to Los Angeles, the house court.

The story of this housing type is perhaps best told as the story of late Sonoratown, during its demise in the early twentieth century. Sonoratown had been the center of the Hispanic population since the days of the early pueblo, and when great numbers of Mexicans came to Los Angeles beginning in the 1870s to work on the railroads, they tended to settle there rather than in Anglo districts where they would meet social and linguistic disfavor.

As is common in slum creation, these immigrants were forced into crowded living spaces, which in Sonoratown were largely made up of shacks erected in the rear courtyards of older, U-shaped Mexican homes.[45] Along the streets were long rows of one-story adobe and frame buildings, and narrow alleyways between them ran back to the former courtyards of homes of the Californios. The original Mexican settlers had "plenty of room for gardening and backyard work, and for the play of big families of children. Now the adobe in front has become a tenement for several families, and the courtyard has been honeycombed with shacks, and tents, and nondescript barn-tenements of one and two rooms."[46]

The native Californios, in the meantime, had begun to leave the area; those remaining occupied the better houses facing the streets and did "not mingle socially with the life of the courts." The older residents

Clark residence, Altadena. This Mission Revival home was designed with sweeping arches fronting the broad veranda and a scalloped parapet in the center. The Mission Revival, however, was only an exterior style.

The interior of the Clark residence was decidedly Craftsman. The library was appointed with "Mission Style" furniture in straight, simple lines, and with handmade rugs on hardwood floors. Indian pottery was also a stylish decoration in the Craftsman home.

were uprooted not only by the Mexican immigrants, however. In the years since the Boom of the Eighties they had lost much of their land to Italian immigrants. "The Italians came with their ability to save and to buy, and have inherited the greater part of the land. Everywhere, where the courts are not, are the homes of the new immigrants."

In 1913 there were 630 such house courts, with 3,700 dwelling units housing about 10,000 people—a considerable portion of the laboring classes of the city.[47]

The courts were variously built, but one thing they had in common: they were in poor condition and overcrowded. In 1906 Jacob Riis had jarred the complacency of the community by stating that Los Angeles possessed congested and unwholesome housing conditions quite as bad, though not as extensive, as any city in the land.[48] Although the Los Angeles Housing Commission, established in 1906, attempted to deal with the problem by demolishing these units, one could still walk in some parts of the city in 1913 and see little else.[49] The city had passed an ordinance attempting to do away with the courts' more glaring evils, allowing, for example, a maximum lot coverage of seventy percent, but it did not specify how the thirty percent open space was to be distributed, and crafty builders could still construct crowded hovels.

As a historical housing type, therefore, the court was a double-edged sword. The best of them, the bungalow courts, compared favorably in many respects to the single-family home. The worst of them

House courts were the subject of much concern by social reformers at the turn of the century. This page is from a 1913 article in the social welfare journal Survey *by William Matthews, entitled "House Courts of Los Angeles."*

Williams house, "Hillmont," 1375 East Mountain Street, Pasadena. View of the exterior and entrance hall, designed in 1887 by Harry Ridgeway.

condemned the poor (at that time, primarily Hispanic laborers) to the worst possible slums. "You may walk in the middle of a 'street' and touch two rows of houses facing each other, or follow a winding path between habitations, tripping over tubs and clothes-poles and outdoor fireplaces, over dogs and cats and children at play and the tinier tots just creeping about."[50]

The vision of Los Angeles as a garden paradise was thus continually plagued by those who were left behind, and their neighborhoods were reminders that the problems of America were brought with the newcomers to Southern California, not left behind in the sooty East. "Almost every week the papers report meetings of groups of people who dream of making their city 'the city beautiful of the world,' of making it a place not only where people of comfortable means may live under ideal conditions, but where every workingman may have opportunity to live and rear his family under fair conditions and wholesome surroundings," wrote William H. Matthews in 1913. "Let her beware of that false civic pride which would believe that everything is best in one's own city."[51]

THE SEARCH FOR A MEDITERRANEAN TRADITION

The Anglo immigrants of the nineteenth century imposed their architecture on Los Angeles as if it had none of its own. To be sure, the adobe forms of the Californios were not very picturesque according to eastern American standards, and their technology was less complex. The Americans brought with them machinery, milled lumber, nails, and glass, while the Mexicans had little more than the natural materials of mud and straw, brea and tule. We now look back upon the architecture of the Mexican period with a new respect, but the early Americans looked upon it as the legacy of a primitive culture, certainly not worth emulating. Even the missions seemed small and plain compared to buildings from the American colonial period, and by the 1880s most were falling into ruins anyway.

Despite the disregard for Mexican culture in the transplanted Midwest of Los Angeles that H.L. Mencken would later call "Double Dubuque," a new architecture arose in the 1890s, calling forth images of the very missions that were collapsing from neglect. Visual elements of an idealized California mission were incorporated into churches, homes, hotels, country clubs, railroad depots, and eventually gas stations, from the 1890s through the 1910s and beyond. The "Mission Style," as it was then called, paralleled the Craftsman movement and shared some of its values, but its forms were quite different.

Mission Revival borrowed from the missions, though it was by no means a composite of their architecture. Architects primarily chose four elements that they evoked again and again in creating the new style. First was the look of adobe. Mission Revival buildings could actually be built of hollow tile, red brick, stone, or wood, but the exterior was usually stuccoed. Some large buildings were constructed of reinforced concrete, a material still experimental at the turn of the century. Others, particularly small apartment houses, were called "Mission Style" merely because they had stuccoed outer walls and a row of red tiles along the parapet above the facade.

Second, Mission Revival structures often included a scalloped parapet rising above the roof, or a *campanario*—complete with bells—which served as an entrance gate or front gable (see p. 82). Third was the tower patterned after the old mission bell tower, often stepped back in tiers and articulated with small, arched windows. The historically correct Mission Revival tower was capped with a small dome, but others had a large, overhanging hip roof.

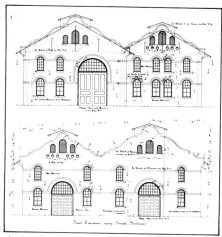

Architect's elevations, Olive Substation, Los Angeles Pacific Railroad, 2798 Sunset Boulevard, 1907.

OPPOSITE:

Villa d'Este Apartments, 1355 Laurel Avenue. The Villa d'Este was typical of many Los Angeles courtyard apartments—a Mediterranean hacienda adapted to the mobile lifestyle of the city. Pierpont and Walter S. Davis designed it in 1928 using rich brick and tile, statuary and, above all, the lush vegetation characteristic of Los Angeles during that period.

The first major building in the Mission Revival style was probably the California Building at the World's Columbian Exposition of 1893 in Chicago. San Francisco architect A. Page Brown modeled its facades after the missions of San Diego and Santa Barbara, complemented by tile roofs and arched windows resembling arcades. The central rotunda had no architectural precedent in the California missions, so Brown borrowed a Moorish roof supported by Moorish colonnades. This style of tile-roofed tower was widely adopted in California Mission Revival architecture as it gained popularity in the late 1890s.

In 1903 William Randolph Hearst began publication of the Los Angeles Examiner, and he commissioned architect Julia Morgan to design his newspaper plant. Her building, completed in 1912, was inspired by the California Building in Chicago. Morgan was the first woman to be trained at L'Ecole des Beaux Arts in Paris, and in the 1920s would be the architect for the Hearst Castle in San Simeon.

Los Angeles Examiner building, lobby.

Fourth was the arcade, often reconstituted as the front porch of a house. On small buildings, a single arch could suggest the entrance to a mission church.

The precise origin of the Mission Revival style has been subject to some debate,[1] but the first major building in the style may have been the California Building for the World's Columbian Exposition of 1893 in Chicago, designed by A. Page Brown of San Francisco. Brown borrowed elements from the Santa Barbara and San Diego missions for the California Building, and on its roof built a semi-tropical garden[2] (see opposite).

If the name of the first architect to put a curved parapet on a house to evoke a mission church has eluded us, the reasons *why* mission forms suddenly became popular are fairly clear. The cataclysmic changes in Los Angeles brought by the Boom of the Eighties may have spawned an exuberant Queen Anne architecture, followed by the rustic Craftsman bungalow, but the rapidity of change also brought forth a surge of interest in California as a romantic landscape—a land not raw and unbounded by tradition as it seemed in everyday life, but a land with a profound history that could serve as an inspiration for a staid society.

This romantic attachment to the past has appeared often in architectural movements, and the value underlying it seems to be that life was different—and better—in earlier times, when people made the things they used and were more satisfied than we are with less than we have. Although accounts of life at the missions hardly bear out the notion that they should serve as a model for modern society,[3] 1890s Angelinos tended to idealize the easy life of the rambling hacienda and incorporate it into their own architecture.

An important contributor to the revival was certainly the novel *Ramona* by Helen Hunt Jackson, published in 1884. The book, which came to be surrounded by a legend that far outstripped its literary merits, was a romance of life in Southern California during the Mexican period, set in rambling adobe homes surrounded by verandas and garden walks:[4]

Cuzner house, 2091 South Harvard Boulevard. The Mission Revival was a popular style for residences, but the link to mission architecture was often only in scalloped parapets and arched windows. This house was built about 1908.

> These verandas, especially those on the inner court, were supplementary rooms to the house. The greater part of the family life went on in them. Nobody stayed inside the walls, except when it was necessary. All the kitchen work, except the actual cooking, was done here, in front of the kitchen doors and windows. Babies slept, were washed, sat in the dirt, and played, on the veranda. The women said their prayers, took their naps, and wove their lace there. Old Juanita shelled her beans there, and threw the pods down on the tile floor, till towards night they were sometimes piled up high around her, like cornhusks at a husking. . . . The benches, which ran the entire length of the walls, were worn into hollows, and shone like satin; the tiled floors also were broken and sunk in places, making little wells, which filled up in times of hard rains. . . .
>
> The arched veranda along the front was a delightsome place. It must have been eighty feet long, at least, for the doors of five large rooms opened on it. The two westernmost rooms had been added on, and made four steps higher than the others; which gave to that end of the veranda the look of a balcony, or loggia. Here the Señorita kept her flowers; great red water-jars, hand-made by the Indians of San Luis Obispo Mission, stood in close rows against the walls, and in them were always growing fine geraniums, carnations, and yellow-flowered musk.

Along with the search for a beneficent heritage, interest in the missions centered on the search for an appropriate Southern California housing type, partly in response to the excesses of the Queen Anne. The great crusader for an indigenous California architecture, and one who carried the Mission Revival into the Craftsman ethic, was Charles Fletcher Lummis, through the pages of his magazine, *Land of Sunshine*.

Charles Lummis and the Crusade for a California Architecture

In 1894 F.A. Pattee began the publication of an illustrated monthly intended for the "people east of the Rockies who are talking and thinking of California."[5] *Land of Sunshine* was a journal in the best booster tradition: it featured articles on the fine streets, beautiful homes, salubrious climate, energetic people, blooming literary talent, rich history, and opportunity for all in Southern California.

Six months after the first issue appeared, Charles Lummis was appointed editor, and he proceeded to guide Easterners to the Southland—and Californians to his interpretation of their own history—for the next fourteen years. Lummis, aged thirty-six when he assumed the editorship, had been born of New England Puritan stock, attended Harvard, wrote two volumes of "Birch Bark Poems" printed on birch bark from the White Mountains, and worked for an Ohio newspaper. In 1884 he decided to go to Southern

California from Cincinnati on foot, which he did in 143 days. His adventure was published in the book *A Tramp Across the Continent*.[6]

During the Boom of the Eighties, Lummis served as city editor of the *Los Angeles Times*, apparently so taxing a position that he suffered a breakdown. He went to New Mexico for recuperation and spent a couple of years living with the Pueblo Indians. He continued writing his impressions of the Southwest, joined Adolf Bandelier on an expedition to South America in 1892, and then returned to Los Angeles and *Land of Sunshine*.

In its pages he was particularly concerned about the appropriate *home*; for the house, its surroundings and its furnishings were crucial to the establishment of the benevolent society of Lummis's vision. He attacked the transplanted Midwestern house in Southern California, writing in 1895 that[7]

> It is broadly true that the average house here is artistically and in convenience an improvement upon the house its self-same tenant occupied in the East. But it is the same architecture—improved only as art has advanced in twenty years. Not one new house in a thousand here has learned anything *locally*. It is still the house of three-foot snows and zero weather, of summer rains, of forest, humid countries—grafted upon a semi-tropic soil whose sky is that of the Arid Lands. Its only adaptation to the new conditions is a pitiful little more of porch and a cheaper construction—since it no longer has to be burglar-proofed against the air of heaven, nor arteried with furnace-pipes.

RIGHT:
Doria Apartments, 1600 West Pico Boulevard, constructed in 1906.

Lummis exhorted his readers to relate to this land in the same way that the Spaniards did: The *adobe house* was the appropriate dwelling for the Southwest. "The adobe was not and is not an institution of

Ivy Substation, Culver and Venice boulevards, Culver City. In 1907 the Los Angeles Pacific Railroad, which operated the electric interurban trains on the west side, erected a number of electric substations and other buildings in the Mission Revival style, including this one in Culver City. A substation reduced high-voltage alternating current to 600 volts direct current for use in the trolley wires. The architect is not known, but may have been a member of the railroad's engineering staff. The Ivy Substation, which was incorporated into the Pacific Electric system in 1911, was in operation until the abandonment of the railroad in 1954. It is on the National Register of Historic Places.

Spain. Garden walls, stables, partition walls, yes—in some little areas of some provinces—but not the adobe house. *That*, the Don learned in America."[8] Mud that could be turned into a dwelling simply by forming it into slabs, piling it up and laying a roof across was found throughout Spanish America. The Spaniard soon learned, according to Lummis, that the adobe house is "fireproof, warmer in winter, cooler in summer, cheaper, more lasting, more comfortable than any other house he could build in any country where adobe still exists."

Many newcomers to Los Angeles simply did not consider building in indigenous materials, and they rejected adobe architecture partly because the things they saw were simple and poorly constructed. That was not the fault of the material, Lummis argued. "The old adobe hereabouts was not often built as workmanlike as we prefer our homes, but neither do the shanties of a lumber camp exactly proclaim all that can be done in wood."[9]

Lummis was not only arguing for the use of adobe as a building material. Rather, he wanted Los Angeles to learn from adobe architecture: thick, insulating walls for comfort, a protected patio for privacy, and a veranda at the front for picturesqueness. He apparently did not view the veranda as particularly useful. The house was not to be a decorated box, but an enclosure that shaded and insulated itself—and looked inward.[10]

Lummis called his readers' attention to examples of domestic architecture he believed to be appropriate to the adobe ethic, and he featured the work of one architect in particular, Sumner P. Hunt. Hunt had written the previous year in *Land of Sunshine* that it was the duty of the new society in Southern

Charles F. Lummis house, "El Alisal," 200 East Avenue 43, Highland Park. Charles Lummis, editor of Land of Sunshine, *founder of the Landmarks Club and the Southwest Museum, and indefatigable crusader for a traditional California architecture, built his own home between 1897 and 1910, using stones from the Arroyo Seco and hand-hewn timbers. Although the house is primarily designed in the Craftsman ethic, it does have arched windows and a curved Mission parapet over the dining room, complete with bell. El Alisal is surrounded by a cactus garden and is open to the public. It serves as the headquarters for the Historical Society of Southern California, and is listed on the National Register of Historic Places.*

California to learn from older civilized societies, and he repeated the then popular refrain that the model for Los Angeles was the Spanish mission.[11] The missions evoked not only a California past; they were linked to the grand Classical traditions of the Spaniards.

As a guide to correct building, the missions were the more important for their imperfect representation of Classical forms. Arthur Burnett Benton wrote in 1911[12] that they possessed "characteristics most admirable in their consistent emphasis of a high ideal in their design and in their very noble use of many base and common materials in their construction"; for "identity and adaptation to environment are fundamental architectural virtues which may, under some conditions, outrank even academic correctness and the niceties of perfected construction."

The mission was the noble savage of architecture. It represented resourcefulness and integrity in the pursuit of a righteous cause. A more apt icon for Southern California could hardly have been found.

Restoration of the Missions

At the same time that buildings looking like old mission churches began springing up all over Southern California, the real missions were still falling into ruins. Apparently many residents of the village of San Fernando in 1895, then a town of "loud saloons," did not even know where the "pile of mud" was situated.[13] A half century of abandonment and the removal of materials for private use,[14] plus to some extent a contempt for what the missions had represented,[15] had taken their toll. The San Fernando mission church

W. F. Holt House, 405 Olive Avenue, Redlands. Designed ca. 1903 by F. T. Harris.

LEFT:

Casa de Rosas, 950 West Adams Boulevard, ca. 1900. Built in 1894 by Sumner P. Hunt, the Casa de Rosas was one of the first buildings in Los Angeles after the Boom of the Eighties to adopt the Spanish courtyard style. The courtyard is beyond the arches to the right. Originally the building was the Froebel Institute, a combination school and residence. Charles F. Lummis saw this building as one of the "fittest and most attractive in Los Angeles," for it paid homage to the Mediterranean architectural traditions he believed were appropriate for Southern California. The construction is cement plaster over metal lath on a frame building.

Beverly Hills Hotel, 9641 West Sunset Boulevard, Beverly Hills, view looking north. In 1912, two years before Beverly Hills was officially founded, Elmer Grey designed this large Mission Revival resort hotel on sixteen acres of open land facing what is now Will Rogers Memorial Park. The hotel and park were landscaped with gardens, palm trees, and grass, which is being watered in this photograph. Originally the hotel was accessible primarily via Pacific Electric interurban trains. Since this photograph was taken in 1920, the hotel has been extensively remodeled and is now hidden among tall trees and surrounding development. In scenes such as this, however, one can see the vastness of the Los Angeles landscape that drew newcomers with unbounded plans, for the land was seemingly limitless.

Granada Shops and Studios, 627 South Lafayette Park Place. Built in 1927, this entire Spanish Revival block is one of the most complete streetscapes of this style in the city and demonstrates the strength of the vision that Los Angeles was destined to be a Mediterranean paradise on the Pacific. It brought a new type of building to Los Angeles—apartments incorporated with shops and studios according to European models. All eighty-four dwellings were reached by exterior balconies rather than interior hallways. The building is one unit, but the architecture was varied for each shop, giving the appearance of many different buildings. It was designed by its builder, Franklin Harper.

Mission Inn, 3649 Seventh Street, Riverside. Mission and Spanish Revival architecture was given one of its most complete expressions in the Mission Inn, built between 1902 and 1931. At the entrance is a campanario complete with bells. The center photograph is of the Rotonda Internacional, built in 1929 to symbolize a desire for world peace.

RIGHT:
Parkhurst Building, 2942 Main Street, Santa Monica. Designed by Norman F. Marsh in 1927, this Spanish Revival store and office building has recently been restored and is listed on the National Register of Historic Places.

was roofless, weeds grew high in the nave, and mounds of debris blocked the doorways (see p. 19).[16] Mission San Gabriel had fared much better because the church was of fired brick rather than adobe and because it had continued in use as a parish church.

The first organized attempt to save the deteriorating missions was concurrent with the earliest Mission Revival period. The Association for the Preservation of the Missions was founded in 1892 by Tessa L. Kelso, head of the Los Angeles Public Library. This group conducted excursions to the missions, gathered pictures showing the need for their protection, and raised funds for preservation. But Kelso left Los Angeles the following year, and the organization languished until 1895, when Charles Lummis assembled its members and formed the Landmarks Club, "to preserve from further decay and vandalism the old Missions of California; to assist in the restoration of such of the Mission buildings as may be found adaptable for uses in harmony with their original purposes; and to safeguard and conserve other historic monuments, relics, and landmarks of the State."[17] The principal organ of the club was Lummis's magazine, whose name changed to *Out West* in 1902. Each month he reported the new members of the club, donations received, the state of the missions, and the progress of the club's works.

The Landmarks Club was concerned primarily with Southern California missions no longer in the possession of the Church. With funds raised through private contributions, it concentrated on the preservation of San Juan Capistrano, San Diego, San Fernando, and Pala, all of which were deserted and in advanced stages of decay. Priority was given to reroofing, clearing debris, and stabilizing the walls of the principal mission buildings, under the supervision of Sumner P. Hunt. Ancillary structures were often ignored, however. The club also sponsored tours to mission ruins and secured leases on several sites to prevent further encroachment.

El Capitan (now Paramount) Theatre and Department Store, 8834 Hollywood Boulevard, 1926. Building designed by Morgan, Walls and Clements; theater by G. Albert Lansburgh.

LEFT:

Million Dollar Theatre, 307 South Broadway. The first major Churrigueresque building in Los Angeles was Sid Grauman's Million Dollar Theatre, designed in 1918 by Albert C. Martin, Sr. The sculpture, by Joe Morra, replaced the religious themes with American whimsy: a bison head, Texas longhorn steer skulls, playing cards, six shooters, and stone maidens. The marquee on Broadway is a later addition. The theater interior, designed by William L. Woollett, borrowed columns and cornices from the Choragic monument to Lycrates. A winged figure representing the West Wind surmounts the proscenium arch, and the walls are covered with Woollett's murals, such as "The Witch Scene from Macbeth."

Religious architecture was not the club's only concern. They worked to save the Los Angeles Plaza and to revive some of the Spanish street names in the city.[18]

Lummis left *Out West* in 1905 to head the Los Angeles Public Library, though he remained as titular editor until 1909. His departure deprived the club of its primary publicity channel, and neither the club nor the magazine recovered from his leaving. By then, however, the missions were the subject of widespread interest, and many were being restored.

The Passing of the Mission Revival

The Mission Revival style lost favor in the teens, though it was occasionally used for at least another decade.[19] Many who experimented with it ended by selecting certain elements and applying them to contemporary buildings, ultimately becoming disillusioned with a basically ornamental approach.

Even admirers of the missions began to admit that emulating their architecture was not an easy road for the designer.[20] The principal frustration was not the style of the missions themselves and the validity of that style for the twentieth century, but the inability of architects to capture the *spirit* of the missions that lay beyond ornamental details. "Ornament is not style," wrote Elmer Grey of the Mission Revival in 1905.[21] "Style is made up of the inherent quality in a building occasioned by its plan, by its site, by local building materials, by the life that goes on within its walls, and only partially by the ornament afterward tacked upon it." If one could only grasp the spirit rather than the ornament of the missions, California would "not need their works as a copy, but could rejoice in them as an inspiration and build our highest aspirations into structures commensurate with our opportunities, as they did with theirs."[22]

The problem seems to have been one that many architects of the period never seemed to grasp: the lifestyle of Anglo California at the turn of the twentieth century was substantially different from that of the Spanish a century earlier. The *spirit* of the missions was the belief in an undefined *better* life in the contemporary period that had little to do with the historical reality of the missions themselves.

Some architectural historians have maintained that the Mission Revival failed as an architectural style. Harold Kirker has written that the open plan and the simplicity of need associated with the mission structures themselves were not adaptable to late nineteenth century building requirements, particularly for commercial buildings.[23] David Gebhard has suggested that it was in fact adaptable (witness the Glenwood Mission Inn in Riverside), but it failed because it was a "naive and puritanical" nineteenth-century style in a period of innovation and mounting aesthetic sophistication.[24] Gebhard believes its longevity was due to its identification with the Craftsman movement, living on its contemporary symbolism rather than its historical identification or its innate qualities. Gustav Stickley, editor of *The Craftsman* magazine, saw it as a contributor to the Craftsman movement, and articles on the Mission Revival began to appear in his magazine. As Earl Pomeroy has suggested, Stickley was "delighted to find a native American tradition of honest craftsmanship, functional and close to the soil."[25]

It is not clear, however, that the style can be dismissed so summarily as a failure. It managed to thrive for a quarter century and to affect the architecture of regions far distant from California. Mission Revival buildings were built in many parts of the United States and elsewhere.[26] Hardly any style has lasted longer in the last century, and indeed many styles that are not thought of as failures (such as Art Deco—see Chapter 6) lasted less than a decade. Mission Revival influenced not only those seeking a revival architecture and provided a thread leading into the Spanish Revival of the 1920s, but it also influenced those looking for new forms. Irving Gill, for example, used mission forms to develop an important precursor to Modern architecture (see Chapter 7). In the long run, Mission Revival has in fact been quite enduring. In the 1980s, it still exerts an influence on architecture in Southern California, in the continuing tradition of red tile roofs and stucco walls.

In the short run, however, it is true that the style did not offer an enduring California architecture hoped for it by its early supporters. It turned out to be primarily a decorative style—and an exterior one at that. "Mission" furniture was actually Craftsman furniture, without reference to the interior decoration of the original missions. In its architecture it hardly lent itself to any significant stylistic development; it

LEFT:
St. Thomas the Apostle Church, 1321 South Mariposa Avenue. Mission Revival architects could make mission elements larger and more precise than could the padres with their crude tools and unskilled labor. St. Thomas the Apostle, designed by the Boston architectural firm of McGinnis, Walsh and Sullivan in 1905, has twin domed towers and a neat stucco facade with an arched doorway and loggia.

BOTTOM RIGHT:
Beverly Hills Water Department, La Cienega and Olympic boulevards. Spanish Revival architecture was applied to a vast array of building types in the 1920s. This tile-roofed cathedral with poured concrete walls, designed in 1927 by Salisbury, Bradshaw and Taylor, is actually the water pumping station for Beverly Hills. Its true function is revealed only when one looks through the rose window above the entrance to find a huge room full of machinery.

Bungalow court, 5740 West Fountain Avenue. One of the most popular styles for bungalow courts in Los Angeles was the Mission Revival, often rendered by a styled parapet capped by a row of red tiles, and a small tile-roofed porch with decorative brackets.

Venice, Cabrillo Canal, early twentieth century.

Venice, California, 1906. One of the grandest statements of the Mediterranean vision of Los Angeles was developer Abbot Kinney's plan to build a Venice of America, complete with canals and gondolas, on the Los Angeles shore. His town was completed in 1905, and the central district along Windward Avenue had the look of an Italian Renaissance street. The arcaded buildings were designed by Norman Marsh and C.H. Russell. Along the canals themselves, however, people generally built small, wooden Craftsman houses. The community was continually plagued by natural and economic disasters, and today only vestiges of its architecture and design remain: the arcaded St. Mark's Hotel on Windward Avenue and the canals south of Venice Boulevard. Venice has long been a center for artists, and this heritage has allowed it to become the center of a new architectural renaissance in the 1980s.

was ultimately static because it focused essentially on certain derivative elements that soon became repetitive and boring. One could make the gable only slightly more ornate than the original mission *espadaña*, or one would risk turning the architecture into Dutch Renaissance, not Spanish. One could pile belfries on top of one another to make a taller tower than the missions ever had, but only at the risk of losing the simplicity that defined the Mission Revival in the first place.

Despite frustration with the Mission style itself in the teens, architects continued to look to Spanish traditions for inspiration, and in 1915 a new patron saint was discovered in the visions of Bertram Grosvenor Goodhue, who brought to California a lavish Spanish baroque style that had also flowered in Mexico. A grand culmination of Hispanic architecture was still to be realized in Southern California. If Junípero Serra had not furnished the inspiration needed to carry on the Spanish architectural tradition, perhaps José de Churriguera, whose spirit was reincarnated by Goodhue in the Panama-California Exposition of 1915, would hold the answer.[27]

California State Building (now Museum of Man), Balboa Park, San Diego. By the 1910s, architects were becoming frustrated with the Mission Revival style, since it was not yielding the true California architecture expected of it. The buildings for the Panama-California Exposition of 1915 in San Diego, by Bertram G. Goodhue, led to a broad revival of Spanish architecture which lasted until the 1930s—and continues to be an important style in Los Angeles today.

TOP LEFT:
Adams Boulevard, looking west from Figueroa Street, ca. 1925. During the 1920s the city spread to the far reaches of the Los Angeles River Basin. Streets became clogged with machines that menaced each other and posed severe hazards for pedestrians, since there was little understanding of the dangers of high speed traffic. The Automobile Club of Southern California building is on the left in this photograph, while St. Vincent de Paul Church, on the right, is still under construction.

BOTTOM:
900 block of State Street, Santa Barbara. In 1925 Santa Barbara suffered a disastrous earthquake. Before then there had been little interest in Spanish architectural traditions, but the Community Arts Association had attempted to instill a public regard for the city's Spanish heritage. After the earthquake, the association turned the destroyed city into a showcase of the Spanish Revival style. State Street was lined with arcades and stuccoed facades that still characterize much of the city.

Panama-California and the Churrigueresque Revival

In 1904 construction had begun on the Panama Canal, a forty-mile channel through the Central American isthmus that, upon its completion in 1914, would bring California 12,500 ship-miles closer to the eastern seaboard of the United States and would open up vast new possibilities for economic growth. San Diego, with a population of 80,000, was the first American port north of the canal on the Pacific. The city decided to promote its advantageous location and to "express the history, resources, prosperity, industries and products, and the golden-lined future promise of the Southwest,"[28] by staging a grand exposition: the Panama-California of 1915.

The theme of this fair was not the usual international Beaux Arts extravaganza, especially since San Diego's rival to the north, San Francisco, was planning that very thing in its Panama-Pacific Exposition. Rather, the San Diego fair would be a statement of local industry, clothed in a Southern California architecture.[29]

Residence, 1498 Sweetzer Avenue. The Churrigueresque was too pretentious for most residential architecture, and a less ornate evocation of Spanish styles was thus chosen for thousands of homes in Los Angeles using red tiled roofs, balconies, arched windows, and stucco facades resembling adobe. The decoration was Spanish, but the house plan was strictly American, yielding a Spanish Revival architecture that would hardly have been seen in Spain.

Hamilton house, 193 North Carmelina, Brentwood. Alongside their work in the Spanish Revival, architects such as John Byers, in the Hamilton house of 1925, were designing in a Monterey Revival style. During the 1930s, when much Spanish architecture fell into disfavor, only the Monterey Revival style continued to be popular. It allowed architects to design in an early California style without perpetuating the Spanish forms themselves. By the 1940s, these styles were so disparaged that owners could hardly find buyers for their Spanish Revival homes.

As overall planner for the spectacle, the architectural firm of John C. Olmsted (son of landscape architect Frederick Law Olmsted) was retained.[30] Irving Gill was early intended to be the principal architect, but the assignment eventually went to Bertram Grosvenor Goodhue, an architect little known in California, but who had visited Mexico and had collaborated on a book about Mexican architecture.[31] He had designed buildings inspired by Mexican styles in Cuba and the Canal Zone,[32] and he saw the San Diego fair as "an attempt to embody the romance of the old Spanish civilization, with its mixture of the spirit of adventure and the spirit of devotion."[33]

The dominant style Goodhue chose was an adaptation of a popular eighteenth-century ecclesiastical architecture, a style born in Spain and brought to florid maturity in Mexico. We call the style Churrigueresque, named after a family of Spanish architects and sculptors who took the Spanish Baroque and transformed it into an almost unrestrained elaboration of ornament that retained only slight suggestions of the Classical forms from which it sprang.[34]

Perhaps Goodhue's greatest achievement at the fair was the California State Building, an exhibition hall in the form of a Churrigueresque cathedral which surpassed anything the real Churrigueresque period actually knew. The opulent stone frontispiece was placed in counterpoint to a 200-foot tower, with three belfry stories surmounted by a tile dome and a great wrought-iron weather vane in the form of a Spanish ship. This magnificent creation stands today in San Diego's Balboa Park as the Museum of Man.[35]

The Churrigueresque was quickly picked up by designers who applied it to large-scale works such as the Million Dollar Theater in Los Angeles (1918; Albert C. Martin, Sr., decorative elements by William Lee Woollett). The niches and escutcheons that would have held saints and angels in their original Churrigueresque incarnation now contained Texas Longhorn steer skulls, with horns attached, and women dangling stone legs over the edge of ornate moldings.

In less ambitious projects, the Churrigueresque was applied to the facades of commercial buildings along many business streets. Today, if one looks to the upper stories along many of the major streets developed during the 1920s, one can see evidence of this exuberant architectural decoration (see p. 127).

Churrigueresque ornamentation was easily adaptable to buildings of any height and type, but it was a bit ornate for most residential structures. Here the interest in Spanish forms created a hybrid domestic architecture of red tile roofs, stuccoed walls, arched entryways, and ironwork balconies that did not follow any particular style. Rather, it was a generic Mediterranean architecture with a Spanish flair that was, in fact, peculiar to Southern California. After the missions, Monterey houses, and Craftsman bungalows, this so-called "Spanish Colonial" style became the fourth major contribution of California to American architecture. In the 1920s it was discussed in the national architectural press as the "California Style," and was exported to other areas of the United States—even to Canada—where there was no pretense of Mediterranean architecture being appropriate for a northern climate. Fine examples of this Spanish style are still to be seen throughout Los Angeles, from the large homes in Palos Verdes Estates to the ornate Spanish apartment houses along streets such as Hayworth Avenue.[36]

The Spanish Revival Institutionalized

The Panama-California Exposition helped to promulgate Spanish architecture as the appropriate California tradition, and soon Spanish forms were adopted as a *leitmotiv* for building types and whole urban districts to which the style had not been previously applied. In 1919, when all of Orange County had a population of 61,000, the city of Fullerton adopted a policy requiring all public and semi-public buildings to follow Spanish styles. The move was a self-conscious statement that the city was established, no longer a desert boom town, and that all matters of public health, safety, and convenience had been ministered to. The new architectural harmony would reflect the "ambition of the people for a more comfortable and beautiful dwelling place."[37]

In 1921, the style was applied to a bank building in Santa Barbara. Hitherto in the United States it was conventional practice to design financial institutions in the style of Beaux Arts Classicism, but suddenly here was a Spanish provincial bank, breaking all norms of form and imagery—and it was heralded. "The building derives directly from the best Renaissance tradition of the church architecture of the Mediterranean countries," wrote Irving F. Morrow.[38] "It realizes the spirit to which the Mission Padres obviously aspired, and which they might have achieved with more competent architectural training and more adequate means of execution."

The institutionalization of the Spanish ethic reached its zenith in Santa Barbara after the 1925 earthquake. Previously there had been some interest in Spanish revival forms in Santa Barbara, but much

Rancho Dominguez, 18127 South Alameda Street, Compton. In 1906 the six Dominguez sisters commissioned architect George Riccard to construct a Mission Revival extension to the original Dominguez ranch house, which had been built about 1827. Riccard designed a U-shaped lath and plaster building facing the Pacific Electric tracks, and used the central court as the setting for landscape gardening. The Dominguez heirs gave the home to the Claretian Fathers in 1924. The grounds are now the Dominguez Memorial Seminary and the house is a museum.

Hotel Green (now Castle Green Apartments), 50 East Green Street, Pasadena, by Frederick L. Roehrig in 1899. In the 1880s, patent medicine magnate Col. G.G. Green invested in an ailing Boom of the Eighties resort hotel project and brought it to completion in 1890. Later that decade he commissioned the architect Roehrig to build an extensive annex to the hotel. The annex stands today as the Castle Green Apartments; the original hotel, which stood across Raymond Street and was connected to the annex by a bridge, was demolished in 1924. The huge Castle Green draws from Moorish architecture in its domed turrets and arched windows, and from the Spanish Renaissance in its balconies and decoration.

Mission Inn, 3649 Seventh Street, Riverside, by Arthur Burnett Benton in 1902. Later additions to 1931 by Myron Hunt, Elmer Grey, and G. Stanley Wilson. The Mission Inn is at once one of the great hotels remaining in Southern California from the turn of the century, and one of the most complete expressions of the Mission and Spanish Revival styles. The first sections of the building, by Arthur Burnett Benton, represent the full expression of the Mission Revival, with curved parapets and mission bells set in niches. Later additions by Hunt and Grey, including the courtyard shown here, borrowed from Spanish Baroque architecture, as the Mission Revival had fallen out of favor by the late teens. Today the building is owned by the Riverside Urban Redevelopment Agency, which is restoring it as a hotel and apartment complex. It is on the National Register of Historic Places.

OPPOSITE:

Powers house, 1345 Alvarado Terrace, by A.L. Haley in 1902. Pomeroy Powers was a real estate developer who laid out Alvarado Terrace and commissioned this Mission Revival home for himself. The style borrowed certain elements from the missions: the arcade; the curved parapet; plus the look of adobe—even though most buildings by the turn of the century were of frame stucco or concrete. Where many Mission Revival buildings were fairly plain in their massing and decoration, in the Powers house the mission elements are taken to fanciful heights.

construction during the Anglo period had followed Eastern architectural styles.[39] The earthquake allowed reconstruction according to a thematic Spanish design plan, and downtown, especially a stretch of State Street, was redesigned with arcaded store fronts. Property owners moved back their facades, constructed arcades along the street—and an old Spanish town arose from the rubble.[40]

As the Spanish look came to dominate much of the Southern California streetscape, however, the inspiration that created the romantic forms seemed to be on the wane. One began to read the same things about Spanish architecture that had been written about Mission Revival a decade earlier. In 1927, Richard Requa wrote,[41]

> If we, of Southern California, are to develop a real architectural style, that will be vital and satisfying and live through the coming generations, we must cease endeavoring to mimic old world styles or contriving tricks, pretenses and shams, just to satisfy the present passion for novelty. We should look to the Mediterranean for inspiration and ideas, but our buildings should express in their design and treatment the spirit of the twentieth century and not of ages that are past and dead . . . ."

The architectural tradition was seen as right; the problem seemed to be the inability of architects to grasp the design lessons believed hidden within the stuccoed walls. Elmer Grey, in his disillusionment in 1929, said that the Spanish style was[42]

> seized upon by untrained amateurs and done and overdone by them almost to death. They construed its adaptability to irregular treatment to mean that almost any arrangement of features would do. They took those which were good in themselves and effective when used in the right places and used them in the wrong places. All sorts of fantastic combinations were strained at in the endeavor to do something new, and that cardinal principle of all good art, namely repose, was either forgotten or never known.

Despite the beauty of its architecture, the city still seemed chaotic, transitory, as though the dynamism of the growing city had overpowered the strength of carefully cultivated traditional forms, had uprooted them and swept them along with it.

Andalusia Apartments, 1471-75 Haven-hurst Drive, by Arthur Zwebell in 1929. Although much of the Spanish Revival was merely decorative, one Southern California housing type made a serious attempt to recreate Mediterranean life-styles. Exotic apartment complexes were built surrounding interior courtyards planted with exotic flora, often with foun-tains and pools. In the balmy Los An-geles climate, the courtyard could serve as an exterior hallway and patio that in colder regions would have to be enclosed.

Spanish Revival apartment houses, Hay-worth Avenue north of Pico Boulevard.

By the late 1920s, Churrigueresque architecture had become as frustrating as the Mission Revival had earlier, but for the opposite reason. If mission architecture could not be further articulated, Churrigueresque elements knew no limits at all. Plain surfaces were necessary to set off the complex ornamentation, and ever greater surfaces of uninhibited decoration would remove any sense of visual organization at all from the building. Architects were thus faced with a dilemma. One could not trace Spanish roots any farther back, and if one crossed the architectural sea to Italy, the search for heritage ended with the Classical forms that had already been blown apart by the overzealous Beaux Arts (see Chapter 5).

The Hispanic architectural symphony remained unfinished. Like a star that burns with blinding brightness before it dies, the architecture of 1920s Los Angeles reveled in a plethora of fantastic forms, all of which were snuffed out with one indiscriminate blow by the economic collapse of the 1930s. Some commissions begun before the Crash were brought to completion, but except for a handful of residential palaces built by movie stars and others who profited from the economic downturn, designers' boards lay idle for five years. When architects picked up their pencils once again, the Mediterranean traditions were hardly to be seen.

In the 1930s, residential architecture continued to look backward for its inspiration, but now to American Colonial and English models. A Monterey Revival arose in those years as well, but it merely allowed architects to design in an "Early California" look without perpetuating the Spanish forms themselves. By the 1940s, unlucky owners of Spanish homes could hardly find buyers for them.[43] In commercial architecture, on the other hand, the look was by then unblinkingly modern.

THE ARCHITECTURE OF HISTORICAL REVIVALISM

Just prior to the turn of this century, central Los Angeles was blossoming into the commercial, financial, and administrative center of a rapidly growing metropolitan area. Los Angeles was no longer a desert boom town, but a respectable city whose population would exceed 100,000 by 1900. As in many American cities, downtown was borrowing its architecture from Classical Rome and the Renaissance, as interpreted by the Beaux Arts movement. With few exceptions it was paying little heed to the Spanish styles popular in other parts of the city.

Downtown in the 1890s

Certain public buildings constructed after the Boom of the Eighties reflected a city confident in its own importance. Whereas the Queen Anne dominated affluent residential architecture of the 1880s and was carried over into bay-windowed hotels and business blocks, public buildings were constructed for the most part in a very different aesthetic. Adopting a respectable style made popular in the East, they tended toward a neo-Romanesque architecture associated with the Boston architect H.H. Richardson.

The major Richardsonian Romanesque monument in Los Angeles, and one of the distinguished architectural creations in the city's history, was the County Courthouse designed in 1888 by Theodore Eisen for the firm of Curlett and Cuthbertson. It was built on a site bounded by Broadway, Spring, and Temple (site of the present Criminal Courts Building), and its red sandstone clock tower stood high over the city on what was then Poundcake Hill. Originally designed with the front facing east, the courthouse was reached by five grand flights of stairs leading to the main entrance under the massive tower. Later, when the population of the city shifted westward, the Broadway side became the front.[1] The building, which proved too small from the time it was opened in 1891, began to dismantle itself in 1918 when stones from the tower started falling onto the pavement below. The top of the tower was removed in that year.[2] The rest of the building was severely damaged by the great Long Beach earthquake of 1933, and was razed in 1935–36.

A Romanesque Revival city hall for Los Angeles was designed in 1888, the same year as the courthouse, by Haas and Caulkin. It stood at the southwestern edge of downtown, on Broadway between

Moorish Revival apartment house, 2627 South Monmouth Avenue, built 1929.

OPPOSITE:
Pasadena City Hall, 100 North Garfield Avenue. Pasadena's city hall of 1927, by Bakewell and Brown, was designed to advertise the beauty of Southern California. It was built in the City Beautiful tradition of monumental public administrative centers, with a domed central tower and cupola supported by Classical Mediterranean pilasters and arched lanterns. Inside, an arcaded ambulatory surrounds a large countyard planted with exotic trees and flowers, with a fountain in the center. The courtyard was built, according to the architects, "on account of the wonderful climate of Pasadena and the possibilities in the way of gardening."

Los Angeles County Museum of History, Science and Art as seen from the Rose Garden, Exposition Park. This Spanish Renaissance Beaux Arts museum opened in 1912 and was designed by Hudson and Munsell as the principal building in what was then Agricultural Park, where local farmers exhibited their bountiful crops. The interior is appointed in fine marbles and a recently restored coffered ceiling under the dome. Today the building is part of the Los Angeles County Museum of Natural History and is listed on the National Register of Historic Places.

Lobby, Fine Arts (now Global Marine) Building, 811 West Seventh Street. Designed in the Romanesque style in 1926 by Walker and Eisen, the building was intended to house artisans. The lobby was "a great exhibition hall of the work of those who will occupy it."

Second and Third. This location helped expand the boundaries of the central city and created a magnet for southward development that would begin in the next decade. The building was razed in 1928, after the present city hall was built (see p. 98).

Today few monuments to this style remain in the area. An exemplary Richardsonian Romanesque residence faced with brown ashlar sandstone and adorned with a crenelated tower and Flemish Gothic stepped gable stands at 2421 Figueroa. Designed by Carroll H. Brown in 1891 as a retirement residence for Chicago lumberman Thomas D. Stimson, the house today serves as a convent. In addition, the old Orange County Courthouse in Santa Ana is a late (1901) building in this style.

Business building facades erected around Third Street after 1890 took on a conservative mantle of brick with reserved, Classical trim. The earliest of those still remaining has a facade mildly reminiscent of the Romanesque, with arched windows on the upper story. It is a transition building combining the Romanesque Revival, the Queen Anne (in the castiron railings and elevator cages of the atrium), and Beaux Arts Classicism (in the castiron Corinthian columns supporting the balconies in its interior space). The Bradbury Building, as it is known, was commissioned by Louis Bradbury as a testament to his social stature and to the fortunes he amassed from his mines in Mexico. He had already hired Samuel and Joseph Cather Newsom to design for him one of the city's most extravagant Queen Anne mansions on Bunker Hill (see p. 176), and he then turned to Sumner P. Hunt to design his business block.

Hunt's design for this building is not known, but apparently Bradbury was dissatisfied with it and asked George H. Wyman, a draftsman in Hunt's office, to amend the plan. According to Esther McCoy, who interviewed Wyman's daughter in 1953,[3] Wyman was intrigued by Edward Bellamy's novel, *Looking Backward, 2000-1887*, which described a utopian civilization of the year 2000. In Bellamy's book, a typical commercial building would be "a vast hall full of light, received not alone from the windows on all sides but from the dome, the point of which was a hundred feet above. . . . The walls were frescoed in mellow tints, to soften without absorbing the light which flooded the interior."[4] (See p. 193).

Wyman apparently created his vision of the year 2000 using the materials and conventions of the 1890s. The central court is not domed but is covered with a pitched canopy of glass. It is surrounded by balconies fronted by ornate balustrades in shaped wood and castiron, with open stairs cascading down each end. Sun reflected from the yellow brick walls fills the entire space with a soft light.

As one steps into the Bradbury's atrium one enters a world unlike anything else to be experienced in the city. The building stands as a unique burst of creative genius, but when it was new, the interior was little noticed, and descriptions spoke primarily of the fine exterior.[5] George Wyman never created another masterpiece like it, and the next year Sumner P. Hunt designed a traditional office block diagonally across the street.[6] He created a respectable facade of fluted Ionic pilasters, but no hall of light, no soaring ironwork. Now called the Pan American, this building still stands much as originally designed.

In 1898 the San Francisco firm of Reid and Reid designed the five-story Douglas Oil Building at Third and Spring. It has a rounded Italianate facade with reserved decor, also drawing no lessons from the Bradbury. These buildings, plus a handful of others in various states of alteration,[7] give us our only glimpse of the commercial architectural trends of the 1890s. Within the next decade, taller and more elegant Beaux Arts structures would move the business center several blocks to the south.

The Los Angeles Building Height Limit, 1905-1957

During Los Angeles's formative years as an American metropolis, as Spring Street and Broadway were becoming the city's financial and commercial centers, not a single tall building rivaled the skyscrapers of eastern cities. Only since the 1960s have true skyscrapers become part of the skyline: downtown, along Wilshire Boulevard, and in Century City. One may imagine that the low profile of the city was the result of abundant available land on the periphery, but in fact the retention of this low scale was a deliberate policy of the city from 1905 to 1957. The building height regulations referred primarily to structural safety, but beneath the pragmatic rationale there may have been a more important motivation— a commitment to maintain an appropriate scale for the city.

At the turn of the century, discussions over preferable architectural styles were accompanied by an uncertainty as to the safety and durability of structural materials. Prior to 1899 there was not even a building code in Los Angeles that set forth standards for safe construction,[8] and subsequently a heated debate among architects ensued over the relative safety of steel frame versus reinforced concrete for tall buildings.[9]

Amidst this debate, in January of 1903, the Los Angeles City Council appointed a committee composed of architects John Parkinson and John C. Austin, and five other building professionals, to amend

Los Angeles County Courthouse, view looking west from Spring and Temple streets. By the Boom of the Eighties, Los Angeles had outgrown the old courthouse in the Temple Market Block. A larger courthouse, shown here, was built in 1891 south of Temple Street between Spring and Broadway, designed by Curlett and Cuthbertson in the neo-Romanesque style then popular in the East. The new courthouse also proved too small, however, and in 1910 a new Hall of Records (on the left) was built to provide additional space. After suffering extensive damage in the Long Beach earthquake of 1933, the courthouse was razed in 1936 and its cornerstone placed as a monument on the lawn of the present courthouse. The Hall of Records was razed in 1959, and today this site is occupied by the Criminal Courts Building. An illuminated sign on the tower in this photo from about 1910 says "Welcome."

the city's building ordinance and introduce appropriate safety standards.[10] The result was a law adopted in December, 1904, and effective in February, 1905, that among other things imposed a height limit of 55 feet for wood frame buildings, 80 feet for Class "C" buildings, 100 feet for Class "B" buildings, and 130 feet for Class "A" buildings. The latter class includes steel-frame and reinforced concrete skyscrapers. Unfortunately, no final report submitted by this committee has come down to us, and the reasons why these limits were imposed—nearly a year and a half before the San Francisco earthquake of 1906—are not known.[11]

The ordinance brought repeated petitions for variances to allow the construction of buildings exceeding these limits.[12] In 1910 the City Planning Committee urged the City Council to deny *all* applications for variances to the height limitations. Structural safety was not mentioned in this appeal, but rather "the development of our great city along broad and harmonious lines of beauty and symmetry."[13] The Legislation Committee recommended that height limits be incorporated into the City Charter "so that any future change shall have to be decided by a vote of the people."[14] This charter amendment, which provided that buildings were not to exceed 150 feet in height, was approved in 1911. Public buildings and monuments were exempted from the regulation, church towers and spires could be exempted by the City Council, but commercial and industrial buildings could be exempted only by a vote of the people.

The charter section was amended in 1923 so that no building could exceed 150 feet in height within the district bounded by Temple, San Pedro, Figueroa, and Pico. Buildings outside this district could be exempted by the City Council, although after 1925 the Council was empowered only to exempt buildings in industrial zones outside the central district.

The height limitation was in effect until rescinded by the voters in 1957—when the city had attained a population of over two million persons. A 1956 report by the Los Angeles City Planning Department stressed the structural safety discussions in reviewing the history of the regulation; it appears that the major earthquakes occurring after the adoption of the law provided a rationale for it that was not intended by its original framers. Although the term "structural" was used in the 1905 regulations, reference to earthquake protection was totally absent. Since the voting public could not be expected to judge the technical merits of an application to exceed the height limitations, it seems that more important to the argument in favor of the electorate being the final judge of variances was the perceived role of building height in affecting the city's visual quality.[15]

Beaux Arts Los Angeles

Following the World's Columbian Exposition of 1893 in Chicago, probably the greatest statement of Beaux Arts splendor ever created, Beaux Arts principles became the standard for large-scale architecture for over three decades. Particularly in institutional and commercial buildings, the Beaux Arts ethic dominated nearly every American city, including downtown Los Angeles.

A Beaux Arts facade was generally styled after the three horizontal divisions of an Italian Renaissance *palazzo*. Traditionally, the *palazzo* rested on a "basement" which was half above ground and faced with smooth or rusticated stone. Above it was the *piano nobile*, the main floor of the house, often recessed slightly from the basement and differentiated in style and facing material. Above the *piano nobile* was the "attic," an imposing roof or upper story, usually more ornate than the features below it and crowned with a Classical cornice. Beaux Arts architects used these elements freely, but maintained their basic relationships.

The decoration of Beaux Arts buildings was derived from a broader historical field within the Western European tradition. Sometimes it borrowed from Imperial Roman architecture: fluted Ionic or Corinthian columns, large arches, surfaces of gray granite. At other times it borrowed from the Renaissance or Baroque, making use of such things as glazed terra cotta facing. These decorative elements were frequently exaggerated or over-elaborated in an attempt to achieve originality and excitement.

The name "Beaux Arts" is taken from the school in Paris, whose teachings strongly influenced American architectural thought at the turn of the century. Students at l'Ecole des Beaux Arts studied the greatest buildings and architectural texts of Roman antiquity and the Italian Renaissance, and from them derived the foundations for an architecture deemed appropriate for the modern city. Even Los Angeles came under the influence of the movement, although of the architects practicing in the city during the early twentieth century, only G. Albert Lansburgh had actually attended the Ecole, in 1906. Later, Stiles O. Clements studied there as well.[16]

Perhaps the most complete statement of Beaux Arts ideals in Southern California is the Riverside County Courthouse (1903–04; Burnham and Bliesner), with paired columns marching across its huge porch and robed figures rising like torch flames from the flanking towers that resemble triumphal arches. In Los Angeles itself, one of the most prominent surviving examples is the County Historical and Art

LEFT:

Herman W. Hellman Building, 354 South Spring Street. Aside from the Hispanic Californios, nearly everybody in Los Angeles at the turn of the century had immigrated there. Herman W. Hellman came from Bavaria in 1859 and started a wholesale grocery business. In 1903 he summoned St. Louis architect Alfred F. Rosenheim to design a Beaux Arts office block on his homesite. The building, with its marble lobby and grand staircase, was restored by the Banco Popular de Puerto Rico in 1974. Photograph ca. 1910.

BOTTOM RIGHT:

Braly Block, 408 South Spring Street. John Parkinson and Edwin Bergstrom designed this building to be the tallest in the city when it opened in 1904. Then, the site was on the edge of downtown, and the ornate attic made the building visually striking from the city center a few blocks to the west. As the Braly Block was being completed, Parkinson was serving on a committee that would draw up a height limit for Los Angeles, leaving the Braly Block one of the city's tallest buildings for half a century.

Fourth and Spring streets, ca. 1900. The Hellman Building replaced several small shops and the Hellman home on the left, built in the 1870s.

Broadway-Spring Arcade Building, 540 South Broadway and 541 South Spring Street; Spring Street facade. Until the early 1920s a small shopping street passed from Broadway to Spring Street at this point. When he designed this twelve-story office building, architect Kenneth MacDonald retained a glass-roofed shopping arcade—a simplified version of the Burlington Arcade in London—where the street had been. The Spanish Renaissance Beaux Arts building was completed in 1924.

TOP LEFT:

Stowell (now El Dorado) Hotel, 416 South Spring Street. The Gothic imagery of the Stowell Hotel, designed in 1913 by Frederick Noonan and William Richards, was unusual for buildings of that period. The twelve-story reinforced concrete building also had colored terra cotta on the facade—Gothic-inspired designs in terra cotta would become popular in Art Deco architecture a quarter century later. White terra cotta molded in leaf patterns is contrasted with green enameled brick. Today the building is part of the Spring Street Financial District listed on the National Register of Historic Places.

TOP RIGHT:

Pantages Downtown Building (now Theatre Jewelry Centre), 655 South Hill Street. A Baroque domed corner tower dominates this former Pantages Theatre of 1920, designed by B. Marcus Priteca.

Museum (1912; Hudson and Munsell), now part of the Los Angeles County Museum of Natural History in Exposition Park. It faces a sunken, formal rose garden, whose axis it shares. Less elaborate than the Riverside County Courthouse, it features two low, tile-roofed wings of red brick, with a central entrance hall surmounted by a truncated dome.

The Beaux Arts skyscraper was an American contribution to the movement. The *palazzo* form could be stretched to include many floors, creating Renaissance palaces of unprecedented height in the skyward-reaching American cities of the early twentieth century. In Los Angeles, a conservative but well executed vision of Beaux Arts Classicism began to unfold along Spring Street after 1900. Two fine buildings still standing at Fourth and Spring began a southward expansion that, by the 1920s, would transform the street into the financial capital of Southern California.

The first of these was not only the first true Beaux Arts building in the city, it was also substantially taller than the buildings from the 1890s to the north. In 1904 John Parkinson completed the Braly Block (now the Continental Building) at 408 South Spring. Its twelve stories soared above its neighbors, and the ornate attic of the two top floors, along with the exaggerated cornice, served as a beacon to attract the attention of persons in the center of town, about three blocks away.[17]

At about the same time, Herman W. Hellman, who had come to Los Angeles from Bavaria in 1859 and had developed a successful wholesale grocery business,[18] hired St. Louis architect Alfred F. Rosenheim to design a bank building on the Hellman homesite across the street from the Braly Block. Rosenheim created an eight-story Italian Beaux Arts office block, the lower stories faced with native gray granite and the upper stories with gray pressed brick. Decorative elements are of cream-colored terra cotta. This building has been restored by the Banco Popular de Puerto Rico, which has retained the original stained glass skylight and marble grand staircase in the lobby.

Rosenheim went on to design other notable Beaux Arts buildings in Los Angeles, including the A. Hamburger and Sons store (now May Company) at Eighth and Broadway in 1907. Faced with ornamental castiron on the lower two stories and cream-colored, glazed terra cotta on the walls above, this building was the first in the city to be designed expressly for a store with many "departments." It included innovations that have become standard, such as escalators, employee lounge, roof garden, and cafeteria.[19]

By the 1920s, Spring Street from Third to Eighth was lined with handsome Beaux Arts buildings, including several more by John Parkinson—certainly the dominant architect of downtown Los Angeles. Today, downtown Los Angeles contains one of the best collections of early twentieth-century Beaux Arts commercial buildings of any city. In the decades following their construction, however, Beaux Arts buildings were little appreciated—they were in fact one of the prime targets for excoriation by Modern Movement architects. Thus, some buildings have been remodeled and their cornices removed. One of the most beautiful Beaux Arts interiors remaining downtown is the elegant bank lobby of the Hellman Bank (now Bank of America) by Schultze and Weaver (1924) at Seventh and Spring streets (see p. 193).

Toward the end of the 1920s, financial institutions began to erect buildings in the "Moderne" styles that were replacing what was by then considered the old-fashioned Beaux Arts. But it is primarily the tall, heavy, elaborately decorated buildings that make Spring Street one of the most interesting architectural districts in the city. In 1979 the rich architectural heritage of the district was recognized when the Spring Street Financial District was placed on the National Register of Historic Places.

Beaux Arts architecture was too monumental for all but the most pretentious residential palaces; thus it is seen infrequently in domestic architecture. There were, however, other evocations of Classical architecture that were widely used. The American Colonial Revival, in particular, had wide currency. It was first seen in Los Angeles in the mid-1890s, and became increasingly correct in its adherence to the pure Classical forms of the Georgian and Federal periods. From bungalows to mansions, houses were built with front porches supported by Doric columns, and roofs ending in crisp pediments. The style flourished until about 1915, when the importance of archaeological correctness began to stifle architectural creativity; it has, however, had a continuing influence on American domestic architecture.[20]

The Civic Center: Crown of the City Beautiful

That the formal space at the nucleus of a settlement serves to identify it has been known in many civilizations. In Los Angeles, for example, the design of the Plaza was the subject of detailed requirements under the Laws of the Indies during the Spanish period. At that time, the plaza was conceived of as a meeting place, a pivot of the social life of the community. In the twentieth century, this central place has often been designed as a center of public administration, as a Civic Center.

Second Church of Christ, Scientist, 948 West Adams Boulevard. Alfred F. Rosenheim's third major commission in Los Angeles, after the Hellman Building and the May Company at Eighth Street and Broadway, was this Italian Renaissance church with a lofty Corinthian entrance portico. The foundation of the reinforced concrete building was sheathed in light gray granite, and the walls were covered with dull glazed white brick and terra cotta. Its copper dome is now weathered to a green patina. The leaded glass windows were designed by the architect.

LEFT:

Pacific Mutual Building, northwest corner, Sixth and Olive streets. Beaux Arts architects applied Classical motifs to their buildings, often in a freehand and exaggerated fashion not appreciated by later followers of Modern architecture. This photograph shows the building as it was originally designed by Parkinson and Bergstrom in 1908. It still stands, but in 1937 Parkinson and his son Donald stripped the Beaux Arts frills from the facade and replaced them with the plain Moderne exterior one sees today. In 1908 this building towered above its surroundings on the edge of downtown, but today it is overwhelmed by the taller buildings around it.

Our modern conception of a civic center was formulated largely within the City Beautiful movement that arose before the turn of the century. Its ideas were partly a response to the crowded, chaotic, and sooty cities that had accommodated themselves poorly to the demands of industrial society. The problems of the cities seemed almost insurmountable to turn-of-the-century planners, but one could at least build dramatic monuments as symbols of municipal order and tranquillity amidst the general disarray.

Large-scale buildings, handsome boulevards, parks, gardens—and, above all, an administrative center for government—were thought of as symbols for a humane society in the industrial era. Architecturally, the City Beautiful was closely linked to the Beaux Arts movement; great fairs such as the World's Columbian Exposition provided a vision of a city inspired by Classical architecture more grandiose than had ever been known in Greece and Rome.

By 1900, Los Angeles was large and unkempt enough to warrant the same attention from City Beautiful builders that larger eastern cities demanded. First, Los Angeles had to live up to the image of an escape from the East that had been created for it in nationwide promotion.[21] Second, there was genuine idealism that Los Angeles could become a wholesome living environment even for those who did not share its prosperity.[22] The first organized City Beautiful effort in Los Angeles was an art committee, established in 1903 to encourage an interest in civic improvement. Two years later this committee was

Proposed Administrative Center for Los Angeles, 1923. City Beautiful proposals for central cities often included a monumental civic center as a focal point. Several proposals for Los Angeles were prepared in the 1920s, including this by Cook and Hall of 1923. The proposed civic center stands along a grand promenade, replacing Spring Street north of First, and is closed at the north end by a towering Hall of Administration. Behind it is a union railroad terminal. The old Los Angeles Plaza is the circular park in the upper middle of the sketch, the Hall of Justice, which still stands, is seen here on the corner of Temple and Broadway, and to the south is the old Hall of Records, now demolished; none of the other buildings was ever built.

Subway Terminal Building, 417 South Hill Street. To provide downtown Los Angeles with rapid transit access from the west side and the San Fernando Valley, a tunnel was built in 1925 from First Street and Glendale Boulevard to an underground station at Fourth and Hill streets. The Subway Terminal Building, designed in 1926 by Schultze and Weaver, was constructed over the station.

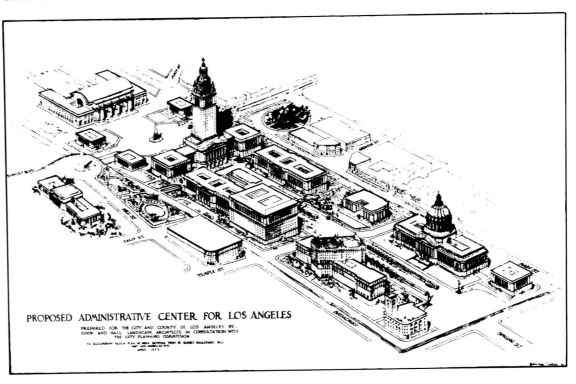

PROPOSED ADMINISTRATIVE CENTER FOR LOS ANGELES

PREPARED FOR THE CITY AND COUNTY OF LOS ANGELES BY
COOK AND HALL   LANDSCAPE ARCHITECTS   IN CONSULTATION WITH
THE CITY PLANNING COMMISSION

formally constituted by the city as the Municipal Arts Commission, whose duty was to review plans for public buildings according to aesthetic criteria. Since 1980 called the Cultural Affairs Commission, this body continues to serve the same function today.[23]

Through the efforts of the Municipal Arts Commission, Charles Mulford Robinson, a planner from Rochester, New York, and spokesman for the City Beautiful movement, was hired to prepare a city plan for Los Angeles.[24] His plan, published in 1909, included a large administrative center at Spring and Temple streets, which would be complemented by an elaborate, colonnaded Court of Honor leading to a public library and museum.[25] Robinson's plan was too costly to implement, but his ideas were not forgotten. In 1918, Mayor Woodman appointed a Civic Center Committee under William Mulholland, Chief Engineer for the city's Public Service Department. The committee, after extended public debate, recommended the site of the old Temple Market Block for the civic center. The Romanesque county court house near the site was to be replaced. In 1923 the matter was taken to the voters, who formally approved a site bounded by First, Sunset, Hill, and Los Angeles streets.

Also in 1923 the City Planning Commission, under the chairmanship of Sumner P. Hunt, commissioned a comprehensive plan for an administrative center by W.D. Cook and George D. Hall, landscape architects.

Hall was a graduate of L'Ecole des Beaux Arts, and his design for the civic center (opposite) was a visionary statement of monumental, Classical order. A long axis north from Spring Street led past the Hall of Records, built in 1910, and the Hall of Justice already being planned. The axis rose to a towered, symmetrical temple of a Hall of Administration, behind which was a large *piazza* serving as the forecourt to a union railroad terminal. Flanking the Spring Street axis were a city hall, and state and federal buildings fronted by Greco-Roman colonnades. The old Los Angeles Plaza was to be preserved as a park next to the Hall of Administration.[26]

Other plans for a civic center were prepared in the 1920s, most notably by the Allied Architects of Los Angeles in 1924.[27] Their Beaux Arts vision for the civic center was partially carried out in their Hall of Justice (1925), a fourteen-story temple in gray granite on North Broadway. It stands today as the only completed Beaux Arts building from any of the early plans. In 1927 a combination of the Cook and Hall and Allied Architects plans was officially adopted, but cost, controversy, and eventually World War II prevented its implementation.

In the meantime a new Los Angeles City Hall was built in 1926–28, replacing the old Romanesque city hall on Broadway. It was designed by a consortium of blue-ribbon architects (John C. Austin, John Parkinson, and Albert C. Martin, Sr., with interiors by Austin Whittlesey). No longer adhering to a strict

LEFT:
Forum Theater, Pico Boulevard at Norton Avenue. The colonnaded facade of this Beaux Arts theater, designed by Edward J. Borgmeyer, contrasts with the small commercial buildings that surround it. In 1924, when the theater was completed, it was in a suburban location, part of the newly expanding development along major new boulevards such as Pico.

Evans house, "Sunshine Hill," 419 South Lorraine Boulevard. Designed by I. Eisner ca. 1910.

Beaux Arts convention, the building combines monumental Classical elements with simple planes and volumes that anticipated the Moderne styles of a few years later.

The main entrance to City Hall from Spring Street is through a colonnaded Greek forecourt with Romanesque arches. Rising up from the building's center is a "glistening-white tower, in appearance similar to a campanile, with its vertical lines and the peristyle at the upper stories, so designed that the effect as viewed from distant points is most impressive."[28] The tower was impressive partly because the Colonel Charles A. Lindbergh Airway Beacon at its apex rose to a height of 452 feet above Main Street, hovering far above the 150-foot height limit imposed on other buildings in the city.[29] John C. Austin wrote in 1928 that the stepped-back tower and the flanking wings were to be regarded as "modern American," influenced by the setback style widely adopted for tall buildings.[30] City Hall, then, was to be Los Angeles's only tribute to the New York skyscraper. It remained the tallest building in the city until the height limit was rescinded in 1957.

The Hall of Justice and City Hall were the only major buildings in the planned civic center to be built in the 1920s. Although more large public buildings were constructed later, the civic center has never attained a sense of unity. It is traversed by major streets, its large public spaces are unrelated to each other, and the architecture of the district is in no respect unified. Subsequent wartime and postwar growth diverted attention from the civic center as a monumental urban space, and eventually the Hollywood Freeway would bisect the district as conceived by Cook and Hall. The buildings of each period seem to stand alone, each making an uncompromising architectural statement of their own time, their own function, and their own designer.

The Movie Palace

Beaux Arts architecture lent itself to a monumental grandeur that could sweep the ordinary city dweller into a fanciful world of beauty and order. In no building type did it lead more easily to uninhibited expression than in the theater. Los Angeles has had five major theater districts in its history; the first is near the Plaza and includes the Merced of 1870. By the 1890s, a second theater district was developing along Main Street.[31] A decade later the two large vaudeville circuits—Orpheum and Pantages—decided to locate new theaters on Broadway; their designs, in 1910, by G. Albert Lansburgh and Morgan and Walls, respectively, were instrumental in creating the city's third and most elegant theater district, along Broadway. The fourth district, from the 1920s, was along Hollywood Boulevard, and the fifth district is today in Westwood.

The Broadway Theater District expanded from Third to Tenth streets in the teens and twenties. The Orpheum built a second and larger vaudeville house south of Eighth Street in 1925, designed by G. Albert Lansburgh. In 1927 S. Charles Lee recreated a small-scale copy of the Paris Opera lobby in the Tower Theater at Eighth and Broadway. In the same year United Artists, a distribution company founded by Mary Pickford, Douglas Fairbanks, Charles Chaplin, and D.W. Griffith, commissioned Detroit architect C. Howard Crane to design the Spanish Gothic United Artists Theatre at 929 S. Broadway. The lobby is in the form of a Spanish cathedral, with vaults and frescoes. The United Artists was the only Broadway theater built as a flagship house by a major studio, since most première theaters were in New York City at that time.

RIGHT:
Los Angeles City Hall, interior.

Los Angeles City Hall, 200 North Spring Street, built in 1928 and designed by John C. Austin, John Parkinson and Albert C. Martin. City Hall combines a monumental Classical architecture with the simple planes and volumes of the Moderne. The main entrance from Spring Street is through a colonnaded Greek forecourt with Romanesque arches. Rising up from the building's center is a glistening white tower similar to a campanile. At its apex the Colonel Charles A. Lindbergh Airway Beacon rose to a height of 452 feet above Main Street, hovering far above the 150-foot height limit imposed on other buildings in the city. The stepped-back tower and the flanking wings were influenced by the New York setback style, making City Hall Los Angeles's only tribute to the New York skyscraper, and the tallest building in the city until the height limit was rescinded in 1957.

Four years later, in 1931, the Los Angeles Theater, the most magnificent of all, opened on Broadway south of Sixth Street. Its lobby resembles a split-level version of the Hall of Mirrors at Versailles. Down two flights of a grand staircase and through the ballroom was a restaurant, and to the side a ladies' restroom with individual rooms rather than stalls, each appointed in a different marble. On the ballroom wall was a periscope screen, where smokers or those waiting for seats could watch the picture being shown upstairs. When it opened, the theater offered such luxury items as electric cigarette lighters, crystal chandeliers, and a crystal fountain at the head of the staircase. For the convenience of patrons, a light board in the lobby showed which seats were vacant.

The Broadway theaters stretched the limits of the Beaux Arts imagination. Their neo-Baroque interiors were not even intended to follow accepted architectural principles; rather they became creative revival styles in their own right.

Extravagant theater decoration was a conscious attempt to provide an environment of escape for a new kind of audience. Before the advent of motion pictures, it had been a luxury to attend the theater, beyond the means of most people. Movies, however, were from the beginning available to all at a moderate price. People of all backgrounds could sit side by side in the darkened auditorium and enjoy the same performance in equal comfort. Designers created theaters that provided thrilling surroundings which ordinary people could never afford in their own lives; where, for brief moments, even the day laborer could "revel in luxury and costly beauty." According to Ralph Sexton in his 1927 book, *American Theaters of Today,* "The design of the average modern motion picture theater is elaborate in the extreme; it is a mass of ornament, rich in color, and gorgeous in decoration. It makes the appeal to the masses to whom it caters because in their eyes it is wonderful, beautiful, and luxurious."[32] The bright marquee beckoned to all those who passed by, and the ticket booth was placed outside, at the center of the entrance near the street, so that to purchase a ticket one never needed to pass through doors or other obstructions that could make one feel unwelcome.[33]

Los Angeles Theatre, 615 South Broadway. The last of the great motion picture palaces built downtown, the Los Angeles was opened in 1931. Its architect, S. Charles Lee, modeled the lobby after the Hall of Mirrors at Versailles, complete with a crystal fountain at the head of the grand staircase. Down two flights of stairs and through the ballroom was a restaurant for theater-goers. Amenities included a ladies' restroom with individual rooms rather than stalls, each appointed in a different marble; a periscope screen on the ballroom wall projected the film being shown upstairs; and an electric light board indicated which seats were vacant.

During the 1920s, however, even as the finest of Broadway's theaters were being built, the city was expanding far beyond its old center. "Hollywood" was becoming the capital of the motion picture industry, and new première theaters were built on Hollywood Boulevard. There in 1925, Morgan, Walls and Clements created El Capitan (now the Paramount) as a Churrigueresque theater and office building, with an ebullient East India theater interior by G. Albert Lansburgh that has since been remodeled. Two years later Lansburgh designed the Gothic-Renaissance Warner Theater (now the Pacific), with two dirigible mast radio towers on its roof. These and other theaters joined with the two expressions of pure exotic fantasy, the 1922 Egyptian Theatre and the 1928 Chinese Theatre, both by Meyer and Holler, and the Art Deco Pantages Theatre of 1930 by B. Marcus Priteca (see Chapter 6), to make Hollywood Boulevard the city's fourth première theater district.

Since the 1960s the première theaters have moved to Westwood, but the movie palace is no longer part of theatergoing. Two of Westwood's theaters are housed in converted supermarkets, and others are in new buildings that offer no competition to the visual spectacle shown on the screen.

Today there remains on Broadway an incomparable legacy of palatial theaters still largely intact. In 1979, the Broadway Theater and Commercial District, including ten of the area's theaters, was placed on the National Register of Historic Places. It is the only historic district in the United States in which theaters constitute a principal theme. Also included in the district are many fine Beaux Arts and Art Deco commercial buildings, along with the Bradbury Building's hall of light.[34]

Exotic Historical Architecture of the 1920s

On October 18, 1922, Douglas Fairbanks in *Robin Hood* opened a new motion picture theater on Hollywood Boulevard. This theater was unlike anything Los Angeles had seen before; in fact it looked unlike a theater at all from the entrance forecourt. A sign over the entrance said "Grauman's," but in all other respects the building was an Egyptian temple, approached through a long, narrow courtyard studded with Egyptian ornament and lined with shops selling exotic merchandise.[35]

Grauman's (now Mann's) Egyptian was not the first exotic building in Los Angeles. In 1913 the architect Franklin M. Small had taken the Japanese influence in Craftsman architecture to its furthest extreme by creating a sixteenth-century Japanese palace called Yama Shiro ("The Castle on the Hill") in the Hollywood Hills.[36] The Egyptian Theatre, however, was symptomatic of the whole development of exotic historical architecture in Los Angeles, and the first to catch the imagination of the city. Why the architects, Meyer and Holler, chose the Egyptian motif is not certain. It was not Howard Carter's opening of Tutankhamun's tomb, for the theater opened more than a month before Carter entered the inner sanctum on November 26, 1922.[37] One might look to events in Egypt itself, for in the teens there had already been notable archaeological discoveries in the royal tombs at Thebes and Lahun. One may also, however, look closer to home for inspiration. Especially in Los Angeles, one may look to the movies. The early cinema showed a fascination for exotic settings and the landscapes of antiquity. D.W. Griffith's *Intolerance* of 1916 depicted the fall of Babylon to the armies of Persia, using the most colossal set that had ever been constructed for a motion picture. Not only could this conglomeration of parapets and towers be seen on the screen by those who could sit through its three-hour length, it could be seen first-hand for years afterward in a lot on Sunset Boulevard. The architecture wasn't exactly Egyptian, or Babylonian, but the effect was a general pharaonic epic grandeur.[38]

Whatever its sources, an Egyptian Revival spread beyond Grauman's during the mid-1920s—to bungalow courts, to apartment houses, and even to a tomb at New Calvary Cemetery, outfitted with battered walls and lotus-flower capitals in bright colors that evoked ancient Egypt.

Other Oriental forms abounded as well. The Japanese Yamashiro was matched by a "northern Chinese" building at 46 North Robles in Pasadena (1924; Marston, Van Pelt and Maybury) to house Grace Nicholson's art objects. It is adorned with green tile roofs, finials, and foo dogs. The greatest pseudo-Chinese monument in Los Angeles was built in 1927 by Sid Grauman and designed by Meyer and Holler. The Chinese Theatre was created to be "totally unexpected and spectacular," and to use "the tremendous possibilities of the style for picturesque and dramatic expression" to develop its "mythical and fairy-like potentialities."[39] The interior was, and is, even more lavish than the exterior, decorated primarily in red. The Chinese motifs are really Chinese Chippendale rather than true Chinese, however. No detail was left untouched: dragons and Oriental plant motifs covered rugs, seats, ceiling, walls—even the water faucets in the lavatories were designed to look Chinese (see p. 195).

Another historical style, the Moorish, had been woven through the entire history of Hispanic architecture in California. It was found in the original missions, as in the interior window arches in the *convento*

Egyptian Revival bungalow court, 1428 South Bonnie Brae. Although the Egyptian Revival was a popular style in the 1920s, it had appeared earlier as in this bungalow court from about 1916. The inspiration was probably Hollywood movies with exotic Oriental settings—not King Tut.

LEFT:

United Artists Theatre, 913 South Broadway, designed in 1928 by C. Howard Crane. Photograph of auditorium, 1928. Theater interiors bespoke elegance, created with inexpensive materials such as plaster. The auditorium ceiling is a gigantic sunburst surrounded by intricate Spanish tracery and includes circular mirrors and crystal pendants which were spotlighted to reflect glittery light patterns on the audience.

Brand Library, "El Miradero," 1601 North Mountain Street, Glendale. In 1904 Nathaniel Dryden designed a Saracenic mansion for his brother-in-law Leslie Brand, a founder of the Title Insurance and Trust Company. Dryden took his design from the East Indian Pavilion of the 1893 World's Columbian Exposition in Chicago. The Moorish theme was carried out in details such as geometrical decorations on wall surfaces, bulbous domes, minarets and horseshoe arches, the interior, however, was strictly Victorian. Today the Brand estate is a public park and library maintained by the city of Glendale.

at San Fernando. In its early days the Mission Revival was often referred to as the Moorish Style, and buildings such as the Philharmonic Auditorium (1906; Charles F. Whittlesey) were elaborate Moorish evocations. It flowered again as an exotic style in the 1920s, perhaps influenced by motion pictures such as *The Thief of Bagdad* (1924). In 1926 the Shrine Auditorium, Al Malaikah, was completed (designed by G. Albert Lansburgh); it was not merely a flamboyant theater with Moorish arches and domes, it was the largest theater in the world. A flurry of stucco-box Moorish apartment buildings were constructed in the late 1920s, and in 1928, architect Hugh Davies designed the Moorish exhibition buildings of the Pacific Southwest Exhibition in Long Beach, where lath-and-plaster stuccoed walls created a North African feudal city for six weeks on the California shore.[40]

A less exotic but certainly as romantic a style, the French Chateauesque, flourished in the 1920s as well. It had been a minor style in Los Angeles since the 1890s,[41] and in 1912–13 Arthur Burnett Benton had designed the Chateauesque Mary Andrews Clark Memorial Home at 306 Loma. According to one architect of the period,[42] it was the First World War that brought the style to a new flowering in the United States. Young architects had returned from France with visions of the Chateaux of the Loire and Normandy, and by the mid-1920s were recreating these castles in Los Angeles. Lofty spires accentuated the height of a building, and the style allowed a freedom in the arrangement of windows and rooms that made the style particularly popular for apartment houses. High above Sunset Strip stands the Chateau Marmont (ca. 1925), and on the shores of Long Beach is the Villa Riviera (1929; Richard D. King), a fifteen-story apartment building surmounted by a steep, pitched roof and a tower.[43]

In one style, architecture left the world of adult fantasy to enter a childhood forest of grotesque witches' homes. One of the first of these "Hansel and Gretel" houses was the Spadena house at Carmelita and Walden in Beverly Hills, designed by Henry Oliver in 1921 as the office of a movie production company. The house is actually quite large, but it looks like a miniscule hut jutting up from the wild overgrowth. Windows appear crooked, although they are not, and the impossibly steep roof sweeps upward to form a caricature of a house that one could find in a fairy tale.[44] Olde English imagery was employed in many other homes of the twenties, where bulbous, irregular roofs rolled down over the walls, suggesting a thatched cottage. Casement windows with diagonal leaded glass panels, simple board

RIGHT:

Spadena house, 516 Walden Drive, Beverly Hills. The English cottage and the brooding Medieval forest were popular images in 1920s architecture, and these images were often taken to the fanciful extremes found in fairy tales. Thus the style is called "Hansel and Gretel." The Spadena house was built in 1921 as the office of Irvin C. Willat Productions, a film company in Culver City, and later moved to this site. The architect, Henry Oliver, "tried to reproduce a tumble-down structure of two centuries ago, " said the newspaper release, "but which will be equipped with the most modern office appurtenances." The house is large but looks small; the windows are straight but look crooked; and an oversized broom sits on the roof.

Aztec Hotel, 200 Foothill Boulevard, Monrovia. Robert B. Stacy-Judd spent much of his professional life in a quest for the true American architecture; he settled on the Mayan as the most appropriate tradition. The Aztec Hotel of 1926 was one of his first opportunities to test his theories, but not knowing the significance of the original Mayan motifs, he applied them to the hotel according to his own fancy. He named the hotel the "Aztec," because the word sounded better than "Mayan."

doors, and rough plastered walls gave a brooding, Medieval look to the simple bungalow.⁴⁵

At the opposite end of the exotic architectural spectrum was Pre-Columbian architecture. The Mayan in particular was the subject of serious interest by Frank Lloyd Wright. Other architects also saw this tradition as the fount of an "All-American Architecture," in the words of the Mayan's greatest crusader, Robert Stacy-Judd. Stacy-Judd designed the Aztec Hotel (1925) in Monrovia, a building not particularly innovative in plan, but which is decorated with a mass of loosely adapted Mayan ornament. Since he was not sure what the significance of original Mayan motifs were, Stacy-Judd "did not duplicate any particular original panel of the temples, but assembled the curious units to [his] own fancy."⁴⁶ His theoretical probes became more intense in subsequent years, as he embarked on expeditions to the Yucatan to find the sources of Mayan architecture, reporting his grueling hardships in *The Architect and Engineer* in 1933–34. The most dramatic example of his work is the First Baptist Church (now the Ventura County Church of Religious Science) in Ventura, completed in 1931.⁴⁷ A stepped, organ-like tower shoots above the front entrance in a fashion dubiously Mayan but clearly Art Deco.

These exotic revival forms leapt back into remote history, but the very act of such daring demonstrated both the freedom of architectural expression that developed during that decade, and the high level of creativity that was allowed to flower in the search for new imagery. The twenties was a period of very little dogma. These exotic styles were all derivative; they were based on some historical architecture or perhaps on folklore, but other than in their exuberance they did not attempt to create wholly new motifs.

A Note on Pershing Square

There are only two public open spaces in downtown Los Angeles that can be called parks. The first is the lawn of the Central Library, and the second is Pershing Square. As noted in Chapter 2, Pershing Square had been left as unsold land from the original pueblo holdings, when all surrounding tracts had been purchased by private landowners. In 1866 concerned citizens interested in preserving this last parcel of open space in collaboration with owners of surrounding property who thought a park would increase their land values, succeeded in having it officially declared a city park.⁴⁸

LEFT:

Samson Tire Factory, 5675 Telegraph Road, City of Commerce. In 1929, Los Angeles was the second largest tire manufacturing center in the world. One of the four major tire plants in the city was Adolph Schleicher's Samson Tire and Rubber Company, built in that year and designed by Morgan, Walls and Clements. It was designed as an Assyrian palace presumably to associate the style of the building with the name of the company. Little was known about ancient Assyrian architecture at the time, but the architects faithfully recreated architectural details from several ancient temples. Not a reconstruction of any one temple, the innovative design created a distinctly twentieth-century building in the Assyrian manner. The factory has been renovated to serve as a contract furnishings design center.

Norman Bungalow Court, 2906 Griffith Park Drive, ca. 1925. One of the popular architectural images in 1920s Los Angeles was that of the medieval forest. Here, eight dimimutive Norman cottages line a winding path leading to a little tower at the rear.

Known as Central Square, plus a few other names in its early years, the park was first used as a campground for travelers entering the city. By 1870 pressure was mounting for its improvement, aided partly by disgust over the condition of the Plaza and partly as an early booster effort to attract new residents. The square was plowed, graded, planted, and fenced. A row of trees graced its perimeter, and axial pathways bisected it, but in general it was, as W.W. Robinson has suggested, a "most casual" plan for a park. Trees and shrubs had been set out in random fashion by well-meaning donors, and the principal use was perhaps as a shortcut for pedestrians and wagons, despite signs at the entrances that said "Heavy Teams are Forbidden to Cross the Park."

In 1886, the city adopted a proposal by Fred Eaton, then city engineer and later mayor. His was the first official site plan, and it incorporated a maze of graveled pathways. These pathways divided ornamental

RIGHT:

Philharmonic Auditorium, 427 West Fifth Street; 1906, Charles F. Whittlesey. The Philharmonic Auditorium was touted as California's largest reinforced concrete building and the largest theater west of Chicago in 1906, when structural systems for large buildings were still experimental. Built to house the Temple Baptist Church, with office spaces on Fifth Street, it was the home of the Los Angeles Philharmonic Orchestra from 1920 until the completion of the Music Center in 1964. Whittlesey, a native of Illinois who had been trained in Louis Sullivan's office, was chief architect for the Santa Fe Railroad and designed a number of Mission Revival hotels and stations in the Southwest. Claud Beelman removed Whittlesey's Moorish exterior in 1938 and replaced it with the Moderne facade seen today. Whittlesey's original theater interior, still intact but hidden by remodeling, is similar to that of Sullivan's Auditorium Theater in Chicago.

plots of grass which were sprinkled with flower beds shaped like crescents and stars. In the center was a scalloped design filled with plantings that was later replaced by a bandstand.

By 1910, the vegetation and trees were becoming closely packed, the lawns were dying, and the trees were decaying.[49] In that year John Parkinson was hired to turn the park into a "broad, well-kept, well-shaded sward." He laid wide paths from each corner and replaced the bandstand with a large bubbling fountain. Tropical foliage was planted along the pathways, trees were thinned out, and ornamental street lights provided nighttime illumination. A decade later, coco palms and banana trees were growing in the park, which had been renamed in honor of General Pershing.

The present design of Pershing Square, by Stiles Clements, dates from 1951, when the park was excavated in order to build a subterranean garage. Today, trees stand in planters, and benches huddle

Pershing Square, 1929. In 1910, John Parkinson had redesigned Central Square, as it was then called. He laid out wide paths, installed a large bubbling fountain, and planted tropical foliage. The park was renamed in honor of General John J. Pershing in 1918. To the far left, the camera looks south on Hill Street. In the center is the original Pacific Mutual Building (1908), to the right of which is the Biltmore Hotel (1923) and the original Philharmonic Auditorium.

LEFT:

Philharmonic Auditorium today. To the left is the Title Guarantee building, designed in 1929 by John and Donald Parkinson.

Villa Riviera Apartments, 800 East Ocean Boulevard, Long Beach. Architect Richard D. King enlarged an English Gothic chateau to create this sixteen-story luxury apartment house on the shore of Long Beach in 1928. It is faced with stucco and art stone.

around a square pool with pipes spraying small shafts of water into the air. Pershing Square is now essentially an underground building with a roof of grass.

The City Expands

Downtown Los Angeles was a successful urban center by 1920, containing more than seventy-five percent of the city's commercial and professional businesses.[50] It was so successful, in fact, that traffic congestion in its streets as early as 1911 reached the point of near immobility. During rush hours, jams of trolley cars covered nearly every foot of trackage in the central city.[51] A decade later the streets had to accommodate heavy automobile traffic as well as trolleys, and by 1924 over a million people per day—more than the entire population of the city—were traveling to and from downtown.[52]

In an attempt to avoid congested streets, the retail shopping center retreated from Broadway to the southwest and by 1930 centered on Seventh and Hill.[53] The financial district, however, remained on Spring Street, and was enhanced by several new Art Deco buildings such as the Title Insurance and Trust and Los Angeles Stock Exchange. These will be discussed in Chapter 6.

Contrasting with the impossible congestion of downtown were the open stretches of the Los Angeles Basin, served by over 1,000 miles of Pacific Electric interurban trackage which could whisk passengers between destinations without hindrance. Trains avoided downtown streets after 1925 by entering a tunnel

Hall of Justice, United States Court House, Triforium.

near First Street and Glendale Boulevard and traveling underground to the Subway Terminal Building at Fourth and Hill streets (1925; Schultze and Weaver), an Italian Renaissance Beaux Arts office building the lobby of which was a huge railroad station concourse.

The juxtaposition of a clogged central area surrounded by accessible open space became particularly apparent in an auspicious period for new urban expansion. Los Angeles was becoming a center for two industries that experienced explosive growth in the teens and twenties: petroleum and motion pictures.[54] New employment opportunities plus the continued promotion of Southern California's year-round balmy climate,[55] led to a new population boom that far overshadowed the Boom of the Eighties. Between 1920 and 1930 over a million people migrated to Los Angeles County, ninety-six percent of whom settled in the cities.[56]

During the 1920s the city began to move away from downtown, reaching out along broad boulevards built for a new public—the automobile driver. Architects increasingly turned their backs on Classical styles to embrace sleek, modern motifs which would dominate architectural practice for the next half century.

6

LOS ANGELES AS THE CITY OF THE FUTURE

Transcontinental automobile travel had somewhat the same relation to the Boom of the Twenties that the completion of the railroads had on the Boom of the Eighties. Southern California was the goal of the first great migration of the automobile age, and in 1923 and 1924 a one-way stream of automobiles could be seen moving westward.[1] The transformation that turned much growth away from downtown accompanied the new acquaintance with the automobile, an acquaintance we now take for granted but which one lifetime ago was unknown.

In the preindustrial city, travel was the privilege of the wealthy.[2] The trains and trolleys, bicycles and ships of the nineteenth century gave a new mobility to those who, in earlier periods, would have had only their feet to propel them, but they had to go when and where the public conveyance went. It was the *auto-mobile*—whose essence was signified in the name itself—that would allow the masses the same privilege of protected, unhampered movement that had previously been reserved for the wealthy. Particularly after 1908, when the Model T Ford was introduced, and as street paving technology provided durable, all-weather roads, barriers to mobility began to fall quickly away.[3]

Even before the automobile became the dominant form of transportation, the open spaces of Los Angeles had been touted as part of the new paradise. In 1911, for example, an article in *Sunset* would boast that[4]

> during September, 1910, sixty percent of the 900 permits to build in Los Angeles were issued for individual homes. Since the average home site in Los Angeles exceeds fifty feet in width, the new residences represented a frontage of four miles and a half, or fifty-four miles of new dwellings in the course of an average year. Cities five times the population of Los Angeles cannot point to an achievement of equal proportions.

New communities were springing up at scenic locations throughout the Los Angeles Basin. Hollywood was developed beginning in 1903 as a carefully planned subdivision. Beverly Hills began as a town in 1906, when El Rancho Rodeo de las Aguas ("Gathering of the Waters") was sold to the Rodeo Land and Water Company, which "planned a city of homes, platted wide streets, picturesque hill roads, large lots, parkways and the leisurely, spacious layout for a village de luxe."[5]

Los Angeles Central Library, detail. Sculpture by Lee Lawrie depicting the allegory of the progress of learning, 1926.

OPPOSITE:
Winnie and Sutch Company, 5610 South Soto Street, Huntington Park; ca. 1935.

The new districts were served by the interurban electric railway system of the Pacific Electric and its predecessors, but by 1920 speculators were beginning to bet on the automobile as the transport of the future. A.W. Ross bought eighteen acres of land along Wilshire Boulevard—then a two-lane country road—halfway between Los Angeles and the beach, at the center of a circle that included the wealthy areas of Hollywood, Beverly Hills, Westlake Park, and West Adams. By the end of the decade, despite a lengthy zoning fight with downtown business interests who rightly saw his development as a threat, Ross created a prestige shopping district called the Miracle Mile. The district was a linear shopping street, but different from its predecessors. Access to the Miracle Mile was to be primarily by *automobile*.

Ross first persuaded Desmond's, an old downtown firm, to open a branch there. Its towered building, by G. Stanley Underwood (1928–29) at 5514 Wilshire, became the flagship of an entire Art Deco retail district which was enhanced in the late 1930s by prestige department stores such as the May Company (Albert C. Martin, Sr. and S.A. Marx), and the Coulter Dry Goods Company. Coulter's had been located downtown at Seventh and Olive, but in 1938 the old store was abandoned and the entire operation moved to the Miracle Mile. Coulter's building, one of Stiles Clements's masterpieces of 1930s Streamline architecture, was demolished in 1980.

A second entrepreneur who saw the potential of Wilshire as a prime shopping district was John G. Bullock, who had opened a downtown store in 1906. In the late 1920s he decided to open a new store

Westwood Village, looking north on Westwood Boulevard from Wilshire, late 1930s. Within a decade the Mediterranean village atmosphere of Westwood had been usurped by the automobile. The city had developed a skyline of tower signs to attract the motorist from afar. In this photograph are seven advertising towers rising above supermarkets, gas stations, and theaters, plus the original Holmby Hall tower in the center background, to the right of the tallest palm tree. The large building with the corner turret in the center of the photograph, originally Ralphs market, is today a restaurant, and the domed building with the arched entrance, to the left of Ralphs, was the sales office for the developers of the tract and is now a savings and loan. Many of the buildings along Westwood Boulevard remain, though most have been remodeled.

on the west side of Westlake (now MacArthur) Park. Wilshire Boulevard did not traverse the park until 1934, so that the new store was isolated from the central city but within easy reach of residents in Hancock Park and other wealthy areas. He commissioned John and Donald Parkinson to create an elegant emporium in the most modern Art Deco style. The result is one of the city's architectural masterpieces. The asymmetrical stepped forms on the exterior are covered with oxidized copper plates and buff terra cotta, and the interior is a stunning display of glittery surfaces and artistic designs. "Every detail, from drinking fountain to clock, ventilator grille, mirror, hinge, has been creatively evoked from the future and not from the past";[6] Beaux Arts revival styles were consciously rejected.

Westwood Village was also developed in the 1920s as an automobile-oriented shopping center, nestled at the base of the new southern campus of the University of California. The shopping center along Westwood Boulevard was intended to look like a Mediterranean town, and an art committee was set up to review all building designs and to control the size and style of signs. Photographs of Westwood from the 1930s show a serene and isolated group of fine stores along a broad boulevard with palm trees and exotic flora.[7]

The automobile allowed new developments like Westwood to be located farther away from the city center and built at a lower density than previously, but it also imposed new constraints on their commercial architecture. First, visibility became paramount. In an effort to put goods closer to buyers passing in their cars, the display of merchandise took on a new importance, and the show window of the commercial shop increased substantially in size. The door no longer bisected the facade but was placed at one end to open up new expanses of glass for display—thereby reducing the space available for architectural decoration. The ultimate showroom was for the automobile itself; the entire facade became a sheet of glass, and the only decoration was a little window trimming and perhaps a tile roof. Spanish and Classical motifs became fairly irrelevant.

One of the most dramatic show window facades in Los Angeles is carried by the E. Clem Wilson building at Wilshire and La Brea (1930; Meyer and Holler). A two-story glass curtain sweeps around the corner, jutting far out from the recessed office tower. At present the glass is partially covered with panels, but in 1930 The Architect and Engineer wrote, "The building being situated at two of the major traffic arteries of the city has made desirable the provision of show window display space for the entire street fronts of the second story, offering an opportunity for the tenants to appeal to the great number of people passing the building in machines. This, in turn, has also resulted in influencing the architectural design of the lower portion of the building along strictly modern lines with large areas of plate glass and small structural members of metal."[8]

A device commonly adopted to lure the motorist close enough to see the window was the tower. The centerpiece of Bullocks Wilshire is a 241-foot tower that took advantage of every provision in the building

LEFT:

Westwood Village, looking south on Westwood Boulevard from LeConte Avenue, 1930. Westwood Village was a real estate development on the old Rancho San José de Buenos Aires, huddled at the entrance to the new UCLA campus. It was designed as a Mediterranean hill town, with red-tile-roofed buildings such as Holmby Hall (1930; Gordon B. Kaufmann), shown in this photo. Palm trees lined the median of Westwood Boulevard, and the bases of the ornamental street lights were clad in colorful Spanish tiles. The photograph is from California Arts and Architecture, *July 1930.*

RIGHT:
Desmond's, 5514 Wilshire Boulevard. During the 1920s, A. W. Ross established a new shopping district along Wilshire Boulevard in what was then open country. He persuaded Desmond's, an old downtown firm, to open a branch there. Desmond's towered Art Deco building of 1929, designed by G. Stanley Underwood, became the flagship for an entire Art Deco retail district which came to be called the Miracle Mile.

E. Clem Wilson Building, 5225 Wilshire Boulevard. Designed in 1930 by Meyer and Holler, the Wilson Building took advantage of its location at a major intersection by providing show window display space for the entire street frontage of the second story.

ordinance to obtain the maximum possible height. It was intended to be visible from afar and was built "for the advertising value such a lofty landmark would possess."[9] In the Pellissier Building at Wilshire and Western (1930-31; Morgan, Walls and Clements) the entire corner building is a height limit tower, with flanking wings containing two-story shops. Even in Westwood, the tower came to dominate the skyline by the late 1930s. Not only did Holmby Hall have a tower, so did gas stations, supermarkets, and theaters, until much of the city became a landscape of towers intended to be seen above their neighbors.[10]

Another effect of the automobile on commercial architecture was on parking. The automobile, unlike the streetcar, had to be parked if the customer were to reach the store. Thus in the late 1920s, the new stores began to turn their backs on the street, placing the main entrance at the rear facing a large parking lot. Shoppers at Bullocks Wilshire drove under a large *porte-cochère* where, protected from rain or sun, they would alight from their machines and have them parked by an attendant. In the next decade, the May Company, Coulter's, and other stores had entrances from the parking lot that were more elegant than their street entrances.[11] The first automobile-oriented shopping center was not in Los Angeles,[12] but these stores contributed to its evolution. The final step was merely to put the parking lot in front,[13] ultimately destroying the urban quality of the street which was still evident in the Los Angeles developments of the twenties.

The Superhighway and the Parkway

Between 1923 and 1931 the population within ten miles of central Los Angeles increased by fifty percent, but the number of people entering downtown increased only fifteen percent.[14] The remaining traffic was headed to other locations. Competing with the Pacific Electric lines in the 1920s were several new "superhighways," as they were called, that traversed the basin. Pico Boulevard was widened to a seventy-foot thoroughfare in 1926 to connect downtown Los Angeles with Santa Monica.[15] Wilshire Boulevard, which began as a dirt road in 1909, was widened and paved from Westlake Park to the ocean in the 1920s, and cut through the park to downtown in 1934. Accompanying the new streets and boulevards were a series of fine bridges such as the Macy Street Viaduct, designed in a Spanish motif with street light standards inscribed with the city seal, or the Hyperion Avenue viaduct joining Atwater and Silver Lake, both spanning the Los Angeles River.

Except for a greater width and more durable materials, these highways were similar to roads extending far back into history. They were lined with homes and businesses, their edges served for parking, and they were intersected by roads and driveways. The automobile would demand a new kind of highway, one that was first developed in Germany during the 1920s:[16] the limited access road, where vehicles

TOP LEFT:

Hyperion Viaduct, by the Bureau of Engineering, City of Los Angeles in 1928. A 24-foot timber trestle produced regular rush-hour traffic jams where Glendale Boulevard crossed the Los Angeles River. The solution was the Hyperion Viaduct which provided a junction with newly constructed Hyperion Avenue. Ornamental pylons marked the ends of the 135-foot arches, and post-top street lights lined the railings.

Plan and Elevation of the Colorado Street Bridge, Pasadena. The drawing is from Engineering News, *July 24, 1913.*

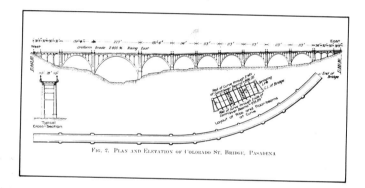

FIG. 2. PLAN AND ELEVATION OF COLORADO ST. BRIDGE, PASADENA

Los Angeles is endowed with a vast array of ornamental street lights from the early decades of this century, when companies would vie for contracts to install distinctive lighting systems in new thoroughfares. Lights from the late 1920s are seen along Santa Monica Boulevard in Beverly Hills (left) and on Wilshire Boulevard near MacArthur Park, from 1934.

BOTTOM LEFT:

Beverly Hills. Cañon Drive, looking southeast, 1910.

entering and leaving traffic would do so at controlled angles at specified points. Early designs incorporated a swath of greenery adopted from City Beautiful ideas to turn the street into a "parkway." In 1940 the first of these in Los Angeles was built along the Arroyo Seco to Pasadena.[17] The Arroyo Seco Parkway, now the Pasadena Freeway, became the first link in a freeway system that would eventually supplant the Pacific Electric as the city's primary transportation network. The parkway was perhaps the ultimate expression of the role of the automobile in urban life, for its green spaces were closed to pedestrians. They served as a landscaped environment for automobile travel in the city.

Art Deco in Los Angeles[18]

The 1920s was a period of tremendous creative energy in architecture, and in Los Angeles it was probably the decade of the city's greatest architectural achievement, given the outpouring of traditional styles, the burgeoning work of the revolutionary modernists (to be discussed in Chapter 7) and the immensely popular and colorful style we call Art Deco. Consciously rejecting historical evocations, the

Samuels-Novarro house, 5699 Valley Oak Drive, designed by Lloyd Wright in 1928. In one of the few Mayan Art Deco houses to be built in Los Angeles, Lloyd Wright turned his father's precast concrete blocks into pressed metal panels to highlight the stucco walls. Lloyd Wright was originally a landscape architect and maintained a deep interest in the relationship between house and ground. This home, once owned by actor Ramon Novarro, straddles a natural ridge.

Art Deco style was founded on a twentieth-century aesthetic and the future promise of the great liberator, the machine.[19]

The sources of imagery used in Art Deco architecture have been extensively studied.[20] They may be traced through cubist and expressionist art and the interest in Pre-Columbian forms, all stylized to give various elements the hard lines of machine-age technology. The great Art Deco exposition itself, the 1925 Paris spectacle of "decorative and industrial arts" that gave its name to the movement, had little to do directly with architecture. However, its requirement that no traditional forms be used either in the buildings or exhibits demanded the creation of a new, modern aesthetic.[21]

Although the path toward a modern aesthetic had already been broken by early masters such as Irving Gill and Frank Lloyd Wright, Art Deco was the first *popular* leap into modernity in American architecture. Characteristic of the style was a totally new look for commercial and multi-family residential buildings. Few single-family homes were designed in the Art Deco style. The Samuels-Novarro house by

Lloyd Wright was one of the rare exceptions. Any resemblance to the Renaissance *palazzo* was swept away. No longer was there a basement, nor a *piano nobile* or attic surmounted by a cornice. The lines of a building, particularly a tall one, soared skyward in an unbroken sweep, often in stepped sequences to a tall central tower. The facades were usually enhanced by decorative zigzags, stylized motifs of plants, geometric forms, and bas-relief sculptures of sinewy human figures.[22] Interiors were clad in marble, glass, and metals in lavish modern designs as well. Art Deco buildings tended to be expensive, reflecting an age of prosperity and material splendor, and many buildings carried this decorative richness to the exterior, using glazed terra cotta, metal, and polychrome designs.

Art Deco stylizations often conveyed an image of motion, which would be fully amplified in the Streamline Moderne designs of the 1930s. This fascination with motion and modern transportation may be seen in the mural under the *porte-cochère* of Bullocks Wilshire. The central figure is winged Mercury, surrounded by a Graf Zeppelin, an ocean liner, railroad train, and a Maddux Airlines airplane, which flew

Garfield Building, 403 West Eighth Street, lobby. The two-story lobby of this tan sandstone Art Deco building, designed in 1930 by Claud Beelman, is appointed in Italian marble, bronze and castiron, with a gold leaf ceiling. The six wall niches are framed in German silver.

from Los Angeles to San Francisco in the late 1920s as one of the earliest scheduled passenger airlines.

In some cases traditional concrete and stucco were used as exterior facing. The Los Angeles Central Library (1926; Bertram Goodhue), the great precursor to Art Deco in Los Angeles, is faced with smooth stucco. The Elks Club at 607 South Park View (1927; Curlett and Beelman), which adopted Goodhue's decorative scheme of cast figures at the upper building corners, is also stuccoed, reinforced concrete.[23] Granite was used in buildings that required an expression of stability, as in the Los Angeles Stock Exchange (1930; Samuel E. Lunden).

The material which could express the full richness of Art Deco motifs was, however, polychrome terra cotta. Especially in the Los Angeles version of Art Deco, highly glazed terra cotta in dazzling colors was applied to highrise buildings in a burst of color never known before or since. The Richfield Building glistened in shiny black, with cast figures in gold adorning the parapets and marching around the first floor. This color scheme was not always regarded as tasteful, but it never ceased to be noticed. Even today, more than a decade after its demolition, it has not been forgotten.[24] Two reminders of black-and-gold terra cotta architecture are the bank buildings at 4300 West Third Street (ca. 1928) and at 5209 Wilshire (1929; Morgan, Walls and Clements).

A spectacular use of polychrome terra cotta which still survives is on the Eastern Columbia Building at 849 South Broadway (1929; Claud Beelman). Its green, blue, and gold facades rise to a huge, neon-lit clock tower that once chimed the quarter hours.[25] One enters the building through a golden sunburst with flamboyant zigzags shooting skyward, originally leading into an interior arcade dividing the two stores on the ground floor. The sunburst is complemented by an Art Deco terrazzo design on the sidewalk. The Pellissier Building at Wilshire and Western (1931; Morgan, Walls and Clements) is sheathed in turquoise terra cotta.[26] Smaller buildings faced in blazing colors include the J.J. Newberry Co. (1928) at 6600 Hollywood Boulevard and the old Hollywood Citizen News Building at 1545 North Wilcox.

Not only was the decorative treatment of an Art Deco building iconoclastic, the entire aesthetic imposition of the building on the street went through a transformation. The Beaux Arts building was earthbound, solidly rooted in a foundation and delineated by the cornice. The Art Deco building looked skyward; its vertical pulsations aspired toward the unknown future and exercised a visual power over the

Eastern Columbia Building, 849 South Broadway, entrance detail. The blue, green, and gold Eastern Columbia Building expresses the soaring pulsation that was a hallmark of Art Deco architecture. The golden sunburst over the entrance peers out from behind vertical bands shooting skyward to the huge clock tower which was originally illuminated with neon. When the building was new in 1930, this entrance led to an interior arcade lined with show windows for the two stores occupying the ground floor. Terra cotta was used extensively as a facing material in Los Angeles partly because the usual materials—marble and granite—were not available locally. The architect of the Eastern Columbia was Claud Beelman.

OPPOSITE:

Los Angeles Central Library, 630 West Fifth Street, rotunda. The entire composition of the Central Library, designed by Bertram Goodhue and completed posthumously in 1926, is an allegorical portrayal of the theme "Light and Learning." Dean Cornwell covered the rotunda walls with over 9,000 square feet of murals depicting the four great eras of California: Discovery, Mission Building, Americanization, and Founding of Los Angeles. The Cornwell murals are important examples of civic mural painting in the pre-WPA period.

streetscape which had not been known before. It was not only the creative power of machine technology, but the power of the built environment, the power created by human design. This power was expressed by the exaggerated verticality which swept the eye upward in awe even with the relatively low Los Angeles skyscrapers such as the Eastern Columbia. The Southern California Edison Company Building (now One Bunker Hill) by Allison and Allison (1930–31) was described in *Arts and Architecture* as "Power Personified in Stone and Concrete." "The white austerity of its massive bulk provides a strikingly effective contrast to the delicate, feathery olive trees, the smooth green lawn" of the "peaceful garden terrace of the Public Library" across the street.[27]

The verticality and the message of power were both expressed through the frequent use of Gothic elements—particularly the heavy towers, sometimes supported by stylized flying buttresses as in the Eastern Columbia or the Title Guarantee Building (1929; John and Donald Parkinson) at Fifth and Hill. "There is a thrilling beauty to the tower; a message in modern tongue, but the same message as in the days of Gothic art."[28]

Bullocks Wilshire, 3050 Wilshire Boulevard. In 1929, when Wilshire Boulevard did not yet cut through Westlake (now MacArthur) Park, John G. Bullock built a branch of his fine department store in this location to attract a wealthy clientele from Hancock Park and other westside districts. The style of the building was the latest trend, Art Deco, which eschewed all historical references. The main entrance to Bullocks is from the rear, under a porte-cochère with a ceiling mural by Herman Sachs entitled "The Spirit of Transportation" (left). The interior, designed by Eleanor Lemaire, Jock Peters, and Feil and Paradise, was planned in a series of boutique spaces. Walls of the elevator lobby (right) are rose marble, with highlights in bronze, copper, and gunmetal. Architects for the building were John and Donald Parkinson.

This sense of power was enhanced through illumination. By day towers served as landmarks, but by night they were illuminated by floodlights to cast an imposing glow over the street. The tower of the Title Guarantee Building with its flying buttresses was lighted at night. The Richfield Building tower was not only illuminated, it was surmounted by an openwork "dirigible mast" with the word "RICHFIELD" in huge neon letters.

The development of neon lighting in the 1920s provided a versatile art form that bathed the viewer in light as never before. Illuminated signs took on fantastic shapes and became much larger than previously possible; facade elements of buildings could be highlighted at night, and the bright neon tubes could even be seen by day. The now demolished Carthay Circle Theater (1926-27; Donald Gibbs) had a "color cap," a basket weave of neon tubes placed over the topmost dome of the floodlighted tower.[29] Even swimming pools could be given a soft neon illumination with underwater tubes.[30] Although most of the original neon from this period is now gone, its evocative power can be seen in films such as Busby Berkeley's *The Gold Diggers of 1933*.[31]

Metal was also embraced in new decorative applications. It was the ultimate machine product, material of the machine itself, of the motor car. Steel alloys, bronze, and aluminum were used as decorative accents for bas-relief sculptures, and most particularly, in screens. Metal screens helped exert the power of buildings by allowing the viewer to see through them but not penetrate them. "Just enough material for protection, just enough material through which to gaze," wrote William Garren in 1930.[32] The parking lot of Bullocks Wilshire is guarded by an ornate metal gate, as is the garage of the W.P. Story Building at Broadway and Sixth, designed in 1934 by Stiles Clements. Grills also cover the narrow windows of the Los Angeles Stock Exchange. Screens were used symbolically as well. The second-story openings of the Title Insurance Building at 433 South Spring (1928; John and Donald Parkinson), in addition to the front entrance, are covered with zigzag floral screens. Grillwork runs around the Cherokee Street facade of the Shane (now Hollywood Center) Building (1930; Norton and Wallis) at 6652 Hollywood Boulevard. Bronze was particularly applicable to monumental doorways, and could be cast in intricate patterns. The Los Angeles Stock Exchange is entered through two twelve-foot-high bronze doors, each weighing one ton and hung on ball-bearing pivots.[33]

Sheet metal found new applications as well. Copper panels, now oxidized, adorn the exterior of Bullocks Wilshire. Since the fifty-foot top of the tower was built as a "sign" under the Los Angeles building code, it is made entirely of metal, and the material with its motifs was carried through all the spandrels of the lower stories, determining much of the design and color of the building.[34]

Despite attempts by architects to reject what were believed to be the tyranny of Classical motifs, by

Coca-Cola Bottling Plant, 1334 South Central Avenue, designed in 1936 by Robert V. Derrah. The interest in speed and streamlining that characterized the depression era was at times expressed literally in architecture. The Coca-Cola plant, a remodeling of an older industrial structure, was turned into a landgoing ocean liner complete with ship's bridge, promenade deck, and portholes. The president of the company was a boating enthusiast, and the nautical motif also expressed cleanliness in an age when the purity of the soft drink was still under suspicion.

the early 1930s one could still see their influence and their incorporation into the Art Deco ethic. In the Los Angeles branch of the Federal Reserve Bank of San Francisco by John and Donald B. Parkinson (1930) at Olive Street and Olympic Boulevard, the piers are fluted Classical pilasters without capitals, but the base of the building is vaguely Pre-Columbian. The interior of the banking room has a stylized Italian Renaissance coffered ceiling. By the late 1930s, many projects supported by the Public Works Admin-istration incorporated flattened, geometricized pilasters. In G. Stanley Underwood's Federal Court House, the Greek temple was evoked in its stripped facade of sheer bulk, whose only articulation is a series of plain but imposing vertical elements which give the composition a monolithic strength. The image of the Court House is absolute, authoritarian, and is not far removed from the buildings being constructed at that same time in totalitarian European states.[35]

The Art Deco of the 1920s was certainly one of the high points in Los Angeles architecture. It was, as the name implies, primarily a decorative ethic that stands as a statement of unbridled confidence in the creative power of the human spirit. During and after the depression, partly out of disillusionment with the 1920s and partly because the purist ethic of the Modern Movement began to dominate architectural thought, Art Deco was rejected and ridiculed.[36] The new acceptance of ornament in architecture that characterized the 1970s, however, has introduced a new understanding of the historical role and aesthetic qualities of Art Deco. It was not truly a modern architecture, but a new form of ornament that in many cases resembled stylized versions of traditional forms, such as Mayan or Churrigueresque. However, the treatment of the building as a unified entity with vertical orientation and the freedom with which the

Commercial buildings, 6554–6600 Hollywood Boulevard. During the 1920s, many Los Angeles commercial districts were turned into Spanish Revival and Art Deco streetscapes, often side by side. In 1927 the architects Gogerty and Weyl remodeled the older building on the left into a Spanish facade with a large Churrigueresque panel and Moorish arches. The next year, a staff architect for the J.J. Newberry Co. designed the colorful Art Deco facade for its store, using turquoise, gold, and yellow glazed terra cotta.

elements were arranged was proto-modern, and the style brought forth a popular acceptance of untraditional forms.

The Streamline Moderne

The upheaval created in the world by the Great Depression affected all realms of human endeavor, and the architecture of the late 1930s—for there was almost none from the early years—was no exception. The first decisive statement of a clearly modern aesthetic to capture the public's imagination was the Streamline Moderne. Its clean, unornamented surfaces, sweeping horizontal lines, and curved corners expressed the new notions of efficiency and modernity without the notion of wealth that Art Deco had

OPPOSITE:

Crossroads of the World, 6671 Sunset Boulevard, designed in 1936 by Robert V. Derrah. The complex has recently been restored and is listed on the National Register of Historic Places.

LEFT:

Wiltern Theater, Wilshire Boulevard at Western Avenue, detail by Morgan, Walls and Clements, 1931.

BOTTOM LEFT:

One Bunker Hill, 601 West Fifth Street, by Allison and Allison in 1931. Originally the home of the Southern California Edison Company, this building is an Art Deco interpretation of Classical architecture. Above the entrance, carved stone panels by Merrell Gage represent hydroelectric energy, light, and power. The lobby in Sienna Travertine marble has high, coffered ceilings with a mural by Hugo Gallin, "The Apotheosis of Power."

Los Angeles (now Pacific Coast) Stock Exchange, 618 South Spring Street. The architecture of the stock exchange represents a massive stability at a time (1930) when the stock market itself was in crisis. Architect Samuel E. Lunden designed the street facade in grey granite with 12-foot bronze doors, heavy grilles, and buttresses.

RIGHT:

Sunset Tower Apartments, 8358 Sunset Boulevard. An Art Deco apartment building designed in 1930 by Leland A. Bryant. The building is on the National Register of Historic Places.

expressed. The world of aesthetics during that decade was transformed by a small group of product stylists called *industrial designers,* who had discovered in the late 1920s that commercial products sold better when they looked better; in particular, when they looked *modern.* By the early 1930s, when consumer spending was down, businesses fought to present more modern and efficient-looking products to corner bigger portions of a shrinking market. The notion of "modern" had been developing in the architecture of the International Style (see Chapter 7) during the 1920s, using plain surfaces with large expanses of glass and sharp corners. Product designers in the United States, however, looked elsewhere for an image of modernity. They looked to the curved form of the teardrop, which was the most efficient shape in lowering the wind resistance of an object placed in the "stream lines" of a wind tunnel.[37]

In Los Angeles, three great streamlined designs of the 1930s caught the popular imagination. In 1934 Donald Douglas of Santa Monica had designed two Douglas Commercial aircraft and, after exhaustive wind tunnel testing, perfected a third design that he marketed as the DC-3. Its long teardrop shape became the classic streamlined design that is still seen in the skies today. Caught by the future promise of the airplane, railroads turned to industrial designers to apply streamlining to their trains. In 1934 the Union Pacific took delivery of its first Streamliner, a sleek, diesel-powered passenger train, and displayed it in Los Angeles. The railroad's *City of Los Angeles* streamlined train began regular runs to Chicago in 1936. The following year artist Leland Knickerbocker designed what may be the classic streamline of all time, when he transformed the nose of a Santa Fe diesel locomotive into a stylized, red Indian head trailed by the silver feathers of a war bonnet in bright stainless steel. He created the imagery

MIDDLE:

Griffith Park Planetarium, north end of Vermont Avenue, designed in 1935 by John C. Austin and Frederick M. Ashley, with interior murals by Hugo Ballin.

Owl Drug Co. (now Julian Medical Building), 6380 Hollywood Boulevard. Designed in 1934 by Morgan, Walls and Clements, this corner building has a curved, asymmetrical pylon tower, a common feature in buildings such as supermarkets during the 1930s.

RIGHT:

Streamline duplex, 754 Harper Avenue, designed in 1936 by William P. Kesling.

for the Santa Fe Super Chief as a "steel arrow," a "beautiful reach of stainless steel" whose prow was a slanted wedge to cut the wind as the train streaked past, and the front was emblazoned with a Zia sun symbol stretched by the wind to sweep back along the sides of the locomotive. The interior appointments were stylized Navajo.[38]

The Streamline Moderne was also applied to architecture; to homes, bungalow courts, and apartment houses. It flourished particularly in commercial architecture, where a building could attract the eye of the passing motorist. Streamline architecture looked efficient in its clean lines; it had an appropriate austerity that reflected the economic hardships of the time, and was in fact relatively inexpensive to build because there was little labor-intensive ornament like terra cotta; exteriors tended to be concrete or stucco.

One of the great manifestations of the Streamline building was the supermarket. Self-service marketing had actually been around for some time by the 1930s; in 1917 Albert Gerrard had changed his Triangle Cash Market to a self-service store, arranged the goods alphabetically on the shelves so that people could find them, and changed the store's name to Alpha Beta.[39] During the depression the lower prices offered by self-service markets were enhanced by the grouping together of several market departments— the butcher, baker, greengrocer—into one "super" market. Here one could not only find everything one needed in a single store, one would be enticed to buy more than one had intended, lured by the "scientific plan" of the supermarket whose aisles were studied by supermarket engineers just as traffic engineers planned movement through city streets. The slogan of Safeway Stores during the early 1930s was "Distribution Without Waste."

Market exteriors were designed in sweeping expanses of glass, with a corner tower beckoning the motorist from afar. The distinguishing feature of one supermarket design was "the huge open-front span which ranges from 75 to 100 feet in width without the encumbrance of supporting pillars." Construction was more expensive than for a supported front, but operators "demanded its heightened display facilities, claiming psychological benefits more than outweigh the costs." As J. Gordon Wright wrote in 1938,[40]

> California architects have vied for the past eight years until a Super market today has many of the earmarks of a modern theater. The latest are employing vitrolite in brilliant hues which catch the sun's rays and dazzle passing motorists into attention. Huge neon-festooned towers, smartly-striped awnings, and varicolored lighting effects for expensive neon signs all have added their bit to make California's markets the beauty queens of the food world.

Frequently, Streamline architecture adopted the literal image of its origins in transportation designs, using porthole windows, steel railings, and curving surfaces. In the 1930s, the ocean liner was still the great marvel of travel and standard-bearer of the machine aesthetic.[41] One of the greatest landgoing ocean liners ever built was the Coca Cola bottling plant in Los Angeles at 1334 South Central Avenue (1936; Robert V. Derrah). The building has rounded corners, porthole windows, doorways that simulate ship's hatches, and is surmounted by a huge sign in the form of a ship's bridge. Offices are reached via a "promenade deck" complete with deck ventilators that are actually hoppers feeding bottle caps to the machines below. The nautical theme may have been chosen because the president of the company was an avid boatman, but it also suggested cleanliness. "After all, what's cleaner than a ship's deck? What,

LEFT:

May Company, 6067 Wilshire Boulevard, designed by A. C. Martin, Sr., and S. A. Marx in 1940. When the May Company was built at the western end of the Miracle Mile in 1940, it loomed as an imposing monument in a district that was still largely undeveloped. Its gold and black corner decoration protruded as a figurehead from the gray walls, attracting the eye of the motorist from afar. The building stands as one of the largest examples of the late Moderne style popular in the 1940s, defined by the horizontal groupings of windows outlined in protruding, bezel-like frames.

therefore, could more aptly express the careful bottling methods of the Coca Cola Company than a ship motif . . .?"[42]

A programmatic nautical theme was combined with exotic architecture in Derrah's Crossroads of the World (1937) at 6671 Sunset Boulevard, designed as a "cosmopolitan shopping center" featuring merchandise from everywhere. The central building is once again a ship, complete with bridge and tower with a rotating globe on top, and it sails down an international street lined with shops designed in Italian, French, Spanish, Mexican, Moorish, Turkish, Scandanavian, and Cape Cod styles.[43] Both of Derrah's creations have been restored and today stand as significant monuments to the Streamline Moderne.

Thomas Jefferson High School, 1319 East 41st Street, by Morgan, Walls and Clements in 1936. The 1934 Field Act, which called for school buildings constructed to resist seismic disturbances, ushered in a period of intense school building in the state. Thus California has a fine array of schools from the 1930s in many styles, including the Streamline.

Modernizing Buildings in the 1930s

One reason so much architecture was created in the 1930s, given the low level of building activity, was the interest in "modernization." With little money to spend on new buildings and with older styles falling into disrepute, it was relatively inexpensive to reface Queen Anne or Beaux Arts commercial buildings with an up-to-date Moderne exterior that may not have been streamlined, but which had clean lines and smacked of newness. Modernization was supported by firms such as the Libbey-Owens-Ford Glass Company in their "Modernize Main Street" competition of 1935. "The shop front with its plate-glass show-windows establishes the character of the store and invites the passerby to stop and shop. The interior fulfills the promise of the front, serving as the setting for the display of merchandise, providing

BOTTOM:

Gerry Building, 910 South Los Angeles Street, designed in 1947 by Maurice Fleischman.

Coulters Dry Goods Company, 5600 Wilshire Boulevard, by Stiles O. Clements in 1938. This huge Streamline department store was one of the most imposing buildings along Wilshire's Miracle Mile. Its central facade was covered with an immense expanse of glass brick, and bands of glass brick swept around each story. A large show window at the corner displayed merchandise to the approaching motorist. The building was destroyed in 1980. Photograph ca. 1938.

the urge to purchase."[44] When less money was being spent by customers, retailers had to spend more to attract them.

The Coca-Cola plant was actually a remodeling of an older factory building, as was the Max Factor Building of 1935 (S. Charles Lee) at Hollywood and Highland. Robinson's Department Store at 600 West Seventh Street had been a Moorish building designed in 1915 by Noonan and Richards, faced with pressed brick and terra cotta with corner towers capped by hip roofs and overhanging cornices. In 1936 Edward L. Mayberry and Allison and Allison removed these outdated elements and replaced them with a sleek facade of light terra cotta Hermosa tile[45] that was partly Moderne but primarily just stripped.

The W.P. Story Building at Broadway and Sixth Street was modernized in 1934 by Morgan, Walls and Clements—the same firm that designed the original building—with no attempt to integrate the modernization into the older fabric of the building. They faced the bottom two stories with Montenelle marble, increased the show window size, and added a bronze marquee.[46] Another major remodeling by the same architect who designed the building was that of John and Donald Parkinson for the Pacific Mutual Building at Olive and Sixth. All of the exaggerated Classical detailing was removed in 1937 and replaced by the sheer Moderne facade seen today.[47] Charles F. Whittlesey's Philharmonic

Auditorium of 1906 was stripped of its Moorish facade and modernized in 1938 by Claud Beelman. Thus, many of the Moderne monuments of the 1930s are really older buildings in a new garb, part of an attempt to keep architectural work going and provide merchants with an inexpensive look of prosperity.[48] It was a cycle of remodeling that continues today.

Architecture as Folk Art: The Programmatic

During the 1920s and 30s, the ultimate in swift visual architectural impact was found in the styling of buildings not according to their function in an architectural sense, but according to what they sold—in particular if they sold food to the motorist. One could drive along the streets of Los Angeles and come across a restaurant called the Brown Derby, in the shape of its name, a chain of chile restaurants in the shape of huge chile bowls, a camera store with its facade a huge camera. David Gebhard has discussed the origins of these forms in his introduction to *California Crazy: Roadside Vernacular Architecture* (1980). Although largely dismissed as an architectural joke, the programmatic was in a sense the culmination of many ideas developing in the 1920s. It was a fantasy style in its own right, usually constructed of stucco over a wood frame, and its images were taken from the business contained therein, rather than from

LEFT:
Academy Theater, 3100 Manchester Boulevard, by S. Charles Lee in 1939. The most magnificent Streamline theater in Los Angeles is the Academy, a series of interlocking cylinders pierced by the hallmark of late 1930s design, glass bricks.

Shangri-La Apartments, 1301 Ocean Ave., Santa Monica, by William E. Foster in 1940, exterior and lobby. This apartment building was designed in an L so that all living rooms and bedrooms could face the ocean. The apartments open out onto rear galleries which replace the conventional hallway.

remote times or exotic places. It was particularly adapted to being seen from the passing car. Programmatic architecture embodied the freedom of expression and creative invention represented in more formal architectural styles such as Art Deco, but it was a populist architecture, often designed by non-professional architects. It was a folk art expression of new lifestyles and of architectural freedom typical of this period in Los Angeles.

The architectural visions of the future city that were brought to completion in the 1920s represented what was perhaps the most creative period in Los Angeles architecture. The constraints of the depression cut short the development of Art Deco, but replaced it with a different expression of the modern. Another architectural ethic, however, more radical than that espoused by the architects who turned to Art Deco and Streamline, would actually come to dominate American—and Los Angeles—architecture by the 1940s. This architecture was that of the Modern Movement, and Los Angeles was an important center of its early growth.

I. Magnin and Co., 3240 Wilshire Boulevard, designed by Myron Hunt and H. C. Chambers in 1939 and interior by Timothy L. Pflueger. The corner of Wilshire Boulevard and New Hampshire Avenue was the heart of the swank shopping district in 1939, and I. Magnin constructed a store clad in 350 tons of Yule Colorado white marble with a black granite base. Inside, even more marble made the interior "an ensemble of impressive refinement and beauty." Photograph 1939.

Channel Heights Market, Coralmont Drive, San Pedro. One of the great inventions of the 1930s, and one of its architectural triumphs, was the supermarket. Facades were designed as clean sweeps of glass, inviting the patron into a large, scientifically planned store that offered nearly everything the food shopper could wish, with ample parking out in front. Many supermarkets were in extravagant streamline designs, but the Channel Heights Market, by Richard Neutra in 1940, was in the Modern style of the Channel Heights public housing. Photograph 1940.

Brown Derby Restaurant, 3377 Wilshire Boulevard; 1926. The Brown Derby was built in this shape, according to legend, because its builder, Herbert K. Somborn, had placed a bet: "If you know anything about food you can sell it out of a hat."

Much of the Los Angeles streetscape in the 1920s appeared rapidly. In particular, Commercial establishments catering to the automobile population were built cheaply, not intended to be permanent. The prefabricated metal gas station appeared about 1924, some with awnings having a bit of sheet metal fringe for decoration. This one is at 1740 Sawtelle Boulevard.

BOTTOM LEFT:

The Tamale (now Casa Garcia), 6421 Whittier Boulevard, Montebello. This restaurant, built in 1928, is a large stucco tamale tied at each end with ropes.

The Darkroom, 5370 Wilshire Boulevard. In 1938, when miniature cameras were becoming the rage, Sigmond Diamond and Robert Marks opened a photo shop on Wilshire. They commissioned architect Marcus P. Miller to design a Vitrolite facade for the shop in the shape of a giant camera.

MODERN ARCHITECTURE IN LOS ANGELES

The sources of twentieth-century Modern architecture can be traced into the nineteenth century, both to the innate styling of straightforward industrial buildings that were not intended to be "architecture" at all and to the attempts by architects to transcend the constraints of traditional forms. The machine was the great vehicle of aesthetic transformation not only for its suggestion of cleanliness and efficiency, but also for the new materials and techniques it introduced.

Traditionally, a masonry building expressed its structure in the application of materials. Strong walls of stone or brick held up the roof; masonry columns supported lintels or arches which spanned open spaces. Decoration of a building continued to have some relation to its structure as well, although the relationship was sometimes tenuous. The European Beaux Arts buildings of the late nineteenth century may have been decoratively too zealous, but they were still based on columns, arches, and masonry bearing walls.

When the steel frame began to replace the masonry wall as the framework of a building, however, it quickly removed any need whatsoever for the aesthetic elements that had been used for three thousand years in Western architecture. In addition, the interior space of a steel-frame building could be planned more flexibly and with more open space than was ever possible before. Today, architects have a century of practice in designing buildings in this new idiom, but a hundred years ago they had an extremely difficult time coping with a problem for which history had no lessons.

One solution, of course, was to maintain a traditional facade over a framework of steel. The Beaux Arts movement applied this solution in an effort to retain traditional architectural values in the face of new technology. The problem was, however, that since there was no structural reason to use Classical decorative elements, the decoration could be moved about and applied merely as frosting on a cake. In Los Angeles, for example, the Pacific Mutual Building (1921; W.J. Dodd), at 523 West Sixth Street, is a typical Beaux Arts highrise building with the traditional attic at the upper stories. This attic is decorated as a Roman temple, but since the columns of this temple have to fit around the wide steel piers, they are split in two and made wider with a flat spacer. Windows of the building are small, but the glass curtain wall

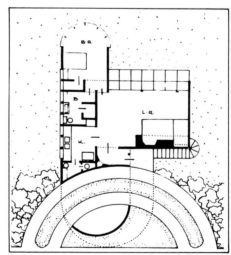

Entenza house, 475 Mesa Road, Pacific Palisades, built in 1937 by Harwell Harris.

OPPOSITE:

Ennis house, 2607 Glendower Avenue. The most monumental of Frank Lloyd Wright's concrete block houses, the Ennis house, built in 1924, uses the dramatic siting of the hill to create the effect of a Mayan temple.

had already been shown possible by the European pioneers of Modern architecture—and even in San Francisco, with Willis Polk's Hallidie Building of 1917. The facades of the Pacific Mutual are of mat glazed terra cotta that looks like carved stone. At the same time, the building had one of the early underground parking garages in Los Angeles, built six years before the introduction of the Model A Ford.

Similarly, the beautiful white terra cotta facade of the W.P. Story Building (1910; Morgan and Walls) at 610 South Broadway has fanciful columns and decorative cornices and brackets which add luster to the streetscape but hold nothing up. They are merely stuck onto the true structure of the building. We now look upon such traditional forms with a new appreciation for their aesthetic qualities and for the sensitivity they showed toward architectural space. However, to innovative architects around the turn of the century, fighting what they saw as the tyranny of the past, the irrelevance of such architecture was intolerable.

The story of the architectural transformation into Modernism has been told at great length, but a part of that story not so well known is the role of Southern California. The architectural exuberance of Los Angeles, which first imported the Queen Anne from the East in the 1880s and nurtured the Mission Revival and Craftsman styles in the following decades, simultaneously supported many architectural ethics. The freedom to build as one wished, particularly in the form of single-family homes which depended little on the context of the street or neighborhood, allowed revolutionary architects to flourish on the fringes of accepted styles. The resulting experimentation in Modern idioms would make Los Angeles a showcase of international significance in Modern architecture by the 1930s.

RIGHT:

Millard house, "La Miniatura," 645 Prospect Crescent, Pasadena. Frank Lloyd Wright brought to Los Angeles his interest in Pre-Columbian architecture and his invention of patterned, pre-cast concrete blocks for building construction. The Millard house, built in 1923, was the first house to employ both. Designed as a massive tower enclosing a two-story living space, today it is hidden among dense overgrowth.

Sowden house, 5121 Franklin Avenue. In this house of 1926, Lloyd Wright borrowed his father's knit-block construction technique and turned it into an imposing sculpture. The house as sculpture is even more pronounced in the interior courtyard, which is designed as a craggy maze of knit blocks. It is on the National Register of Historic Places.

Modern Pioneers in Los Angeles

The Modern Movement finds its roots largely in designs associated with engineering and technology. Southern California, however, harbored a unique precursor in the Mission Revival movement—a movement that attempted not to reach out into modernity but to reach back into tradition. In the hands of an innovative designer such as Irving Gill, the Mission Revival could express the same clean lines and planes that were seen in the work of Louis Sullivan and, in particular, Frank Lloyd Wright.

Frank Lloyd Wright worked for Sullivan in the early 1890s, and in his office at the same time was a young New Yorker, Irving Gill (1870-1936). Gill moved to San Diego in 1893 and designed homes in the English and American Colonial styles then popular, but in the next few years he moved away from these norms and began to develop a very personal aesthetic. He began to flatten the roof lines of his houses and to use arches and pergolas in the Mediterranean fashion. His exteriors became a series of cubes, their flat walls punctured by frameless windows. Thin interior walls featured flush woodwork. Gill's idiom was primarily the Mission Revival, but he cleaned it of ornamental detail, leaving smooth forms in white stucco. In 1916 he wrote that if architects "wish to do great and lasting work [they] must dare to be simple, must have the courage to fling aside every device that distracts the eye from structural beauty, must break through convention and get down to fundamental truths. . . . Any deviation from simplicity results in a loss of dignity."[1] The line, the arch, the cube, and the circle were the four principles of architectural beauty.

The most striking of Gill's buildings that remain today is probably the Women's Club in La Jolla, built in 1913, with its sheer stucco facade fronting the street. The walls are of pre-cast concrete, formed in molds on the ground and tilted upright. Nearer Los Angeles, his Miltimore house (1911) at 1301 Chelten Way in South Pasadena demonstrates the cubic form he was developing, with hints of a Mediterranean influence in the trellises extending from two sides of the house. Construction materials are stucco over a wood frame. Similarly, a smooth stucco plane with simplified Doric columns fronts his Pacific Electric Railway Station (1913) in Torrance, at 1200 Cabrillo Avenue.

Gill's Horatio West Court (1921), at 140 Hollister Avenue in Santa Monica, is based on the Southern California innovation of the bungalow court. It is designed as a block of four white stucco cubes with what was originally an open porch on the second story. Perhaps because the sea breeze proved too crisp, the porches were enclosed in the 1920s, probably by Gill. The entrances to the dwelling units are under smaller cubes with arched openings off the interior courtyard.

Sharing the fate of many innovators, Gill was little appreciated in his time. He was a strong individualist developing his own blend of traditional and modern styles, and by the 1920s the tide of architectural fashion had swung to the more ornate Spanish Revival styles. Gill retired into obscurity that has only recently been reevaluated. In the intervening years much of his finest work has been destroyed, including

LEFT:

Wayfarers' Chapel, Portugese Bend. Built by the Swedenborgian Church as a memorial to its founder and as a center for meditation and prayer, the Wayfarers' Chapel stands high above the ocean on the Palos Verdes Peninsula. Designed by Lloyd Wright in 1949–51, the church embodies the architect's vision of building enveloped in nature. The visitor is sheltered by blades of glass on the roof and looks out to evergreen trees towering above the chapel.

Wayfarers' Chapel interior. Photograph 1951.

Lovell beach house, Thirteenth Street, Balboa. The first architect to bring the new International Style to Los Angeles was R. M. Schindler; his 1925 commission for the Lovells resulted in one of America's most notable monuments of the early Modern Movement.

Buck house, 805 South Genessee Avenue, built in 1934, is one of Schindler's early designs that adhered to International Style principles of glass walls and an open plan. It is shrouded by hedges from the street, but juxtaposed roof lines and clerestory windows suggest the transparency of the house that would be the subject of much interest by architects in the 1950s.

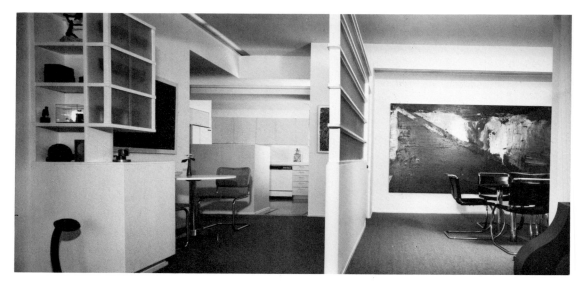

Buck house, interior. Innovations included recessed ceiling lights—but using incandescent lights that were too hot for practical use. Photograph 1979.

Baldwin Hills Village, 5300 Rodeo Road. Of the several planned communities in the Los Angeles area, perhaps the most successful is Baldwin Hills Village, an eighty-acre community of 627 homes built in 1941. Clarence Stein developed the site plan based on his greenbelt concept first carried out in Radburn, New Jersey, elements of which appear here: a superblock of houses surrounding a "village green" which becomes the heart of the community and complete separation of pedestrian and automobile. Homes face pedestrian walkways through the village green, and auto garages are located at the periphery of the site. By 1941, Los Angeles had an average of one automboile per family, and Baldwin Hills combined convenience in its use with a peaceful escape from its dangers. The houses themselves are typical Los Angeles tract dwellings, designed by Reginald D. Johnson and Wilson, Merrill and Alexander.

the Dodge house on Kings Road, probably the most complete embodiment of his architectural principles. Its last owner, the Los Angeles Board of Education, auctioned it to the highest bidder and it was demolished for an apartment complex, despite an intense effort by preservationists to save it.

The Lewis Courts (1910) at Mountain Trail and Alegria Avenue in Sierra Madre still stand, but they have been extensively remodeled.

Irving Gill was not the only architect to suffer from the waning interest in innovative forms that characterized the late teens. Frank Lloyd Wright had been able to find work only in Japan for some years when he received the commission to design a home for Aline Barnsdall in Hollywood. Wright had previously sought inspiration for architecture in Pre-Columbian traditions and had applied them in earlier buildings.[2] The "Hollyhock House" he designed for Barnsdall, completed in 1920, has traces of the Mayan combined with a sophisticated plan blending interior and exterior spaces. One of Wright's major contributions to architecture was to eliminate the room as a mandatory box. He created interior spaces that flowed along the ground and gave subtle hints of an unfolding to infinity. This innovation found its beginning in his Prairie School work and was continued in Los Angeles as well. As exterior decoration of the Hollyhock house, he placed a salient brow of stylized hollyhocks—Barnsdall's favorite flower—around the entire facade above the windows. The house is built of wood frame with a stucco exterior, presenting at first a monolithic, enclosed mass that belies the interplay of interior and exterior spaces.

By 1923, Wright had discovered another structural system that could provide a rich surface texture as well as suggest the Pre-Columbian: hollow, pre-cast concrete blocks that were patterned or perforated, and reinforced with steel rods. Since the blocks were reinforced, they could be used for all purposes—to span openings as well as support weight—so that the structural concrete forms and decorated wall surfaces became one.[3]

His first project in this material was the Millard house (1923) at 645 Prospect Crescent in Pasadena. The house is a two-story tower faced with concrete blocks perforated with star shapes, reflected in a quiet pool. In the Storer house (1923), 8161 Hollywood Boulevard, the concrete blocks are piers fronting a two-story living space protected by a glass curtain window. The most monumental of all his concrete block houses is the Ennis house of 1924, at 2607 Glendower Avenue. It is also the most Mayan of his homes partly because the dramatic siting uses the hill as the base of the temple. Here the cubistic massing of the blocks is not only applied to the imposing facade of the house, but also to the long wall along the street. Inside, hints of infinite space are realized through corridors and chambers, each carrying the feeling of a vast temple by the arrangement of concrete blocks.

Lloyd Wright, Frank's eldest son, came to Southern California as a landscape architect with the firm of Olmsted and Olmsted to help plan the Panama-California Exposition of 1915 in San Diego, and he stayed to supervise the construction of several of his father's works. In the 1920s he moved from landscape design to building design, bringing an intense interest in the harmony of man-made and natural environments. This harmony is evident in the broad spectrum of his work in Southern California, from his Taggart house (1922–24) at 5423 Live Oak Drive, which clings to a steep hillside, to his Wayfarers' Chapel (1951) on the Palos Verdes Peninsula, a glass-enclosed, transparent church set in a grove of trees which now tower over the building itself.

Lloyd Wright has been shown less appreciation than his work deserves, the fate of one who lives in the shadow of a great father. His style was a personal one and remained undefined by any of the major movements. Other notable examples of his work include the Samuels-Novarro house of 1928, at 5609 Valley Oak Drive, one of the few Mayan Art Deco houses in the area. The Mayanesque concrete blocks are actually of pressed metal. His Sowden house of 1926, at 5121 Franklin Avenue, has a dramatic street facade which may be interpreted as highly stylized Churrigueresque, Pre-Columbian, or anthropomorphic.

Both Wrights continued to build in Los Angeles for many years, Lloyd settling there and building his own house at 858 North Doheny Drive in 1928. It retains the monolithic enclosure of the Mayan ethic, with stylized Joshua trees as the decorative motif. A major later work of Frank Lloyd Wright is the Sturgis house (1939) at 449 Skyewiay, where only the cantilevered balcony can be seen from the street.

The Early International Style

The first architect to transport the vocabulary of the International Style to Los Angeles was Rudolph M. Schindler.[4] Born in Vienna in 1887, he studied architecture, painting, and sculpture, and in 1914 he went to work in Chicago, eventually entering the office of Frank Lloyd Wright. In 1920 he came to Los Angeles to supervise the construction of Wright's Barnsdall house. The following year he built his own house on Kings Road and established his own practice. The Kings Road house is a unique blend of the

Strathmore Apartments, 11055 West Strathmore Drive. Richard Neutra built this Modern version of a bungalow court in 1938. The eight units are grouped around a landscaped central court. An important part of the Modern look was the flat exterior wall with elements recessed rather than protruding. Here the balconies are inside the outer walls, emphasizing the clean, square lines of the building. Photograph ca. 1939.

Miltimore house, 1301 Chelten Way, South Pasadena. The Mission Revival style was intended to look back to California traditions, but in the hands of architect Irving Gill it foreshadowed the Modern Movement. Gill's Miltimore house, built in 1911, is a large white cube with only hints of traditional styles. It is listed on the National Register of Historic Places.

Nesbitt house, 414 Avondale Avenue, 1942. This house marked the beginning of a new phase of Richard Neutra's architecture, away from the International Style. Choice of materials became less important than the general transparency of the whole. Here he employed redwood, brick, and glass, and surrounded the house with luxurious vegetation beginning to grow in this 1942 photograph.

International Style and Craftsman architecture; it is of post-and-beam construction with glass curtain walls facing the rear courtyard, and the solid walls to the front are of tilt-slab concrete, a technique developed by Irving Gill. The house is built of redwood, all of which was left unpainted, and the floors were of raw concrete. Access to the courtyard was via sliding canvas doors. The house was built for two families—the Schindlers and the Chaces—and contains five studio spaces, one for each adult and one for guests. The two families shared a common kitchen. Today the house is being restored and is open to the public for tours.

Schindler's next renowned work is the 1925 beach house for P.M. Lovell on the Balboa Peninsula. The house is suspended high above the beach on five vertical, concrete fin-like frames, and the two-story living space looks out to the ocean through a glass curtain wall. During the next fifteen years he designed a number of homes that are classics of the Modern Movement, including the Oliver house (1933), Buck house (1934), Walker house (1935), and Rodakiewicz house (1937).[5] Although his primary aesthetic was the International Style of plain white stucco surfaces and flush bands of windows, his later work incorporated complex forms which gave his houses a certain picturesque idiosyncracy. He continued to design houses until his death in 1953.

Richard J. Neutra was also a Viennese, born in 1892, who knew Schindler as a student in Vienna. The two maintained a correspondence until Neutra emigrated to the United States in 1923, to what he called a "fantastic living culture of some yet unknown people."[6] He worked briefly in Detroit and Chicago, and in 1925 came to Los Angeles to work with Schindler. Two years later he set up his own practice.

BOTTOM

Dunsmuir Apartments, 1281 South Dunsmuir Avenue. Gregory Ain, the first architect raised and educated in Los Angeles to work in the International Style, built this apartment house in 1937 on a forty-foot lot. The north facade is composed of a series of closed, white cubes in a sawtooth pattern, with a continuous band of narrow windows on each story. The south facade, largely glass, opens to small private gardens.

Lipetz house, 843 Dillon Street. Raphael Soriano combined elements of the Streamline Moderne and the International Style in this 1935 house. The house, which sits on a high lot overlooking Silver Lake, was designed for music, with the centerpiece a grand piano.

With his second major commission,[7] a residence built in 1929 for the same Lovell for whom Schindler had designed the beach house in Balboa, he created a major monument of the International Style. The Lovell Health house (so called because Lovell was a naturopath) at 4616 Dundee Drive is built with a steel frame and white stuccoed walls of ready mix concrete poured in place.[8] The expanses of windows hover over a cantilevered balcony and look down a long canyon through a mesh of rich foliage. Along with other architects of the Modern Movement, Neutra was interested in the application of new technology to architecture and at the same time believed that a building should be in harmony with the natural environment. The interior is a celebration of openness, rather than a group of boxy rooms enclosed by walls. This "open plan," pioneered by Neutra and others, constituted a major contribution of the Modern Movement to architectural space. The Health house was built when the Model A Ford was the latest automobile, and Neutra embedded a Model A headlight in the stairway wall. Unlike the Model A, however, the house looks as modern today as when it was built.

During the depression Neutra, along with Schindler and others, directed his energies toward using technologies that could provide inexpensive, flexible, yet graceful accommodations for the middle classes. In 1936 he designed an experimental house of plywood that could be easily transported; the home has in fact been moved a few times and now stands at 427 South Beloit Avenue. Two years later he created two modest apartment houses in Westwood: the Strathmore Apartments at 11055 West Strathmore Drive are a Modern version of the bungalow court, and the Landfair Apartments at Ophir Drive and Landfair Avenue are a series of glass and white stucco cubes in a sawtooth configuration. In 1941–43, Neutra

Kaufmann house, 470 West Chino Canyon Road, Palm Springs. Built by Richard J. Neutra in 1947 for the same client as Frank Lloyd Wright's Falling Water, the Kaufmann house demonstrates the potential for transparency and clarity of form that could be achieved by post-and-beam construction. The carefully defined horizontal and vertical planes give the house an imposing man-made appearance in contrast to the mountainous desert landscape. Photographs ca. 1947.

designed the 600-unit Channel Heights Public Housing project on Coralmont Drive in San Pedro, clusters of dwellings on a hillside which commands a view of San Pedro and the ocean. Between the clusters, deep arroyos were left in their natural state. In this project, Neutra anticipated by thirty years the concept of clustered housing in a natural landscape which was frequently applied to planned unit developments of the 1970s.

Other experiments in clustered housing were being designed at the same time, usually in more traditional architectural styles. One of the most notable is Baldwin Hills Village, a complex of 627 attached homes on an eighty-acre site at 5300 Rodeo Road (1941; Reginald D. Johnson; and Wilson, Merrill and Alexander; Clarence S. Stein, site planner). The concept of the village was "complete convenience in the use of the automobile and a peaceful escape from its dangers."[9] The homes are arranged around a central landscaped field which is free of automobiles, and parking garages are provided at the perimeter of the site.

Neutra continued to apply advanced technology to his designs, but the Nesbitt house of 1942 marked a move away from concrete and the steel frame. Here he used redwood, brick, and glass: non-strategic materials during wartime. Glass was the key to his new aesthetic, and from 1942 onwards he concentrated on transparency in his domestic architecture. "Privacy was achieved by planning; interior and exterior merged; the site entered the house and vice versa."[10] This vision reached maturity in designs such as the Kaufmann house (1947) in Palm Springs, where the interior of the home is barely separated from the

Case Study House #22, 1635 Woods Drive. In 1959 Pierre Koening designed a steel-frame house on a 150-foot wide, 86-foot deep lot on the edge of a precipice. Solid walls face the street; all other sides of the house are of glass, allowing a 240-degree view of 100 square miles of Los Angeles County. All rooms of the L-shaped house are oriented toward the swimming pool, and eight-foot overhangs protect the glass walls from the western sun.

rugged mountains behind it by a single pane of glass. The indoor-outdoor lifestyle nurtured by California's climate may have been embodied in the patios and courtyards of the Spanish Revival styles of the 1920s in Los Angeles, but nowhere was it realized as fully as in the architecture of the Modern Movement.

Neutra and Schindler were joined in the 1930s and 1940s by a group of European and American architects who produced a new generation of Modern architecture which lasted until well after mid-century. Gregory Ain was the first local architect to work in the Modern idiom in Los Angeles. He had been born in Pittsburgh in 1908 and came to Los Angeles as a child, studied architecture at USC, and worked briefly with both Neutra and Schindler.[11] As with many other Modern architects, Ain's crowning achievements tended to be his early works, in particular the Dunsmuir Apartments (1937) at 1281 South Dunsmuir Avenue. He designed four two-story housing units which march up a gentle hill in a sawtooth pattern, each of the two stories marked by a continuous band of narrow windows along the entire front and side.

Some local examples of the 1930s merged the International Style with the Streamline Moderne in an interplay of cube and curve. In the Entenza house of 1938 by Harwell H. Harris at 475 Mesa Road, the driveway and carport are designed as interlocking curves. The Lipetz house (1935) by Raphael Soriano at 843 Dillon Street has a semicircular, glass-enclosed living room whose centerpiece was originally a grand piano. Outside, a wide, overhanging flat roof and metal railings lend a hint of the nautical.[12]

These and other early Modern houses in Los Angeles were constructed for individual clients amidst the overwhelming dominance of Spanish and other traditional styles. The Modern Movement, however,

was soon to gain a public outlet when, in 1938, John Entenza became editor of a regional magazine called *California Arts and Architecture*. The magazine had already shown an interest in Modern architecture, devoting its January 1935 issue to the work of Neutra and others. Entenza dropped "California" from the title and turned the magazine into an outspoken supporter of Modern architecture, stressing the work of Southern California architects to what would become an international audience. Entenza's influence was felt dramatically in the late 1940s, after the hiatus of the Second World War brought new attention to the plight of cities and to the need for housing.

Postwar Los Angeles: City Planning and Case Study Houses

The United States returned from war in 1945 to find a set of urban problems of unprecedented magnitude. The economic downturn of the 1930s followed by the demands of the war effort resulted in a neglect of city planning and residential construction for a decade and a half. Although small stucco apartments had been built in the coastal areas of Los Angeles to house employees of the aircraft industry, the housing shortage was acute. In addition, central cities across the country were suddenly found to be in a state of decay that demanded immediate attention.

Arts and Architecture had published a series of articles in the early 1940s decrying the state of the cities and of Los Angeles in particular, calling for renewed planning efforts and the provision of affordable housing. The city was characterized by "obsolescence and disorder" and suffered from the "total disintegration of form, space, and structure in the urban pattern."[13] City planning of the 1940s in Los Angeles

Goldwater Apartments, 3212 El Segundo Boulevard, Gardena. Designed by Carl Maston in 1964, these fourteen two-story units each have a private courtyard and share two larger interior courts. Here the post-and-beam ethic reaches almost constructivist proportions, with the slat used as the ubiquitous unifying design element.

LEFT:

Perkins house, 1540 Poppy Peak Drive, Pasadena. By the mid-1950s, post-and-beam architecture in Los Angeles was testing the limits of transparency. In the Perkins house, designed in 1955 by Richard Neutra, a closed street facade shields the house, but to the rear, the home is totally open to the outdoors.

had already sought to institutionalize the automobile as the primary means of transportation. In the 1941 plan for the region, downtown had been supplanted as the city's central core by a number of commercial and industrial centers throughout the basin, with the single-family home as the dominant housing type. Unrestrained access to home, job, and recreation was to be provided by a network of freeways so that everybody would be within four miles of an interchange. Following the opening of the first section of the Arroyo Seco Parkway in 1939, the Cahuenga Pass Freeway (now the Hollywood Freeway) was opened in 1940. A right-of-way for Pacific Electric trains was originally provided in the median but was later replaced with additional freeway lanes.[14]

Amidst the debate over postwar housing which raged before any new housing was being built, John Entenza decided to demonstrate the potential of domestic Modern architecture in what would become one of the country's most ambitious experiments in architectural progress: the Case Study House Program.[15] Entenza had two primary concerns when he announced, in 1945, that *Arts and Architecture* would become the client for eight nationally recognized architects to design eight houses, "each to fulfill the specifications of a special living problem in the Southern California area."[16] First, he feared that the hoped-for postwar building boom would turn away from Modern architecture and return to eclectic historical styles that had dominated the 1930s.[17] The Case Study houses would demonstrate that Modern architecture was not merely for the avant-garde, but could provide aesthetically pleasing Modern housing as a general standard. Second, he hoped to find the best materials, new or old, to provide high quality housing at a reasonable cost.

The first Case Study house was Modern in style but conventional in materials, partly because war restrictions had not yet been lifted. J.R. Davidson's "minimal house" (1946) at 540 South Barrington Avenue used wood framing, fir siding, and plaster. By 1950, when thirteen houses had been completed, architects such as Charles Eames and Eero Saarinen were moving away from traditional materials to steel frames and glass curtain walls. They adopted the International Style as interpreted in particular by Mies van der Rohe, and demonstrated the enduring beauty of spare Modern forms in achieving a synthesis of privacy and openness.

As the program continued into the 1950s, more architects were invited to participate, and the interest turned more consciously to the use of steel framing, especially by architects Pierre Koenig, Craig Ellwood, and Raphael Soriano. More than ever before they opened up the interior of the house to the exterior, they made solid walls subordinate to floor-to-ceiling glass, and they finished their houses with exposed steel beams.

The Case Study houses were more than aesthetic statements, however. Davidson's house no. 1 had a floor plan without halls, a design that would become extremely popular in the 1950s. The emphasis was on family living—most houses had two or more bedrooms and two baths, for servantless families with children. Complete kitchens, as well as Modern furniture and floor coverings, were part of the package.

During the 1960s the program moved away from the single house, of which twenty-two were actually completed, to embrace the larger environment of tract housing. But the program lost its visionary leader when Entenza sold the magazine in 1962, and by then the program had made its statement. It ended formally with cessation of the magazine's publication in 1967.

Entenza's vision brought to wide public attention the possibilities of Modern design in domestic architecture—over 360,000 visitors toured the first six houses when they were opened for viewing.[18] Most of the later homes were built of steel with glass curtain walls; steel framing was strong and it imposed a minimum of interference of structural members with the transparent wall and open plan. But steel framing was also expensive, and it required skilled technicians for its construction. Thus the Case Study house type itself was picked up only seldom by the architects it influenced. Other Modern architects designing housing during the 1950s followed many of the stylistic innovations of the Case Study houses as well as those of the earlier International Style architects, but they developed a somewhat different approach.

The typical Modern home of the 1950s and early 60s was of post-and-beam construction in wood, with glass walls looking onto private outdoor spaces. This structural system was fairly simple to build, was relatively inexpensive, and could utilize more readily available construction skills. Stylistically it could make a small house seem bigger, thrusting walls out into space and bringing the garden inside through the windows. The visual connection between the house and garden was through the wooden beams—often left natural—of the house frame. In this architecture even the modest house could become a pavilion, to celebrate as never before the Southern California climate, its exotic flora, and the freedom of its space. Post-and-beam architecture was unflinchingly Modern, but it had its roots in the open plan of Japanese

Maston house, interior of living room. Photograph 1962.

Maston house, 1657 Marmont Avenue. Following the Second World War, architects working in the Modern idiom developed a style of domestic architecture characterized by post-and-beam construction, glass curtain walls, rich wood finishes, and open plans. One of the early examples is this 1948 house designed by architect Carl Maston for himself. The slab walls and roof express the structure in a fashion similar to that simultaneously being forged in highrise commercial architecture.

architecture and the horizontality of the Craftsman bungalow. It influenced, in turn, a whole generation of developer-built homes called the California Ranch House, with their low and rambling open plan, natural wood, glass sliding doors leading to the patio, and a flat or shallow pitched roof.

In the Los Angeles area, the principal architects working in the post-and-beam idiom included Ray Kappe, Conrad Buff, Carl Maston, Thornton Abell, A. Quincy Jones, Harwell H. Harris, Whitney Smith, and Wayne Williams. This architecture, however, has largely been neglected in architectural history. Further research into this period is needed to bring it the recognition it deserves, for it is one of the major contributions of California to American architecture and lifestyles.

One architect who has been active in Los Angeles since 1939 has cast his personal stamp on residential design, but remained on the edge of mainstream styles. John Lautner began working for Frank Lloyd Wright in 1933 and came to Los Angeles to supervise the construction of Wright's Sturgis house. In 1941 he built for himself a plywood house with a concrete frame supported by I-beams on a forty-five degree slope at 2007 Micheltorena Street. After the war he experimented with steel and reinforced concrete using industrial technology. His most noted house is probably the Malin "Chemosphere" house (1960) at 776 Torreyson Drive. It is a single-story, octagonal saucer held up on the edge of a cliff by a

Malin house, interior. Photographs 1961.

single concrete column. The clear-span roof leaves the interior space open—1300 square feet of living-dining-kitchen area is uninterrupted. He created this house on an essentially unbuildable site without destroying it: there was no bulldozing, no large holes dug, and no retaining walls.

In the mainstream of the postwar Modern movement, the goal shared by many architects—to build moderately priced homes—continued to be elusive. Most of the latter Case Study houses were quite expensive, sometimes perched on the edge of high hills with breathtaking views of the city through their glass walls. Post-and-beam houses tended to become larger and more challenging for architects as well, spanning ever larger distances between posts. One of the last houses in this tradition, for example, Ray Kappe's Sultan house (1976), has 7,000 square feet and stands on a steep slope and is supported on redwood towers. As this construction became less of a challenge during the 1960s, architects began to lose interest in it, and architectural publications turned to more dramatic, high-technology buildings. In the mid-1960s, Charles Moore's Sea Ranch Condominium No. 1 and other new approaches to the house had turned the next generation of architects away from the post and beam, and by the 1980s this change culminated in an avant-garde Los Angeles architectural movement of nearly unbounded forms, colors, and materials.

Malin "Chemosphere" house, 776 Torreyson Drive. John Lautner has set a strong personal stamp on Los Angeles domestic architecture while remaining on the edge of mainstream styles. His Malin house of 1960 is a single-story, octagonal saucer held up on the edge of a cliff by a single concrete column. The clear-span roof leaves the interior space open—1300 square feet of living, dining, and kitchen area is uninterrupted. Lautner built the house on an essentially unbuildable site without destroying it; there was no bulldozing, no large holes dug, and no retaining walls.

In the broader view of postwar residential housing in Los Angeles, however, what happened was quite different from what was envisioned in the Case Study House program or by the post-and-beam architects. Los Angeles had known population booms before, but the Boom of the Fifties was of unprecedented magnitude. The population of Los Angeles County rose from 2.8 million in 1940 to 4.2 million in 1950, 6.0 million in 1960, and 7.0 million in 1970. The city of Los Angeles doubled in population during that period, from 1.5 million to 2.8 million; much of the growth was in the San Fernando Valley. In Orange County the boom spilled over into the 1960s, as the population rose from 200,000 in 1950 to 700,000 in 1960, and 1.4 million in 1970.

In this growth the key phrase was "tract home," inexpensive single-family dwellings constructed assembly-line fashion, purchased with little or nothing down with a VA loan, and spreading like a blanket over the remaining empty spaces of Los Angeles. One of the largest tract home developments of the early 1950s was Lakewood Park, where[19]

great power diggers gouged out a foundation trench for a house in fifteen minutes. Lumber arrived pre-cut for each home. Conveyor belts carried shingles to the roofs. Carpenters used automatic nailing machines and powered door-hanging machines. Expediters with radio cars moved from one home to another looking for bottlenecks. On some days as many as 100 new homes were started; 10,000 were finished in the first two years. Mass construction was matched by mass sales; by late 1950 the volume reached 107 sales in a single hour.

In their design, most of these homes paid little heed to the Modern ethic, or even to the California ranch house. This was populist architecture—small, square, and traditional, with slight hints of the New England house. Whatever their form, these mass-produced houses did realize for millions the American dream of a single-family house on a private lot which characterizes much of the Los Angeles streetscape today.

RIGHT:

Mirror Building, Second and Spring streets, 1948. The Mirror was an afternoon tabloid of the Los Angeles Times. The architect, Rowland H. Crawford, combined horizontal bands of windows in the International Style with a vertical Moderne facade on Spring Street. The building has concrete exterior walls faced with Indiana limestone, trimmed in granite, bronze, and extruded aluminum. At the top of the Spring Street facade are figures representing Culture, Justice, Faith, Progress, and Equality. Photograph 1948.

General Petroleum Building, 612 South Flower Street. The late Moderne style of the postwar period was characterized primarily by protruding, bezel-like window outlines that gave a sense of closure to a building, in contrast to the openness of the International Style. Wurdeman and Becket's General Petroleum Building, the first large office building designed by the firm, is clad in beige terra cotta, and the primary exterior feature is a bank of vertical aluminum fin sunshades that protrude from three facades. At the corners are small horizontal bands of bezeled windows.

Commercial Modern Architecture and the Late Moderne

The first non-residential International Style buildings in Los Angeles appeared in the late 1930s, a decade after their counterparts in domestic architecture and after the path to Modernism had been cleared by Art Deco and Streamline commercial buildings. The International Style CBS Building (1938; William Lescaze and E. T. Heitschmidt), at 6121 Sunset Boulevard, is raised on free-standing columns, leaving the ground floor open. Here, visitors could watch technicians in the glass-enclosed main control room route radio programs over the network in the pre-television era. When the building was opened, *Arts and Architecture* commented that its reinforced concrete exterior was "stark in its simplicity, yet the beautiful strength of functionalism is immediately apparent." Bands of continuous lateral windows run along the east and south walls. Lescaze explained that "although people are vertical forms themselves, they move in a horizontal plane and therefore horizontal lines tend toward visual comfort and away from nervous strain."[20] (See p. 203.)

The Second World War halted the construction of commercial as well as residential buildings, and the first postwar designs began to appear about 1948. During the hiatus in construction, the aesthetics of architecture had changed considerably. Late versions of the 1930s Moderne style reappeared in buildings such as the Carnation Company (1948; Stiles O. Clements), at 5045 Wilshire Boulevard, which stands in pure whiteness, the color and cleanliness of milk, and in the Carnation Research Building, 8015 Van Nuys Boulevard, a very late Streamline Moderne design of 1952. The Moderne was combined with the International Style in the Mirror Building at Second and Spring streets (1948; Rowland H. Crawford), with horizontal bands of windows set off against the accentuated vertical facade.

The late Moderne style which lasted from the mid-1940s until the late 1950s was descended from the Streamline, but the curve and teardrop were replaced by sharp angularity, and the smooth stucco

LEFT:

Lever Brothers Company, 6300 Sheila Street, City of Commerce. The corporate version of Modern architecture during the postwar years was primarily concerned with expressing the structure of a building in its outward appearance, a trend similar to that of the post and beam style in domestic architecture. In this 1951 design by the Bechtel Corporation, the four-story office building is constructed with a concrete frame and cream-colored spandrels. Large reddish-brown cement tiled concrete slabs at each end of the building, as well as the slab roof, visually float away from the building core, emphasizing the role of the frame in holding the entire composition together.

Citizens National Bank, 5780 Wilshire Boulevard. Even Stiles Clements, brilliant visionary of the Churrigueresque and Streamline, worked in the late Moderne bezel style in the late 1940s. The facade of his Citizens National Bank of 1948 is dominated by a large, outlined block of windows and corrugated glass panels. The west side of the building (right in photo) is of architectural concrete finished with mica flakes, and the front is highlighted in rusticated stone.

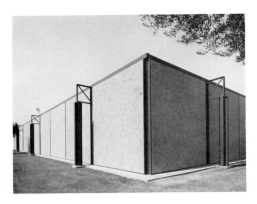

SDS (now Xerox) Building, Aviation Boulevard, El Segundo. Craig Ellwood brought to maturity in Los Angeles the Modernity envisioned by Mies van der Rohe. In his SDS Building of 1966, Ellwood placed the piers outside the exterior walls and hung tilt-slab precast concrete panels from the trusses. Here is the flying buttress of the Gothic cathedral adapted to an uncompromisingly Modern aesthetic.

RIGHT:

Milliron Department Store (now Broadway), 8739 Sepulveda Boulevard, Westchester. Designed by Gruen and Krummeck in 1949, this large department store is the anchor for one of Los Angeles's early shopping centers. The Sepulveda and 88th Street facades are of brick articulated with Moderne vertical fins and surmounted by a sweeping white roof ledge that frames the automobile entrance at one end of the building. Since parking space was limited, the architects added roof parking and provided access via two interlocking ramps that were left exposed. There are no show windows along Sepulveda, but this function is given to four freestanding display buildings set at an angle to the street so that motorists "can get a glimpse at the goods displayed without turning their heads and distracting their attention from safe driving."

walls were often replaced with brick. The most readily identifiable facade element of this period is the bezeled window. Like the crystal of a pocket watch, windows were outlined in a protruding, bezel-like flange, often in a material and color that contrasted with the wall. Frequently the bezel would extend beyond the windows to wrap around corners or dive into the ground in an inverted L-shape, giving the facade a look of tautness. This treatment seemed to express a steadfastness and rootedness that in actuality the country had not experienced for nearly two decades.

Los Angeles Orthopedic Hospital, 2400 South Flower Street. Another structure-expressive building is this hospital by A. C. Martin and Associates, built in 1959. The design juxtaposes external piers with protruding horizontal plates that define the floors and serve as sunshades for the next lower story. The aesthetic of the slab in construction is emphasized by the use of varying colors. This period of Modern architecture, like the late Moderne, has largely been disregarded in subsequent years, but it was an important stylistic development.

LEFT:

Union Bank Plaza, 445 South Figueroa Street. This 1967 highrise by A.C. Martin is a late example of the structure-expressive period of the Modern Movement. Recessed windows alternate vertically with black spandrels, and the protruding steel piers are sheathed in grey metal and accented in white. Situated in the middle of a formal garden with concrete planters and benches, the building is linked to the complex of highrise buildings across Figueroa Street by a pedestrian bridge.

Tishman Building, 3325 Wilshire Boulevard. During the 1950s and 60s, the glass curtain wall made its appearance as a major style within the Corporate Modern Movement. The most notable early example in Los Angeles is the Prudential Building, illustrated on page 205. During the 1950s, the walls were not left exposed as in the skin buildings of the 1970s, but were usually shrouded by sunscreens. The 1957 Tishman Building by Victor Gruen and Associates has a vertical metal screen of slanted fins covering the east and west walls and horizontal screens covering the south facade on Wilshire Boulevard. Sunscreens had practical value and also gave interest and complexity to an otherwise plain glass facade.

OPPOSITE:

Sultan house, 744 Brooktree Road, Pacific Palisades,exterior. By the 1970s, the challenge of the typical post-and-beam house had been met with great elegance and its architectural problems solved. Some architects moved away from the style, while others, such as Ray Kappe in his Sultan house of 1976, began to capitalize on the possibilities of large spans. In this 7000-square-foot house, Kappe substantially opened up the interior both horizontally and vertically, and expanded the glass walls into the ceiling to maximize the surrounding forest view. It is set on a steep hillside, supported on redwood towers.

One of the buildings to adopt this idiom partially was the first large postwar building in downtown Los Angeles and the first major office structure designed by a firm that would become one of the world's principal designers of large-scale architecture. The General Petroleum Building (now Lloyds Bank), designed by Walter Wurdeman and Welton Becket and completed in 1949, stands at 612 South Flower Street.[21] The building was actually innovatively light in weight, but its cubic form lends a feeling of density and enclosure. Corners are accented by a horizontal group of bezeled windows on each floor. The architects attempted to cut air conditioning costs by installing aluminum fin sunshades that also provided a nominal exterior decoration for each facade.

Even an architect such as Stiles O. Clements, the brilliant stylist of prewar Art Deco, Churrigueresque, and Streamline, moved toward the bezel treatment in his postwar work. The facade of his Citizens National Bank (1948), 5780 Wilshire Boulevard, was designed with plate and corrugated glass panels, aluminum, and limestone in a huge, square composition which juts out from the body of the building.[22] Marsh, Smith and Powell's Founders Hall (1950) on the University of Southern California campus incorporates poured concrete "earthquake bands" extending the length of the building and emerging through the facades, which are of variously patterned red brick. One of the bands whips around the main entrance in an L-shape, to create a three-foot-deep reveal.[23] Numerous buildings in this style, most with brick facades and horizontal bands of bezeled windows, are found along Wilshire Boulevard east of MacArthur Park. Many postwar factories also adopted the style; it was an inexpensive way to add flair and color to a basic building, in an era when the construction industry was still recovering from a long period of little activity. Almost no research has been undertaken regarding this style, and the architectural significance of these buildings has remained unappreciated. Future investigations will, it is hoped, bring the postwar Moderne greater recognition as a significant architectural period.

Beyond the late Moderne, within the Modern Movement itself, two trends emerged after the war, the second of which has, by the 1980s, emerged into a substantial school of thin-skinned architecture. In the first postwar trend, the emphasis was on the expression of a building's structure, in an idiom analogous to the post-and-beam residential architecture of the period. An early postwar design in this style is the Lever Brothers Factory (1951; Bechtel Corporation with Welton Becket and Associates) at 6300 Sheila Street in the City of Commerce. The four-story office building, set in landscaped grounds in front of the soap manufacturing plant, is built of a concrete frame. Large concrete slabs at each end of the building, as well as the slab roof, visually float away from the building core, emphasizing the role of the concrete frame in holding the building together.[24]

The Los Angeles Orthopedic Hospital (1959; Albert C. Martin and Associates) at 2400 South Flower Street juxtaposes external black piers with protruding white horizontal plates which define the floors and serve as sunshades for the next lower story. On the north end an external flying staircase serves as a fire escape.[25] A late structure-expressive highrise is the Union Bank Plaza (1967; Albert C. Martin) at 445 South Figueroa Street. Here, recessed windows alternate vertically with black spandrels, and the salient steel piers are sheathed in grey metal and accented in white.

This architecture was busy visually, and unsound economically since the external structure restricted the potentially leasable floor space. Thus by the 1970s, a second trend in corporate architecture, the building sheathed in a thin curtain wall, became the dominant form for all but prestige office towers. Curtain wall development can be seen in Los Angeles beginning with buildings such as Wurdeman and Becket's Prudential Building (1948) at 5757 Wilshire Boulevard. The dominant feature of the facade is a central windowless shaft, but flanking it are two ten-story office wings with facades largely of glass. The glass wall was not yet totally exposed, however; the facade of the Prudential has horizontal aluminum sunshades running the length of the office wings. At night the building becomes an illuminated negative of itself, with light from the windows reflecting off the central shaft. The period of its construction is indicated by the east facade, which is articulated with bezeled Moderne windows.

During the 1950s the glass facade was further asserted as the entire exterior of a building, but the facade tended to be protected by great quantities of sunscreen, in materials such as gold anodized punched aluminum. The Tishman Building (1957; Victor Gruen and Associates) at 3325 Wilshire Boulevard has a vertical metal screen of slanted fins covering the east and west walls, and horizontal screens covering the south facade on Wilshire. A nearly identical building at 3540 Wilshire Boulevard also has horizontal sunscreens on the Wilshire facade, but this time it faces north. Thus the sunscreen was as much an aesthetic device as a practical one, to enhance an otherwise plain glass wall. The image was similar to that of the 1950s sunburst wall clock, where simple forms were enhanced by bright metal eye-catchers. Like the wall clock, the Tishman Building is now a period piece, but it is a forerunner of the commanding aesthetic of the 1980s.

Crystal Cathedral, 12141 Lewis Street, Garden Grove, by Philip Johnson and John Burgee, 1980. For the expansion of his drive-in church, Dr. Robert Shuller wanted a building that interfered as little as possible between "your eyeball and the infinity of space." Thus the architects created an immense glass tent in the shape of a four-pointed star, with a tapered, glass roof. Behind the pulpit, two ninety-foot-high airplane hangar doors open to welcome the automobile congregation. The church is not air conditioned, but is cooled with cross ventilation from the doors, windows, and a clerestory at the top. Reflected in the glass walls of this photograph are the original Garden Grove Community Church of 1961, by Richard Neutra, and the Tower of Hope, designed by Dion Neutra in 1967.

By the 1950s, the totally exposed glass curtain wall had been developed in the work of Mies van der Rohe, as in his Lake Shore Apartments (1951) in Chicago. The artistry of making this curtain wall appear extremely thin was brought to a scintillating maturity in Los Angeles during the 1950s and 1960s by Craig Ellwood.[26] Ellwood's specialty, both in his domestic and commercial architecture, was to leave only the slightest hint of a transition through the facade between outdoors and indoors, even when he worked in the aluminum sunscreen period of the 1950s. In his first major commercial design, the South Bay Bank (1958) in Manhattan Beach, his modular sunscreens were placed in perfect proportion to the large facade windows so that one could view the entire interior as one approached the entrance. His Carson/Roberts Building (1960) at 8322 Beverly Boulevard presents an entire street facade of glass panels which shade

The Crystal Cathedral interior is completely covered with space trusses in the form of three-inch white pipes. Its shape was intended to pull all 1890 seats in as close as possible, resulting in a shortened nave and tapered transepts. On a sunny day, natural light streams past the piping, and at night the interior is bathed in white latticework. Johnson saw the building as a modern version of Sainte Chapelle in Paris, where the enclosure is principally glass and the structure seems to disappear. Above the chancel, the green bamboo tubes in this photograph were in the place of the pipe organ being built in Italy by Fratelli Ruffati.

small office balconies, all hovering above an open ground floor. His SDS (now Xerox) Building (1966) on Aviation Boulevard in El Segundo incorporates a flying buttress support system that allowed plain curtain walls of concrete and glass. This building shows Ellwood's penchant for tight modularity in an industrial building that needed large windowless expanses.

During the 1970s, the pure glass curtain wall was applied to large-scale buildings in an even sheerer skin, and architects still pursuing Modern forms in domestic architecture turned away from wood to steel and high tech. These recent trends, as well as the reaction to the Modern Movement that has brought Los Angeles once again to the forefront of architectural innovation, are discussed in the following chapter.

RECENT TRENDS
IN LOS ANGELES ARCHITECTURE

Several times in the history of Los Angeles, new waves of architectural sentiment have swept across the city, expunging old styles and introducing new ones, and changing the scale and materials of the city. The Italianate and Queen Anne swept away the adobe houses of the Californios, and the Craftsman and period revivals swept away the Queen Anne in turn. In the 1920s and 30s a handful of young, revolutionary architects planted starkly Modern homes among the Spanish and Tudor Revival streetscapes of the city, and by the 1950s they had fairly succeeded in removing period architecture from Los Angeles drawing boards.

Today, however, the city is witnessing an outburst of architectural intensity wherein all these tendencies are evident at once. There is a thriving Modern tradition in commercial architecture, and to some extent in residential architecture. The interest in traditional styles has been rekindled in yet another Tudor Revival. There is also, for the first time, a growing awareness of the city's architectural heritage in the burgeoning historic preservation movement. *Arts and Architecture* magazine was revived in 1981, under the editorship of Barbara Goldstein. On top of these waves, a handful of young architects are once again building starkly individual creations in the city, bringing Los Angeles to the forefront of architectural innovation in the 1980s.

Corporate Architecture: the Thin Skin

The glass-sheathed facade of the 1960s, following in the tradition of Mies van der Rohe, was an absolutely flat surface, sharply delineated in a travated system, and covering a building invariably shaped like a rectangle. In the individual building, this form could be beautiful, but when it was uniformly applied to a streetscape, the results were often a whole urban district of monotonous form and silhouette. The skyscraper canyons of large cities were partly the result of repetitions of good architectural solutions. Good solutions repeated too many times, however, become bad solutions.

Thus in the 1960s, architects of large-scale buildings began to turn away from the Miesian aesthetic to more sculptural forms that presented the building not as a rigid rectangle but as an enclosure sensitive both to the street and to differing interior spaces. The aesthetic vehicle for this transformation was the

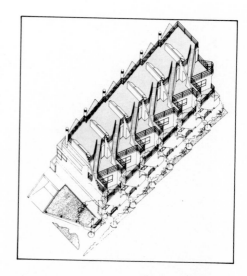

Condominiums, 831 Pacific Street, Santa Monica, designed in 1981 by David Cooper and Michael Folonis.

OPPOSITE:

Delmer house, 15th Place, Venice. Remodeling in 1977 by Thom Mayne and Michael Rotondi.

thin skin of glass which was moved to the outside edges of the mullions, enclosing the entire structural system of the building. The development of the thin-skin building, which by the 1980s has become the norm for many commercial buildings, is represented in the designs of two architects working together in Los Angeles during the mid-1960s: Anthony Lumsden and Cesar Pelli.

Working for Daniel, Mann, Johnson and Mendenhall from 1964 to 1968, Lumsden and Pelli began to search for an architecture free of the old constraints placed by masonry construction—in particular the heavy exterior wall of a building in which the interior was determined by traditional notions of office spaces. If the interior spaces could be freed up, and if the exterior walls were totally devoid of structural responsibilities, then the exterior could be handled as a skin—thin and pliable.

The first building to which they applied a thin skin was the Century City Medical Plaza at 2080 Century Park East, designed in 1966 and completed in 1969. The seventeen-story tower and adjacent four-story building are still Miesian rectangles, but they are entirely sheathed in black glass joined by narrow mullions whose exterior faces extend about an inch beyond the surface of the glass itself. In two other projects designed the same year, Lumsden and Pelli moved away from the rectangle, beginning the evolution toward the sculpted office building which continues in the 1980s. Their Teledyne Laboratories, completed in 1968 at 19601 Nordhoff Street in Northridge, is a black glass groundscraper where the rectangle is broken by triangular extensions so that the building reflects itself in its own mirrored windows. The Federal Building in Lawndale, 15000 Aviation Boulevard, completed in 1973, is clad in silver reflective glass and aluminum panels and mullions, taking on a neo-Streamline look.

Shelton house, 1211 Linda Flora Drive. This redwood house, designed in 1977 by Charles Moore and Ron Filson, is set on a hillside of rich foliage, combining visions of the California ranch house and the formal villa. One enters the long house through a courtyard containing a swimming pool fed by a waterfall, and from inside one looks out a series of windows that climb the uphill side of the living room to frame treetop views. Different planes are different colors, subtly varied to extend and restrain spaces, and slant-topped arches remove the feeling of being inside a long house.

Of Pelli's buildings in Los Angeles, certainly the masterpiece is the Pacific Design Center (1975), 8687 Melrose Avenue. The blue glass skin of this display center for the contract furnishings industry stretches for 530 feet along Melrose, around a semicircular protrusion on the front which holds banks of escalators, and up over a barrel vaulted galleria on the top floor, whose shape is expressed in the roof line of the building. The interior layout belies one's expectations, as the passageways are floored in red tile and generally lie in a diagonal to the facade. On the upper floors, narrow passageways wander like Medieval streets past the showrooms, and the galleria above borrows from the enclosed European shopping street.

If the image of the 1930s was speed, the image of the 1970s was the cool, quiet competence of electronic technology, represented in architecture by the smoked-glass exterior. After Pelli left in 1968, Lumsden and his associates at DMJM began to play with the skin in an effort to enhance the character of the tall building. DMJM's One Park Plaza (1972), at 3250 Wilshire Boulevard, has glass-skin towers at each corner, and the Century Bank Plaza of the same year, at 6420 Wilshire, is one of the first faceted tall buildings—an angular, sculpted form which has been much copied. Not so much copied, but perhaps still a portent of the future skyscraper, is the Manufacturer's Bank of 1973, at 9701 Wilshire Boulevard in Beverly Hills. The frame of this building is trapezoidal, but the smoked-glass skin undulates around it, obscuring any hint of the building's actual structure.

As energy-conscious designs began to call for the maximum reflective power of the skin during the 1970s, the smoked-glass skin gave way to mirrored glass. The forerunner was the CNA Building at Sixth

Warner Brothers Office Building, 3903 West Olive Avenue, Burbank, by the Luckman Partnership, 1981. The ultimate thin-skin building is where no mullions at all protrude beyond the exterior surface. In the Warner Brothers Building the curved exterior glass is glued in place with silicone adhesive instead of being set into an aluminum frame. The building features exterior balconies and three three-story atriums.

Street and Commonwealth Avenue (1972; Langdon and Wilson), which mirrors the landscaping of La-fayette Park and the neo-Gothic First Congregational Church (1932; Allison and Allison) at 540 South Commonwealth. By the 1980s the mirrored building is seen frequently in office districts throughout the city. Visually, the surface building gives its surroundings back to the street, the building becoming an invisible mass; its success depends heavily on its context.

The ultimate mirrored building in the Los Angeles area is the Crystal Cathedral (1980; Philip Johnson) in Garden Grove. From the interior one looks out through a space frame of oversized white pipes covering both ceiling and walls. At night the image is reversed, and the soft white glow of the interior illumination can be seen from afar, while from the inside the glass skin turns black and one is surrounded by a delicate mesh of white. The building dwarfs the original drive-in church beside it, designed in the structure-expressive ethic of 1962 by Richard Neutra.

Innovation in corporate architecture of the 1960s and 70s created a building type that is flexible and inexpensive to construct. This new architecture has taken the Modern ethic in a full circle from the Beaux Arts treatment of the facade. The Miesian tradition held that the structure of a building should be its dominant aesthetic feature; today, by contrast, the thin skin is consciously divorced from a building's structure in the same way the Classical motifs of the Beaux Arts period were divorced from the steel frame. Skin buildings in the 1970s were generally conservative, following in the tradition of their International Style forebears, but, with the growing acceptance of skin as divorced from structure, new forms, styles, and colors for the corporate highrise of the 1980s hold the promise for a new era in architectural design.

Late Modern Residential Architecture

The Los Angeles hillsides lent themselves to the cubical Modern designs of the 1920s and 30s, as well as the post-and-beam architecture of the 1950s. Here the house could jut out from the slope and, through its glass walls, command the hill and the views of the city below. Two architects who have returned to the steel frame in the 1970s and have developed a high industrial ethic in domestic architecture are Peter de Bretteville and Helmut Schulitz. De Bretteville's double house, built in 1976 at 8071 Willow Glen Road, is essentially composed of two two-story cubes separated by a concrete stairway, with walls of windows facing the private hill away from the street. The street facade is composed of a nearly windowless wall of corrugated metal siding, so that the house can be mistaken at first for a prefabricated industrial warehouse. The facade is painted a soft green, however, to blend with the wooded canyon in which it sits. De Bretteville has retained the interior of his own house in a hard, industrial look, with exposed wood and steel trusses, while that of his neighbor has been appointed in rich woods and filled with loft spaces.

Helmut Schulitz's interest in building industrialization led him to rethink the role of custom and ready-made elements in construction. "We seem to find nothing wrong when traditional housing is built from ready-made standardized floor plans with custom-made building techniques," remarked Schulitz. "I prefer the opposite approach: to use custom designs that respond to special situations and user needs and then to build the houses with ready-made standardized parts as industrialized systems."[1] Using this technique he built a house for himself in 1977 on a nearly unbuildable site at 9356 Lloydcrest Drive in Beverly Hills. He compiled a ready-reference catalog of off-the-shelf components. Then he developed a set of rules by which the components could be combined in different situations. As applied to his own house, the system yielded an exterior steel frame with corrugated metal siding and glass walls, with a thirteen-foot cantilevered terrace (see p. 163).

Alongside the steel-frame house, the post-and-beam tradition has been brought forward by architects such as Conrad Buff. His own house, built in 1980 at 1229 Linda Rosa Avenue, employs a symmetrical plan organized around a tiled walkway that begins at the motor court, passes over a swimming pool and through the house. The house itself is built of redwood, with stucco walls and teak appointments.

The Freedman house (1981; Kappe, Lotery, Boccato), at 533 Ninth Street in Santa Monica, brings the indoor-outdoor tradition into the house itself. The three-story home, plus tower, has grey stucco walls built around an exposed F-shaped steel frame, and a central skylighted atrium is crossed by bridges on the upper floors. A field of baby's breath is planted in the middle of the first floor, between the open kitchen and the sunken living room. From the outside the house has an enclosed look, but interior spaces are often separated only by waist-high partitions.

These and other architects continuing work in the Modern idiom have been paying little heed to the constraints imposed by its early masters. They are breaking away into personal statements that probe

OPPOSITE:

Conrad Buff house, 1229 Linda Rosa Avenue. Post and beam architecture has been brought forward by architects such as Conrad Buff. His own house, built in 1980, employs a symmetrical plan organized around a tiled walkway that begins at the motor court, passes over a swimming pool and through the house. The house itself is built of redwood, with stucco walls and teak appointments.

Century City Medical Plaza, 2080 Century Park East, Century City. Cesar Pelli and Anthony Lumsden, working together in the late 1960s, sought a way to free the exterior of a highrise building from its structural elements. They developed the notion of the thin skin, where the mullions lay inside rather than outside the windows, thus creating the possibility for sculptural exteriors that could move away from the frame. The first skin building was their Century City Medical Plaza, completed in 1969. It is composed of two buildings entirely sheathed in black glass, and the mullions protrude only about an inch beyond the exterior surface.

Federal Building, 15000 Aviation Boulevard, Lawndale. Cesar Pelli's Federal Building, completed in 1973, is an early skin building in mirrored glass and dull aluminum panels. The complex curvature at the corners exceeded the capacity of the materials to express smooth transitions, giving the composition an intriguing bulkiness, unlike the sleekness of the Teledyne Labs.

RIGHT:

Manufacturers Bank, 9701 Wilshire Boulevard, Beverly Hills. The potential for the skin to be placed independent of the steel frame was tested by Anthony Lumsden in his Manufacturers Bank of 1973. The frame is trapezoidal, but the glass skin undulates around it, obscuring any hint of the building's skeleton. Where speed was the image often evoked in the 1930s, the image of the 1970s was the cool, quite competence of electronic technology expressed in the "black box" look of smoked glass.

Teledyne Laboratories, 19601 Nordhoff Street, Northridge. One of Cesar Pelli's contributions to large-scale architecture has been the flexible interior organization system based on circulation spines. His first spine building, the Teledyne Labs of 1968, is organized internally as a city street bordered by various divisions of the aerospace firm. The exterior incorporates protruding bays that allow the two-story building to reflect itself in its bronze glass sheathing.

new aesthetic values while attempting to grapple with questions of appropriate architecture. In recent years, however, they have been joined by a group of architects following a quite different path and approaching these questions from a different perspective. They use unorthodox materials to create unorthodox spaces, offering basic challenges to the formulations of Modernism and reaching out to draw from other architectural ethics.

Charles Moore and Frank Gehry: Beyond Modernism in Los Angeles

The Modern Movement, as it released architecture from the tyranny of the past, created for many architects its own tyranny of the present. Its rigid dogma rejected any reference to architectural style other than that created by the materials and structure of the building itself. Major architects who were able to work outside its bounds by mid-century, for example Edward Durrell Stone, were often viewed as romantics who played on sentiment and the inner longing for Classical order. The watershed design by Charles Moore, Sea Ranch Condominium No. 1, legitimized a whole new school of thought countering the Modern Movement. Built in 1965 north of San Francisco, it is probably the single most influential building for recent architecture in California. His shed roofs reintroduced the roof as an architectural element, whereas most roofs of Modern buildings were flat and therefore unseen. Moore also reintroduced

LEFT:

CNA Building, 600 South Commonwealth Avenue. As energy-conscious designs began to call for the maximum reflective power of the skin during the 1970s, the smoked-glass exterior gave way to mirrored glass.

the enclosed house of solid walls using the traditional material of stucco, and brought new attention to the window as an element of form that could be played with by the architect, rather than serving as a diaphonous curtain between indoors and out. His writings, particularly *Body, Memory and Architecture* (1977), written with Kent C. Bloomer, have offered a theoretical framework within which to question the tenets of the Modern Movement. He formulates his discussion around the question of how buildings affect individuals and communities emotionally, how they provide people with a sense of joy, identity and place rather than around the Modernist notion of architecture as a Cartesian grid.

Moore has succeeded as perhaps no other twentieth-century architect in understanding why the long history of Western architecture has created certain enduring spaces and how we respond to them, and he has brought this understanding to his own work. His basic supposition is that the best way to design something that will be used and enjoyed is to start with something we enjoy already. In his Los Angeles work he has reached back to the Hispanic heritage of California and Mexico, to the Shingle Style of New England, to the Hollywood stage set, and to the Italian Renaissance.

Moore's first Los Angeles commission was the Burns house (1974) at 230 Amalfi Drive in Pacific Palisades. The three-story house strains for a view of the Pacific, but as viewed from the street its pitched roofs respect the context of the neighborhood's bungalow scale. The transition from the street side to the

Schulitz house, 9356 Lloydcrest Drive, Beverly Hills. Architect Helmut Schulitz reconsidered the role of custom- and ready-made elements when he built this house for himself in 1977. Where housing has traditionally been designed with standardized floor plans using custom-made building techniques, Schulitz prefers to use custom designs that respond to special situations, and then to build with standardized parts.

TOP:

Danziger Studio, 7001 Melrose Avenue. As an accomplished architect in the Modern idiom for many years, Frank Gehry's interest in art led him to the notion of architectural minimalism.

villa scale of the downhill face is marked by color variations in the stucco walls: 28 colors to be exact, of orange, mauve, and ochre. The courtyard, with its zigzag pool, is actually a small space, but its lush planting and bright colors send the viewer's attention through a carefully placed cutout to a piece of the ocean beyond. Inside, his tall, small spaces make both the people and the objects inhabiting it seem big and important. The rich texture of the house has inside windows looking out, outside windows looking in, enclosures within enclosures, outside materials inside, and inside materials outside, making a unified and nurturing environment of the entire parcel of land.[2]

The same nurturing environment is created in other of Moore's works using quite different materials and evocations. His Shelton house (1977), 1211 Linda Flora Drive, is built of redwood and is set in a hillside of rich foliage, combining visions of the California ranch house and the formal villa. One enters the long house through a courtyard containing a swimming pool fed by a waterfall, and from inside one looks out a series of windows that climb the uphill side of the living room to frame treetop views. A vista makes us feel that our body has expanded, according to Moore. Different planes are painted different colors, subtly varied to extend and restrain spaces, and slant-topped arches remove the feeling of being inside a long house.

A third distinctive vision is Moore's Rodes house (1979) at 1406 Kenter Avenue. The home evokes a Palladian villa, its striking formal facade set against a steep hill. The drama of the house is in its public face, and it incorporates many of the aesthetic values that impressed Moore in Frank Lloyd Wright's very first commission in Chicago.[3] In paraphrasing Moore's comments on Wright's Winslow house, we find the character of the Rodes house as well. The house has a tremendous presence, an impression due in no small part to the treatment of the site itself. A step up at the elliptical terrace makes a low podium of the front and sets it apart from the surrounding grounds. The public face of the Rodes house appears to rest on this terrace, from which rises a tough protective skin of pink stucco. The act of penetrating the stucco

RIGHT:

Duplex, 6672 Vista del Mar, Playa del Rey. This sculptural duplex, designed by Eric Moss and James Stafford in 1977, received an American Institute of Architects award as a "whimsical tour de force." The white and yellow curvilinear facade is purely an aesthetic device.

Cabrillo Marine Museum, 3720 Stephen M. White Drive, San Pedro. Gehry was bothered by the tendency of owners to construct an ugly chain-link fence around a beautiful building for security purposes. Thus, for his Cabrillo Marine Museum of 1981, he designed a group of inexpensive detached buildings surrounding a central courtyard completely covered by a mesh of chain link. Chain link is continued in the interior, where it doubles as security fencing and a surface for hanging exhibits.

skin is celebrated by edging the window and door openings in white. An amphitheater is formed from the front of the house and its terrace where plays and concerts are staged by the owner (see p. 208).

Frank Gehry is probably the second most influential Los Angeles architect in the 1980s. He comes from a quite different point of view than Charles Moore, however, and from a less theoretical basis. Gehry was an accomplished architect in the Modern idiom for many years, but his interest in contemporary painting led him to architecture as art, and in particular to the notion of architectural minimalism. In an early work at 7001 Melrose Avenue, the Danziger studio (1965), the street facade is a pure closed cube in mysterious grey stucco, broken only by an open cube at the roof, encasing a window, and a recessed rectangle of a garage door directly below. To the rear, a glass curtain wall opens to an enclosed courtyard.

During the early 1970s, Gehry began to move away from constrained forms to explore both the medium of Modern architecture and its symbolic content. He began to experiment with architectural volumes using ordinary, mass-produced building materials. The results were what he has come to call a "cheapskate architecture"; since it was often necessary to cut costs with inexpensive materials, believed Gehry, the architect should understand their potentials and find ways to make them beautiful.

Gehry was bothered, for example, by the tendency for owners to construct an ugly chain link fence around a beautiful building for security purposes once it had been completed. Thus he explored the aesthetic qualities of chain link, culminating in a project he calls the "Chain Link Extravaganza by the Sea," the Cabrillo Marine Museum (1981), 3720 Stephen M. White Drive, San Pedro. Here he designed a group of inexpensive detached buildings surrounding a central courtyard completely covered by a mesh of chain link. Chain link is continued in the interior, where it doubles as security fencing and a surface for hanging exhibits. He arranged the volumes of the buildings so that visitors follow a planned sequence of events, guided by architectural clues such as angles, differing materials, and architectural cutouts.

Gemini G.E.L. Building, 8365 Melrose Avenue. During the 1970s, Frank Gehry turned from the Modern movement to explore other realms of architecture as art. Two of his themes are clashing volumes and forced perspective, executed in inexpensive, unfinished materials such as chain link and unfinished plywood. His Gemini G.E.L. Building of 1976 employs architectural cutouts and exposed studs to tear away visually accepted architectural conventions such as "wall."

LEFT:
Gemini G.E.L., interior

In other projects he has concentrated on the art of architecture, forcing perspectives and revealing structure. In this aspect of his work, however, he pursues risk rather than beauty, testing the notion of organized chaos and the aesthetic results of colliding forms. Gehry's addition to the Gemini G.E.L. studios (1976) at 8365 Melrose Avenue bends the cornice line from the old building downwards, away from its edge, and inserts a raw plywood staircase between the old and new buildings which runs unexpectedly but fittingly to Gehry's personal sense of order. Above it is a skylight that sits at an angle—another favorite Gehry element presenting exactly the opposite of what one expects to see.

The Arnoldi Triplex (1981), 322 Indiana Avenue in Venice, is composed of three free-standing cubes sheathed in clashing, unexpected materials. One is in dark green asphalt shingle siding, the second in unpainted, exterior plywood, and the third in bright blue stucco. Each unit has a signature as well, in an oversized stairway cascading down the first unit, a huge New England fireplace chimney—not real—on

Delmer house, 15th Place, Venice. The seaside community of Venice has long been a haven for individual lifestyles and architectural visions and since the 1970s has been the site of many innovative designs. In 1977 Thom Mayne and Michael Rotondi remodeled Fred Delmer's old bungalow, sheathing it in corrugated aluminum for protection against the corrosive sea breeze. Atop the house, a low wall around the sun deck screens out both street noises and the wind.

the second, and a miniature fractable gable on the third. The signatures, coupled with windows designed as cutouts and the buildings' irregular shapes, create pieces of abstract sculpture.

His penchant for exposing raw materials such as plywood and house framing, his carefully orchestrated unfinished looks, his cutout walls of windows that serve as stage sets, have been accompanied by his desire to expose whole rooms as free-standing forms scattered about a parcel of land. By disassembling his architecture he asks basic questions about what a room is and what are appropriate links between spaces. His raw aesthetics force the investigation of what should be seen in a building and what should not. Charles Moore has suggested the importance of a building's public face, whereas Gehry has asked why the public face should belie the working spaces of a building—a Modernist question for which he provides a very personal answer, often by making the opposite of an expected decision.

To some extent Gehry answers his own brash questions in smooth work such as the Santa Monica Place shopping center (1980). Chain link and the exposed, inexpensive structure is present in abundance, but he has created a welcoming address to the street at the main entrances, and the diagonal pedestrian shopping street through the center uses his conventions of superimposed grids and the feeling of passage marked by bridges and columns to provide a small-scale environment in a large space (see p. 210).

New Architecture in Los Angeles

Today Los Angeles finds itself a rich seedbed for young architects who are asking very personal architectural questions and thereby bringing architecture in the city to the forefront of architectural innovation. The new Los Angeles architecture does not easily fit into a style or school, since there is no common dogma among the practitioners, and a precise overview of this work will only be possible with

the perspective of time. Despite the differing forms coming from their drawing boards, however, and despite the immediacy of this new unfolding, some observations can be made about what they believe and about the aesthetic in which they work.[4]

In general, this group of architects works from the point of view that the Modern Movement has few lessons to teach them. The ideology of the Modern Movement, with its notions of social reform, long ago was bleached from its architecture, leaving the forms but without convincing content behind them. The Centre Pompidou in Paris stands as the ultimate negative image of the vision of super-technology without content, where function, structure, and mechanical systems determine the form of the building. Thus it is now important to reinvest architecture with meaning no longer present in the remaining shell of the Modern Movement which asks only how to express the structure or how to make the skin smooth.

Delmer house, view looking upward through the skylight.

Architects are searching once again, as the Modern pioneers did nearly a century ago, to rediscover the fundamental truths of what architecture is, what is the nature of buildings in an urban context, what is style, and what is appropriate technology. Charles Moore's admonition that architectural structure be left aside as the basis for building design has been taken seriously, but the path for the young architects has not been clearly drawn. The negative influences on their work seem to be stronger than the positive ones—the architects know what they don't want to do, but there are few models to suggest what they do want to do. Society has no direction today, so architecture doesn't either.

Innovations in the new architecture are more aesthetic than structural, partly because many of the new architects tend to be artists as well. Coy Howard has a background in graphics, set design and film; Frederick Fisher has worked in collage and is interested in drawing; Robert Mangurian and Craig Hodgetts are interested in film. There is a new interest in architecture as craft but the desire to explore new materials is thwarted by the lack of them; thus the new architecture tends to be executed in traditional materials such as stucco or in industrial materials that are utilitarian, inexpensive, and durable. Some work, such as Frederick Fisher and Thane Roberts's Caplin house (1979), 229 San Juan Avenue in Venice, tends to follow Frank Gehry's unfinished look, creating with it the image of the house as the ocean wave. Whereas Eric Moss has designed a five-unit condominium (1981) at 475 South Euclid Avenue in Pasadena in well-finished stucco. Its south wall has a window distribution to suggest five faces—two double hung windows on the third floor for the eyes, two casement windows below for the nose, and a row of six double hung windows on the bottom story for the teeth.

Industrial materials have often been chosen as architects attempted to look at the utility of each item in a building rather than choose elements because of a style. Steve Wiseman's Suntech Townhomes (1980) at 28th and Pearl streets in Santa Monica is hardly high tech in execution, with its pastel stucco

RIGHT:
Caplin house, interior

Caplin house, 229 San Juan Avenue, Venice. This house by Frederick Fisher and Thane Roberts is a painterly nautical metaphor responding to the owner's childhood on a boat. The roof is arched as an upside-down hull, but is distorted to one side as a wave. From the exterior, the house is reminiscent of a blue rolling wave. The front is the most important composition. It is an abstract collage to look not like a house, but like an assemblage of elements, including eleven types of windows, tile, a glass bib over the front door, and a bathroom ventilator as part of the design. The exterior yields no hint of the interior.

walls. Entering the interior passageway between the units, however, is akin to walking through the Hoover Dam powerhouse: tubular steel railings, industrial gooseneck lighting fixtures, galvanized stovepipe chimneys, modular windows, and flat walls resembling turbine housings—or perhaps grain elevators on the Midwestern plains.

When remodeling Fred Delmer's old bungalow in Venice (1977), Thom Mayne sheathed the entire house in corrugated aluminum which is maintenance-free and would resist the corrosive climate of the beach air. The potential for humor in such applications has not gone unnoticed—when it was mentioned that the remodeled house looked like a semi-trailer, Delmer installed amber truck running lights around the top corners of the house.

Aesthetic conventions normally serve to define an architectural style. With the new Los Angeles architecture, however, a set of aesthetic conventions is not being forged. In fact, the pursuit of beauty is not necessarily part of the process at all for some architects like Gehry. Robert Mangurian and Craig Hodgetts, on the other hand, create simple but dramatic surfaces and bold colors. They even audaciously apply traditional ideas, for example the formal space of a central, circular atrium in their Gagosian Gallery (1981) in Venice. Most of the other new architects tend to be more interested in the aesthetics of spaces rather than the aesthetics of surfaces—a pursuit they have adopted from the Modern Movement.

Part of the aesthetic derives from the interest in probing fantasy, a human quality, rather than efficiency, a structural quality. Thom Mayne and Michael Rotondi's 2-4-6-8 house is a study in how buildings communicate to us; it originated as a child's sketch of a house, and it attempts to discern the meaning of house as an allegory to the time span of growing up. Frederick Fisher has designed fanciful environments to explore not only the sensuous contribution of architecture to the ritual of bathing, but also to reaffirm the relationships between humans and their natural environment.

LEFT:

2-4-6-8 house, Amorosa Court, Venice. Thom Mayne and Michael Rotondi conceived of this small studio-house as a hobby kit one might buy in a model shop. The windows in the four walls of the one-room house progress from two feet to eight feet square. By standing in the middle of the room and turning to look out each window sequentially, one can create the illusion of growth or shrinking. Outside, bright blue vents mimic beams above each yellow-framed window, and above the vents are red scuppers to keep water out of the vents. The garage walls are constructed of grey and pink concrete blocks.

Condominiums, 831 Pacific Street, Santa Monica. By David Cooper and Michael Folonis, 1981.

Solar One, 2065 North Sycamore Avenue. Extensive use of solar energy is one of the hallmarks of new architecture in the 1980s. The south front of this 1981 home by Frances Offenhauser is dominated by a solar greenhouse, which in cool weather serves as a passive heating element. At more temperate times it becomes a sheltered living space. Space heating and hot water are provided by an active solar system. Dining room, kitchen, den, and bedrooms are on the ground floor, and the living room is upstairs to take advantage of the vistas offered by the site.

TOP LEFT:
Condominiums, Barrington and Brookhaven avenues. The trend in the 1980s is to vertical living spaces in response to high land costs. These condominiums, designed in 1980 by Michael Folonis and David Cooper, are each three stories high above a garage, and they share a common roof terrace. The towers conceal stairwells.

RIGHT:
Office building, 1750 Fourteenth Street, Santa Monica. The rose colored cutout facade of this office building by Steve Wiseman, designed in 1980, is sited dramatically overlooking the Santa Monica Freeway.

The looseness of this architecture forces the readdressing of two architectural questions—integrity and context. Since the new architecture is not to be identified by stylistic conventions, the bounds of integrity within a work are unclear. That is, future remodeling may well go unnoticed because there were no conventions to be broken. This freedom does relieve the potential problem of how to respect an architectural creation in future remodelings, but it also supports the rapidly changing Future Shock atmosphere of Los Angeles which is sometimes taken as the entire architectural reality of the city.

Testing the question of what is context, the new architecture sometimes attempts to relate to the neighborhood by borrowing certain of its elements. Eric Moss took a chimney shape from the bungalows in the neighborhood of his condominium at 475 South Euclid Avenue in Pasadena and applied it as a silhouette on the front facade, and he made suggestions of a bungalow roof on the front of his building, which is essentially a box, to try to relate his taller building to the lower surrounding scale. In general, however, the traditional notions of architectural context—scale and harmony of line, color, and form—are loosely treated. Things out of context themselves eventually form a context, and in an area such as Venice which has a history of architectural innovation, there are so many off buildings that offness has become the new context. Aesthetics are thus allowed to run free, unhampered by a tie to functionalism. The architect can create forms that are merely to be looked at and enjoyed. You don't just put in a gutter, goes the saying, you play with the gutter.

Although no regional style as such is filtering through this work, there is a community of place and spirit, and a Southern California that puts up little resistance to architectural adventure. There is physical space to build on, and that space also allows an independence to create new forms, particularly in Venice, where there is a tradition of artists' studios and kindred spirits. Unlike the Modern masters, who intended their work to serve as paradigms for others, the new architects create each new design specifically for a time and circumstance. The essence of this architecture is thus the creative event more than what is created.

Whether the new architects can find new answers beyond the aesthetic realm is still unclear. What remains unasked are the hard social questions of affordable housing, neighborhood context, or the need for increased urban densities in the 1980s. Several architects have been working with passive solar

energy systems, but more effort has been concentrated on creating expensive pieces of architectural art. An exception is Glen Small's Green Machine project for the median strip of Venice Boulevard in Venice. This low-cost housing scheme calls for a three-story pyramid of housing space composed of new and recycled elements, with special attention to environmental conservation features. Another exception is Frederick Fisher's extremely low-cost artists' residence and studio in Venice. In general, however, if the pioneers of the Modern Movement developed social theories of architecture that could never have been borne out in their work, the new architects tend to pursue an atheoretical approach. If their answers are not always clear, perhaps it is because their questions aren't either.

Revival Architecture of the 1980s

The avant-garde work in Los Angeles is set against a background of traditional forms that still represent appropriate architecture to many of its consumers. In much developer-built housing, styles from the European Renaissance and early America are still in vogue. Rather, the symbols of these periods are in vogue, to decorate conventional houses of the American builder's vernacular. Such symbols have been part of most revivals in the last century, but in the 1980s they are copied with less fidelity and probably in thinner suggestions than previously as rising costs force builders to spend less on decoration.

The Hispanic tradition is still with us, in red tiled roofs and earth-colored stucco walls. In addition, American Colonial and French Renaissance decor is enduring, and neo-Victorian architecture is beginning to appear now that most of the real Victorian architecture has been removed. The period style reigning supreme in the 1980s is, however, the English Tudor.

The Barry Tarlow Law Building (1981; Warner and Gary) at 9119 Sunset Boulevard is designed as an eighteenth-century law office such as those found on Boston's Beacon Hill; it has round dormer windows, clay tile roofing, and huge brick chimneys topped with stork shields. The residential condominium development in Century City called Le Parc (1980; Casper Ehmcke for Maxwell Starkman and Associates) is a French country chateau set in waterfalls and grassy walks behind high, guarded walls. The building facades have suggestions of Mansard roofs and sparse Renaissance detailing enlivened by pastel colors. In Canoga Park, a neo-Victorian office building at 19725 Sherman Way (1981; Tom

Verdugo Hills subdivision, Camino de Villas, Burbank. The Spanish Revival lives on in Southern California, but the symbols of traditional styles become thinner. The large homes in this 1981 subdivision have stuccoed exteriors and red tile roofs, and are appointed with Mediterranean elements such as Italian floor tile, wrought iron railings, and wine cellars. Every home, however, is set atop a stucco box pierced by a garage door and plain main entrance.

TOP RIGHT:

The Oaks subdivision, Mulholland Drive at Topanga Canyon Boulevard. The English Tudor is the most popular revival style in the 1980s. Half-timber and brick facades lend an association with English aristocracy. Homes in "The Oaks" offer crown moldings, vaulted ceilings, paneled doors and hardwood cabinets.

LEFT:

Pages Victorian Court, 444 South Los Robles Avenue, Pasadena. Since much of the Victorian heritage has been demolished, new Victorian buildings are being constructed in the 1980s. Thornton and Fagan's Victorian Court is a typical 1980 multi-family dwelling, but it attempts to recapture the Victorian spirit through shingled siding, spindlework under the eaves, and brackets under the balconies.

Layman) is built of more than a thousand original artifacts rescued from real Victorian buildings razed in recent years. The all-new Pages Victorian Court at 444 South Los Robles in Pasadena (1980; Thornton and Fagan) has "the once traditional Victorian flavor with all the comforts of twentieth-century technology and design."

Tudor Revival has been a recurring trend in American domestic architecture. A few Tudor mansions still stand along West Adams Boulevard from the turn of the century, and many from the 1920s may be found in Hancock Park and other wealthy districts of that era. During the 1950s the Tudor waned, as people turned to vernacular Modernism for a vision of the bright new future, but once again in the 1980s the Tudor is the most popular traditional style for residential architecture. It has been the most popular choice in every western United States city except Seattle during the late 1970s according to one real estate marketer, who said that "people probably tend to associate cross-timbers with permanence and that's one reason why they like Tudor whether you call it Tudor or not. They also might associate Tudor with a move-up since it is difficult to build a low-end one."[5] The Tudor suggests wealth, partly in its association with English aristocracy. In expensive homes it lends itself to intricacy and surface ornamentation in its brick and wood beams, half-timbered walls, diamond-paned glass, and steeply pitched roofs.

The enduring value of some traditional architecture, when executed sensitively and with modern uses in mind, is seen in the J. Paul Getty Museum (1972; Langdon and Wilson), 17985 Pacific Coast Highway. The museum building is modeled after the Roman Villa de Papyri, to house the Getty collection of classical art. A Roman road leads through a Roman gate, and the building is resplendent in its reflection in a long courtyard pool.

The competition for public acceptance between period vernacular architecture and modern design remains strong and is now complicated by the attempts of some avant-garde architects to find a role for historical ideas once again. The opportunity for a new synthesis of these countervailing factors is offered in the 1980s by another important architectural trend: the interest in the preservation of the historical urban environment itself. No longer confined to an interest in great historical monuments, the preservation movement encompasses neighborhood preservation and the broad goals of urban conservation. Beyond

RIGHT:

Restored Spanish Renaissance lobby, Biltmore Hotel.

Platt Building, 19725 Sherman Way, Canoga Park. Parts of demolished Victorian houses live again in this neo-Victorian office building designed in 1981 by Tom Layman. Over one thousand original Victorian artifacts, including stained-glass windows, doors, banisters, columns, plumbing fixtures and decorative elements, were rescued by owner Dennis Platt from buildings about to be razed and incorporated into his new building.

an interest in the aesthetics of historical buildings, the movement now embraces the values of urban amenities, energy conservation, neighborhood stability, and human scale in the city—most of which are pursued by the avant-garde architects as well.

Historic Preservation in Los Angeles

Unlike the interest in conservation of the natural environment, which has been of concern in the United States for over a century, the conservation of the physical environment was largely disregarded until recent years. In fact, the assumption in American building practice was that physically or economically obsolete buildings would be removed and replaced by a new generation of more modern structures.

In a handful of cases public sentiment or a private donor would call for setting aside a building of particular historical merit and preserving it as a monument in the middle of a changing urban scene, but the notion of urban conservation—the intrinsic value of conserving the urban environment—was not part of the American ethic. Today, however, Americans have begun to take a second look at the cityscape. They have begun to value the sense of continuity and the link with past time and place that is forged only through a sensitive interplay of new and old.

The interest in conserving architecture and streetscape has extended far beyond the aesthetic qualities of historical architecture. Real estate developers and the business community have begun to see the sensitive rehabilitation of older buildings as opportunities for investment. The preservation of a building as a cost-efficient and resource-conserving alternative to new construction has in many cases become economically advantageous to investors. At the same time, there has developed a new appreciation for the amenities of many older buildings—the quality of materials and the fine craftsmanship of an earlier era—so that unlike one or two decades ago, it is common to see older interiors restored to a former elegance rather than remodeled to the latest architectural style.

In Los Angeles, a major impetus in the revitalization of the Pershing Square district of downtown has been the restoration of the Biltmore Hotel. The Biltmore had been the largest hotel west of Chicago when it opened in 1923, with 916 rooms. Designed by architects Schultze and Weaver, who had also designed the Waldorf Astoria in New York, the Biltmore interior evoked a lavish Renaissance palace with a Spanish main lobby and highly ornate public rooms with coffered ceilings and tapestried walls. By the early 1970s, however, the hotel had followed the economic decline of the central city and was badly in need of repair.

The architects Gene Summers and Phyllis Lambert were designing a new hotel complex on Bunker Hill in 1973 when they learned of the Biltmore's pending sale. Summers and Lambert changed their plans and purchased the Biltmore, renovating the building into one of the city's most elegant hotels. The public spaces were restored to their earlier elegance; the hand-painted galeria, originally by Giovanni Smeraldi, was retouched by his former apprentice A.T. Heinsbergen; and the guest rooms were fully modernized.[6] To date the project has proven a financial success and has demonstrated that a restored historical landmark can become an important center for downtown renewal.

At about the same time that Summers and Lambert purchased the Biltmore, the owners of the Pacific Mutual Building (1922; W.J. Dodd), a block away at 523 West Sixth Street, undertook the preservation of their building as well. When Pacific Mutual moved its headquarters to Newport Beach in 1969, they listed the old building for sale. When no buyers appeared by 1974, the company decided to keep the Beaux Arts building and began a major renovation. The ornate main lobby, with its measured spatial sequence and ornate marble staircase, was refurbished and appointed with new light fixtures. Upstairs, the spacious marble office corridors and the original marble and iron stairwells were preserved.

Also nearby, at 617 South Olive Street, is a renovated Art Deco masterpiece. The Oviatt Building (1928; Walker and Eisen) was built as an elegant men's clothing store, above which was James Oviatt's sumptuous Art Deco penthouse. When the store closed in 1969, the building fell into disuse. It was purchased by Ratkovich Bowers, Inc., in 1976 and refurbished as office spaces. The ground floor has been turned into a restaurant that preserves the original clothing shop decor—the oak cabinets formerly used to store shirts and ties now house wines, tablecloths, and silverware. The building is appointed in rich materials such as Lalique etched glass, French marble, and hand-carved oak elevators, most of which have been restored. Much of the Lalique glass in the lobby marquee was lost and has been replaced by a modern facsimile (see p. 207).

Elsewhere in the city, in an attempt to preserve examples of historical Los Angeles architecture that would otherwise be demolished, the private, non-profit Cultural Heritage Foundation has established a ten-acre site in Highland Park called Heritage Square. The foundation has moved to the site a number of residences and other buildings constructed in the late nineteenth century and is restoring them for

One of the most important architectural trends in the 1980s is the rediscovery of the values of older buildings. In Los Angeles, a major impetus in the revitalization of the Pershing Square district has been the restoration of the Biltmore Hotel, 515 South Olive Street. The Biltmore was the largest hotel west of Chicago when it opened in 1923. Designed by Schultze and Weaver, the interior evoked a lavish Renaissance palace with a Spanish main lobby and ornate public rooms with coffered ceilings and tapestried walls. By the early 1970s, the hotel had followed the economic decline of the central city. In 1973 architects Gene Summers and Phyllis Lambert purchased and renovated the old hotel. While the rooms were modernized, the public spaces were restored to their former elegance.

public viewing. Heritage Square is being rebuilt as a replica of a nineteenth-century village, with historic residences such as the Hale house (see p. 56), parks, and commercial buildings.

Heritage Square was planned in a period before the importance of maintaining the historical context of the city was realized. Today it is believed vital to retain buildings in their original locations where possible. One of the largest collections in the region of Queen Anne homes remaining in their original location is in Angeleno Heights, where a group of residents formed the Carroll Avenue Restoration Foundation in 1975 in order to preserve the architectural integrity of the street. The residents, through the foundation, have restored nine Queen Anne homes and have moved two into the neighborhood, replacing previously demolished homes. Recent installation of vintage street lights recreates a street of early Los Angeles, circa 1905 (see p. 240).

In the early 1980s one of the most significant older urban districts now on the threshold of revitalization is Spring Street. Already a National Historic District, Spring Street is the former financial center of the city. Its Beaux Arts and Art Deco office buildings, many of which are intact, often remained tenantless after the major financial institutions relocated to the Flower Street and Wilshire districts beginning in the 1960s. However, new owners and the Los Angeles Community Redevelopment Agency (CRA) are bringing new life to this historic street. The CRA has financed the rehabilitation of the I.H. Van Nuys Building (1911; Morgan and Walls) at Spring and Seventh streets into subsidized housing for senior citizens (Edward C. Barker and Associates, renovation architects). The CRA's program calls for mixed commercial, residential and cultural uses in other buildings along the street.

Two important buildings on Spring Street were pioneering renovation and restoration projects. The H.W. Hellman Building (1905; Alfred F. Rosenheim) and the Title Insurance and Trust Building (1928; John and Donald Parkinson) have been refurbished and restored in recent years by private owners, the former by the Banco Popular de Puerto Rico, and the latter by architect Ragnar C. Qvale. These buildings now offer modern office spaces that are reached through lobbies and corridors with marble stairways, bronze doors, coffered ceilings, stained glass skylights, terrazzo floors, mahogany wainscoting, and gold leaf detailing.

Historic preservation and urban conservation in Los Angeles are still in early stages, several years behind similar activities in other major American cities. The late start in Los Angeles is less a reflection of its potential for urban conservation than of the traditional attitude toward this city as a place of constant change and growth. Neighborhoods developed after the turn of the century are only now coming to be

Pacific Telephone Building, 716 South Olive Street. This four-story building was originally constructed in 1911 and remodeled about 1930 by Morgan, Walls and Clements into the Art Deco style. In 1979 Timothy Walker and Associates began a renovation of the building to retain its Art Deco features while modernizing its mechanical equipment. The central open staircase was preserved by enclosing the entire lobby for fire safety. Marble stairs were discovered beneath a vinyl surface and were restored, as were the wrought iron and wood banisters and the original cage elevator. Plaster moldings and cornices were repaired, and variations of paint color were used to accent period decorative motifs.

appreciated as historical entities, and Los Angeles has an incomparable legacy of Craftsman, Spanish Revival, and other architecture from the teens and twenties, as well as extensive Art Deco and Moderne commercial streetscapes which have until recently remained largely unnoticed. The current trend in urban conservation is not being lost on Los Angeles, however, and in the coming years the city will certainly see a broadening interest in the preservation of its urban past.

Los Angeles as an Urban Palimpsest

Nearly 7.5 million people live in Los Angeles County today, and the region continues to grow. In the last two hundred years the builders of this city have created many different environments, bringing with them from around the world their traditional styles and their new ideas. Each generation moved outward beyond the limits set by their forebears, so that today Los Angeles is woven with a dense fabric both unified and diverse. One can look to the city's past as a remote agricultural village in a Spanish colony reflected in the Plaza and its restored relics and then to the towering new skyscrapers of Flower Street, the pulsing center of the modern city. Stately Queen Anne mansions beaming their virtuosity toward the street stand beside courtyard homes facing inward to private spaces.

Long commercial thoroughfares speak of the Boom of the Twenties, reaching to the sea and to the eastern valleys. Similar streets beyond the Santa Monica Mountains tell us of the boom of the Fifties, when the San Fernando Valley turned from fields to homes. Cantilevered balconies, private elevators, and homes on giant stilts in the surrounding hills speak of our desire to be high, to see far; while neat rows of bungalows remind us of the American neighborhood that followed many here from their homeland in the East. Not only the architecture of Los Angeles speaks to us, but the context of that architecture as well: its scale, styles, materials, and colors. In the Los Angeles streetscape can be read the pursuit of the American dream and the desire to create a Mediterranean paradise on the Pacific.

When we contemplate a beautiful city, we see not only the latest architectural trends, but also the images of history which lend a sense of continuity and an intensity of place that comes only through time. Los Angeles is not yet an old city, but much of what stands today speaks of generations no longer with us, and of periods earlier in this fast-moving century that lived by different ideals. The city's vastness often hides its treasures, but a careful look between the freeways and behind the modern buildings reveals glimpses of previous generations. Los Angeles is an urban palimpsest; like the reused parchment on which the old writings are still faintly visible, the city retains vestiges of each period in its history.

Petroleum Building, 716 West Olympic Boulevard. Currently the object of a major historic preservation effort is the Petroleum Building, originally the business office of oil magnate E.L. Doheny. It was designed in 1925 by Meyer and Holler, architects of the Chinese Theater in Hollywood. The marble vaulted lobby will be restored, with its cast bronze elevator doors and stonework Gothic decor, and the false ceiling in the bank lobby will be removed to expose the plaster arches. Upstairs, the elevator lobbies and marble restrooms will be restored as well. Some of the marble flooring and wainscoting in the corridors will be retained, but since the U-shaped building is too narrow for many tenants today, some of the marble and wood appointments will be relocated to create larger office spaces. New mechanical systems will also be installed. The new owners plan to nominate the building to the National Register of Historic Places.

CODA: BUNKER HILL

Bradbury house, Court and Hill streets.

Third Street looking west toward Bunker Hill from Spring Street, 1888.

Etchemendez house, 237 North Hope Street, built in 1886. Demolished.

The story of Bunker Hill is a microcosm of the story of many American central city districts. In less than a century it went from raw land to fine mansions to derelict housing and back to raw land, where it now awaits a second future.

Real estate interest in Bunker Hill began in the late 1860s, when it was still some distance to the southwest of the city proper. As a speculative enterprise, the land was bought and subdivided by Stephen Mott, George Hansen, Prudent Beaudry, and others; but even though the lots offered an expansive view of the entire Los Angeles River Basin, they were quite unbuildable because no groundwater was available for domestic use.

In the 1870s, Beaudry franchised with the city to construct two reservoirs and fill them with water from a steam-driven pump and to distribute this water through iron pipes to the lots.[1] He also established a marketing program to sell properties on the hill to incoming Anglo residents, under a scheme to make land ownership feasible for middle-class families before they had become prosperous in their new surroundings. By the late 1870s, Bunker Hill was dotted with angular, white frame dwellings, usually two stories high and rising from a square floor plan; porches, store rooms, and kitchens were later tacked on to the cubes, and structures were topped with high-pitched roofs with ornate mouldings. This early architecture on the hill was a total Anglo import, and the simple hacienda forms of the indigenous adobe were largely deprecated.

Beaudry's enterprise and political connections, along with the Boom of the Eighties, made Bunker Hill a desired residential neighborhood by the 1890s, as the white boxes gave way to extravagant Queen Anne homes. It was not the most prestigious neighborhood in the city perhaps, but the home of substantial professional people: doctors, lawyers, merchants. According to Patricia Adler (1963)[2] "mechanics and day laborers had homes that delight the artist's eye" on Bunker Hill, where the new styles reached a concentration and exuberance scarcely to be matched. Houses were decorated by corner towers, spindled verandas, second- and third-floor balconies, stained glass, diagonal strips of siding, whorls of round-ended shingles, parti-colored roofing, English chimneys, and exterior walls painted brown or grey, according to the taste of the period.

As urban development leapfrogged over Bunker Hill and headed west, the hill was in a strategic location. During the Boom of the Eighties there was pressure for hotel construction, and soon elegant hotels such as the Melrose, Richelieu, Lincoln, and Belmont began to squeeze out the fine single-family residences. In those days there were no zoning laws to protect neighborhoods from encroaching development. Then came the commercial buildings: 136 of them were built on the hill by 1914. The intense land use and the new construction on the hill rendered it an architectural crazy-quilt, and many of the large old houses were divided into multiple units as the families moved on to newer, more elegant, or more secluded neighborhoods.

Looking north on Grand Avenue from
Fourth Street, Bunker Hill, 1913.

Bunker Hill Towers, 800 West First Street,
designed in 1968 by Robert E. Alexander.

Population pressures on the hill increased as it became easier to get to the top. One of the early problems in its development had been the steep climb to the top from Hill Street, and although cable railways had been attempted in the 1880s, successful public transit access to the hill was afforded only in 1901, with the construction of Angels Flight inclined railway at Third Street. Three years later, Court Flight [3] was constructed at the northern end of Bunker Hill, and operated until 1944.

At the same time that the cable cars began to run up the side, a tunnel beneath Third Street was blasted from Hill to Hope streets, carrying traffic under the hill and beginning to isolate it from the pulse of the city. By 1924, two additional tunnels carried traffic under Bunker Hill.

Crocker house, Olive and Third streets,
built in 1886, demolished in 1908.

After World War I, Bunker Hill became predominantly a refuge for pensioners, transients, and derelicts, as the area followed the economic decline of downtown as a whole. Construction literally ceased after 1920. According to the 1940 census, the mean date of construction of Bunker Hill buildings was 1895—the oldest for any census unit in the city. By 1955, eighty-two percent of the dwellings were substandard, most were owned by absentee landlords, the crime rate was double the city average, and city tax revenues from properties on the hill covered only fourteen percent of the city's costs in providing services to its population—predominantly low-income, elderly males.

In 1948 the City Council adopted a resolution declaring the need for a redevelopment agency, and by 1955 a plan had been prepared and adopted that called for the demolition and redevelopment of the entire hill. The derelict old mansions-turned boarding houses would be replaced by modern apartment towers and landscaped plazas. The proposals were controversial, but ten years later the land had been cleared, its population removed, and Angels Flight was dismantled amidst promises that it would be rebuilt as part of the redevelopment plan.

Portions of Bunker Hill have been redeveloped with highrise buildings set in landscaped malls and pedestrian walkways which have largely separated Bunker Hill from the surrounding city. One can walk from the Atlantic Richfield Plaza (1972; Albert C. Martin and Associates) south of Bunker Hill, through the Los Angeles Bonaventure Hotel's lobby (1976; John Portman and Associates), which is reminiscent of the movie sets in H.G. Wells' *Things to Come,* and from there either to the residential complex of Bunker Hill Towers (1968; Robert E. Alexander) or to the landscaped open areas of the Security Pacific Plaza (1973; William L. Pereira Associates) without ever entering the space of one of the streets surrounding these buildings.

At this writing, a mixed-use development called "California Center" is proposed for the remaining vacant land west of Hill Street. It will include highrise office space, a museum of modern art, theaters, shops, and residences. If these plans are realized, Bunker Hill will become the most intensely urban district in the city.

SEVEN TOURS OF LOS ANGELES

Along the streets of the city, buildings of many different periods and styles exist side by side; many are remnants of historical streetscapes that were once more unified. The image often held of Los Angeles, however, is one of freeway landscapes and extensive reaches of single family homes—and at freeway speeds one easily misses the rich urban character of the region. In Los Angeles the streetscape reads as a catalog of trends in Spanish, Mexican, and American urban development over the past two centuries. Although many older buildings have been demolished, the past hundred years of the city is still well represented. New development has tended to move ever outward, filling up empty land which seemed to be endless in the Los Angeles River Basin and San Fernando Valley. Thus, contrary to the refrain that Los Angeles is a city without a past, it turns out the city has an extremely rich architectural heritage from the perspective of the 1980s, when urban conservation has become a dominant theme in urban planning.

This book has highlighted buildings that still exist and has given their addresses where possible, to show the architecture of Los Angeles as a living history, and to encourage readers to explore the city's neighborhoods. The seven tours presented here supplement the discussion in the book by serving as a brief guide to some of this heritage. The last tour also offers a look at the latest architectural trends.

Please note that many of the buildings are privately owned. These should be viewed only from the street. The interiors of many of the city's fine houses may be viewed during house tours given from time to time by the Los Angeles Conservancy and other organizations. Self-guided walking and driving tour brochures to the architecture in many areas of the city are available from the Los Angeles Conservancy.

Interior, Bradbury Building

TOUR 1

OLD LOS ANGELES

Two Franciscan missions remain in the Los Angeles area from the Spanish colonial period, plus numerous adobe houses that were originally residences for the large ranches that once covered the Los Angeles Basin. This tour also includes vestiges of architecture introduced by the Americans prior to the Boom of the Eighties.

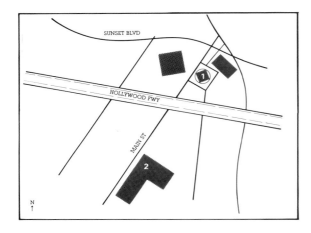

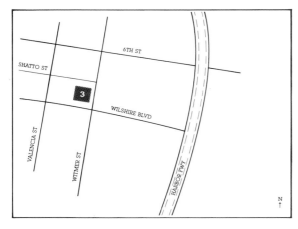

1   El Pueblo de Los Angeles State
Historic Park
North of the Hollywood Freeway on
Main Street

The center of the Spanish pueblo was the plaza. Now the centerpiece of this historic park, the Los Angeles Plaza is not the first for the city, but it has existed at this location since the early 1800s. Buildings of particular note in the park are the Plaza Church, built as the center for worship for the small village in 1822, and the Avila adobe, originally constructed in 1818 and now the oldest existing residence in the city. The Pico House hotel (1870; Ezra F. Kysor) and several buildings along Olvera Street are examples of early architecture introduced by the Americans. Tours of the park and a descriptive brochure are available from the park office.

2   St. Vibiana's Cathedral, 1876
Ezra F. Kysor
114 East Second Street

St. Vibiana's was built at the southeastern edge of downtown in the 1870s, and replaced the Plaza Church as the city's principal Roman Catholic church. In 1922 its facade was removed and replaced with a replica of its former self, but in Indiana limestone rather than its original red brick. It was also moved closer to the street. One of the most graceful vestiges of early Los Angeles architecture is the bell tower to the rear.

3   Foy House, 1873
633 South Witmer Street

One of the few remaining examples of Italianate architecture, which was popular in the 1870s, this house was originally on the site of the downtown Hilton Hotel. The front porch, formerly open, has been enclosed.

4   Italianate House
2624 Portland Street

Little is known about the early homes of the city, but this one certainly predates the construction surrounding it. The Italianate style borrowed details such as brackets and cornices from Italian villas, but in Los Angeles they were constructed of wood rather than stone.

5   San Gabriel Mission, 1771
537 West Mission Drive
San Gabriel

The fourth of the California missions to be founded, San Gabriel was established in 1771 further to the south of its present site and was moved here in 1776. The church dates from about 1805, and stands today much as it was originally designed. The exterior buttresses supported the original vaulted roof. A self-guided tour brochure is available at the mission.

Nearby is the Lopez de Lowther adobe, a long, low building that was originally part of the mission's west wall. It is now a museum.

6   San Fernando Mission, 1797
15151 San Fernando Mission Boulevard
Mission Hills

This mission was founded in 1797, in the middle of a vast grassy valley which provided water for crops and lime for mortar. The buildings were constructed around a central courtyard, and the most salient architectural feature is the long arcade that fronts the old *convento*. The mission church itself was destroyed in the 1971 earthquake and has been rebuilt as a copy of its former self. It is quite plain on the outside, but the interior shows the attention paid to decorative details of the mission churches by the Spaniards. The mission is open to the public.

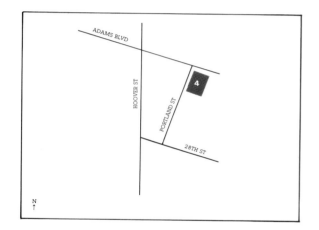

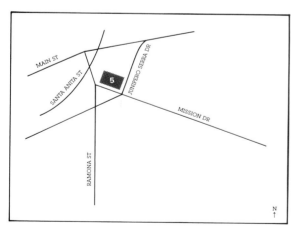

1   *Plaza Church, ca. 1940*

8   *Leonis adobe*

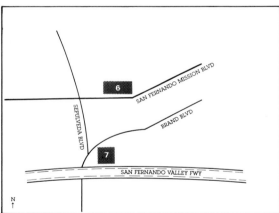

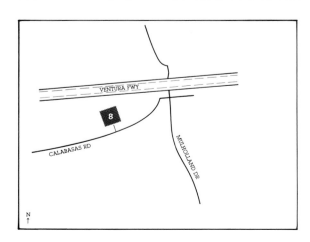

7   Andres Pico Adobe, 1834
10940 Sepulveda Boulevard
Mission Hills

The central part of this house was built in 1834 by former neophytes of the San Fernando Mission; the second story was added in 1873. Like many buildings from the early period, the Andres Pico house has several rooms in a row, joined by an exterior *corredor* or veranda rather than a central hallway, as in early American houses. It had fallen into ruins by the 1930s and was extensively restored. It now serves as the headquarters for the San Fernando Valley Historical Society.

8   Leonis Adobe, ca. 1844
23537 Calabasas Road
Calabasas

Originally constructed about 1844, the house was remodeled in 1879 to add the two-story veranda in the latest Queen Anne style which was being introduced by the Americans. The interior adobe walls were also covered with wood paneling at that time. The Leonis Adobe Association has restored the home as a museum. Interpretive placards in the various rooms lend much insight into the life and architecture of the period. A most unusual feature is the functioning 1880s bathroom.

9   Los Encinos State Historic Park
16756 Moorpark Street
Encino

Two buildings serve as the centerpiece for the park. An adobe home built by Don Vicente de la Ossa in 1849 is in the typical configuration of a row of rooms fronted by an open veranda; de la Ossa actually constructed two verandas, one on each long side of the house. In 1870 the Frenchman Eugene Garnier bought the property and, since the original home had no kitchen, he constructed a French Provincial farmhouse out of limestone next to the Ossa adobe, containing a kitchen and sleeping quarters for the ranch employees. The site is maintained as a museum.

10   General Phineas Banning Residence
Museum, 1864
401 East "M" Street
Wilmington

Phineas Banning was the developer of Wilmington harbor, and he hired ships' carpenters to build this mansion in 1864. The style is taken from the Greek Revival, popular in the eastern United States a couple of decades earlier, but the somewhat unsophisticated forms such as posts rather than real columns supporting the front porch attest to the difficulty of creating elegant architecture when Los Angeles was accessible only by ship and stagecoach. The City of Los Angeles maintains the home as a museum.

Tour 2-5 Craftsman house, 1186 West 27th Street.

1   Sepulveda house, 1887, in El Pueblo de Los Angeles State Historic Park.

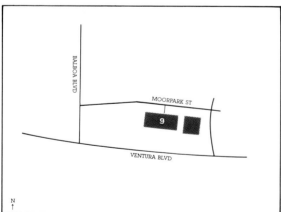

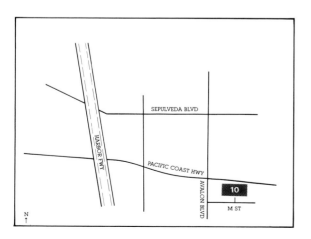

TOUR 2

QUEEN ANNE AND CRAFTSMAN ARCHITECTURE

During the Boom of the Eighties, the thousands of Anglos coming to Los Angeles brought with them the picturesque Queen Anne architecture they had known in the East. This style celebrated the decorative qualities of machine-turned wood and was starkly different from the plain adobe homes of early Los Angeles. By the turn of the century, the Queen Anne style had succumbed to less ornate styles such as the Craftsman. It avoided the use of ornate sawn-wood patterns and towering house designs, to create an architecture of unpainted wood and arroyo stones that seemed to hug the ground.

North University Park, one of the early neighborhoods in Los Angeles, was built in the 1890s with ornate Queen Anne homes on large lots. Several fine homes in this style can still be seen in the neighborhood, and some are being restored. The Los Angeles Conservancy and North University Park Community Association have prepared a detailed walking and driving tour of the area, a few highlights of which are included here.

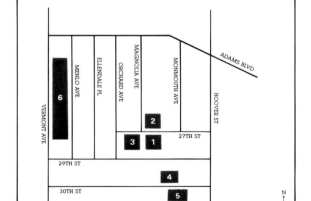

1 House, ca. 1890
Bradbeer and Ferris
1160 West 27th Street

The largest Victorian on the street, this home has the towers, gables, shingled walls and wide veranda that are hallmarks of the Queen Anne style.

2 House, ca. 1890
Bradbeer and Ferris
1163 West 27th Street

A lofty Victorian with a Chinese Chippendale balustrade and a moon gate (spindlework arch) on the upstairs balcony. The home has survived twenty-seven owners in ninety years and is now being restored. It is listed on the National Register of Historic Places.

3 Craftsman House, ca. 1912
1186 West 27th Street

The bungalow officially had only one story, but many two-story homes in the bungalow style of overhanging eaves and shallow pitched roofs were built as well. Craftsman architecture often included arroyo stones and brick in the foundations and chimney, as in this house, blending the connection of house and ground.

4 Bungalow Court
627 West 30th Street

The bungalow court was a series of small cottages built around a central courtyard, often on a regular house lot. Many were built for rental occupancy by winter visitors, and they were probably the forerunners of the motel. This bungalow court is still intact, probably from the teens.

5 House, ca 1890
626 West 30th Street

A few years after these Queen Anne homes were constructed, the fashion turned to less picturesque Craftsman architecture which appeared primarily in the bungalow but also in two-story homes resembling Dutch styles.

6 Craftsman Houses
Menlo Street south of Adams Boulevard

The remainder of this tour leads beyond North University Park to other districts of the city.

Craftsman bungalow, 2650 South Magnolia Avenue, 1908.

6   *Craftsman house, 2654 South Menlo Avenue, ca. 1900.*

RIGHT:

9   Gamble house, dining room

8   Lewis house

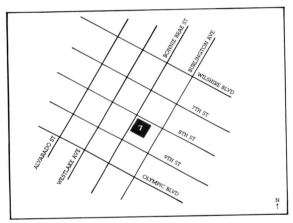

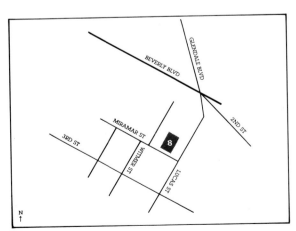

7   **Mooers House, 1894**
    818 Bonnie Brae Street

Unlike most homes in the Queen Anne style, this one has a Moorish flavor. Frederick Mooers purchased this house after having discovered the Yellow Aster gold mine in Kern County.

8   **Lewis House, 1889**
    1425 Miramar Street

Many Queen Anne homes were built by contractors and carpenters whose names have been lost to us. The Lewis house, however, was designed by the San Francisco architect Joseph Cather Newsom, who, with his brother Samuel, designed some of the most pretentious of all homes during the period.

9   **Gamble House, 1908**
    Greene and Greene
    4 Westmoreland Place
    Pasadena

This house is one of Southern California's architectural masterpieces, where every element from porch beams to interior woodwork to furniture was designed as a unified art object. The architects, Charles and Henry Greene, transformed the humble Craftsman bungalow into a high art, incorporating fine woods and Tiffany glass. Every visible surface is smoothed and rounded, and no hint of the nails used in construction was left visible. The house is open to the public, and guided tours are available.

10 **Houses**
    Wilton Place near Beverly Boulevard

During the 1920s, many Los Angeles streets were lined with Craftsman bungalows, but today Wilton Place retains one of the few intact streetscapes. The low homes with shallow, overhanging pitched roofs and exposed beams exemplify this style of architecture which was indigenous to Los Angeles.

11 **Catholic-Protestant Chapel, 1900**
    J. Lee Burton
    Sawtelle Veterans Center

Established in 1887 as the sixth national soldiers' home in the United States, the Sawtelle Veterans Center originally contained a number of large wooden dormitories with verandas, turrets, and ornate gables. The only building remaining from this period is the chapel, constructed in 1900. The building actually houses two chapels, each with separate entrance and tower with belfry.

Dormitory, Sawtelle Veterans Center, 1887. Demolished 1975.

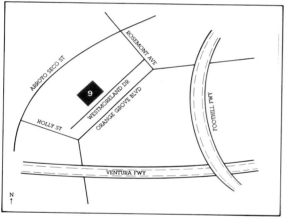

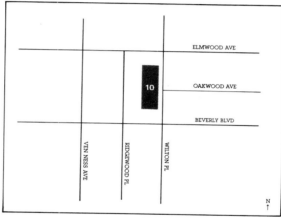

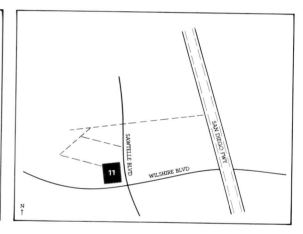

11   Catholic-Protestant Chapel, Sawtelle Veterans Center

TOUR 3

THE MISSION AND SPANISH REVIVALS

In the 1890s the architecture of Los Angeles paid little heed to the Spanish and Mexican heritage of the region, but during that decade there suddenly arose a new interest in the missions and their architecture. The Mission Revival spawned homes, schools, churches, and other buildings that evoked old mission architecture, in a movement that lasted through the teens. The Panama California Exposition of 1915 in San Diego turned the movement toward a broader interest in Spanish forms, especially the Churrigueresque, which lasted through the 1920s. This Spanish Revival was Spanish in detail, but Californian in spirit.

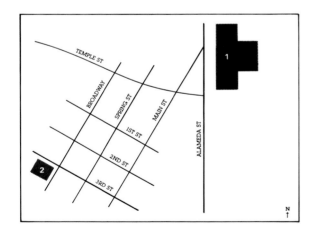

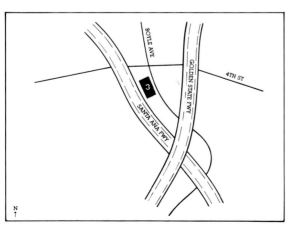

1 **Union Passenger Terminal, 1939**
John and Donald B. Parkinson
800 North Alameda Street

Union Station was the last large railroad passenger terminal built in the United States. On the outside, the building incorporates huge arched windows and a bell tower in the Spanish idiom. The interior waiting room measures fifty-two feet high, and its decor combines Spanish and Moorish influences with the Moderne styles of the 1930s.

2 **Million Dollar Theater, 1918**
Albert C. Martin, Sr.
307 South Broadway

The building is a basic office block designed by Albert C. Martin, Sr., but the decoration and theater interior by William L. Woollett is something to behold. The style is derived from the Churrigueresque, a Spanish Baroque architecture widely adopted in eighteenth-century Mexican churches. The frontispiece around the Third Street entrance did not incorporate angels and cherubs, however, but Texas longhorn cattle skulls with horns attached and other symbols of the American West. High above, two stone women dangle legs over the edge. The fanciful Churrigueresque is carried to the interior of the auditorium as well in statuary, ornate ceiling, and large organ screen.

3 **Hollenbeck Home for the Aged, 1896**
Morgan and Walls
573 South Boyle Avenue

One of the city's earliest and finest examples of Mission Revival architecture, the original portion was designed by Morgan and Walls in 1896. The building was enlarged in 1908 and again in 1923 in keeping with the original style. The Hollenbeck Home is the state's oldest retirement home, founded in 1896 by the widow of a wealthy real estate investor.

4 **Examiner Building, 1912**
Julia Morgan
1111 South Broadway

The first major statement of the Mission Revival was probably the California Building at the World's Columbian Exposition in Chicago of 1893, and the *Examiner* Building, with its massive central tower fronted with two Mission belfries and an entrance surmounted by a huge curved parapet, is modeled from it. Julia Morgan also designed the Hearst Castle in San Simeon.

3   Hollenbeck Home for the Aged

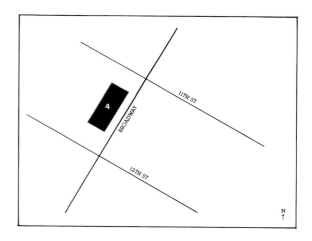

1   Union Passenger Terminal

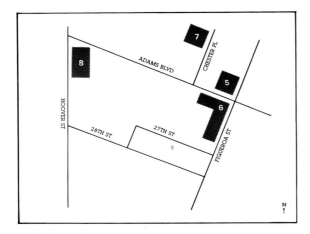

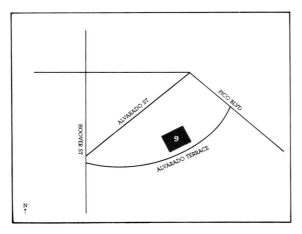

11   *Baine Building*

5   St. Vincent de Paul Roman Catholic Church, 1925
Albert C. Martin, Sr.
621 West Adams Boulevard

Dramatically sited at a forty-five degree angle to the intersection, this church is the major example of Churrigueresque Revival in Los Angeles. The church was a gift of Mr. and Mrs. Edward L. Doheny. Interior decoration is by John B. Smeraldi.

6   Automobile Club of Southern California, 1923
Hunt and Burns
2601 South Figueroa Street

The original portion of this building was designed by the architects Hunt and Burns who were noted for their work in the Mission Revival style. The plain surfaces and large arched windows foreshadow the Modern architectural ethic in a building innovative for its simple forms. The interior of the rotunda is, however, in fine Spanish decor.

7   Wilson House, ca. 1897
7 Chester Place

Chester Place was originally a private residential enclave laid out in 1895, and includes the English Gothic mansion for the Doheny family, designed by Eisen and Hunt in 1898. Of interest for this tour is the Wilson house which faces it. Built about 1897, its facade is a magnificent embellishment of the Mission Revival curved parapet.

8   Casa de Rosas, 1894
Sumner P. Hunt
950 West Adams Boulevard

This house is one of Sumner P. Hunt's early works. It is not particularly Mission Revival in its styling, but it was one of the first Los Angeles homes to be designed around an interior courtyard. Thus it was a precursor to the indoor-outdoor lifestyle that has become characteristic of much Southern California architecture.

9   Powers House, 1902
A. L. Haley
1345 Alvarado Terrace

Pomeroy Powers, the real estate promoter who developed the exclusive residential street of Alvarado Terrace, commissioned A.L. Haley to design this house. Here one can see the arcade, towers, and scalloped parapet of the Mission Revival turned into playful architecture.

10   Chapman Park Market, 1929
Morgan, Walls and Clements
3465 West Sixth Street

In the late 1920s, before the advent of the supermarket, entrepreneurs developed the "drive-in market." Specialty stores which had previously been located at random along a street were grouped around a parking lot to offer the advantage of one-stop shopping. The drive-in market did not work very well, because patrons who had already parked tended to be hemmed in by those trying to enter the parking lot. Hence, the supermarket as we know it today was developed in the early 1930s—where the patrons park in a lot near the store and enter the large market building to shop. In the Chapman Park Market, Los Angeles is fortunate to have an intact drive-in market, an important milestone in American entrepreneurial history. One can still enter the auto courtyard from Kenmore Avenue through an arched entryway, and the old storefronts still stand around the court. The Spanish Revival was a popular style for drive-in markets.

11   Baine Building, 1926
Gogerty and Weyl
6601 Hollywood Boulevard

Much of the Los Angeles commercial streetscape of the 1920s is lined with buildings in the Spanish Revival. One particularly colorful example is the Baine Building. It is a virtual catalog of Spanish devices such as arched, ornamented windows, wrought-iron balconies, scalloped, corner entrance reminiscent of the Moorish, a tower with balcony, Churrigueresque decoration, and red tile roof.

10   Chapman Park Market drive-in facilities, 1929

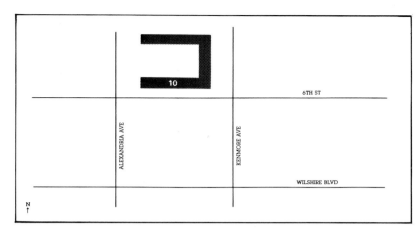

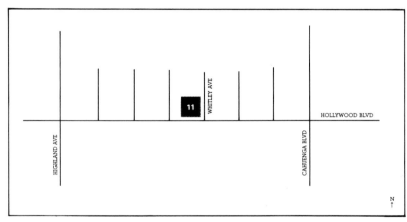

10   Chapman Park Market today

6   Automobile Club of Southern California

TOUR 4

HISTORICAL ECLECTICISM

Los Angeles architecture showed an interest in other historical revival forms along with the Hispanic during the early decades of this century. Downtown in particular was embellished with many Beaux Arts buildings, adopting their style from Roman Classicism and the Italian Renaissance. During the 1920s, perhaps the city's most creative period in architecture, styles from more exotic periods and places were adopted with exuberance in other parts of the city. This tour offers a glimpse of the fanciful streetscapes of those years.

Detailed walking tour brochures of downtown Los Angeles are available from the Los Angeles Conservancy.

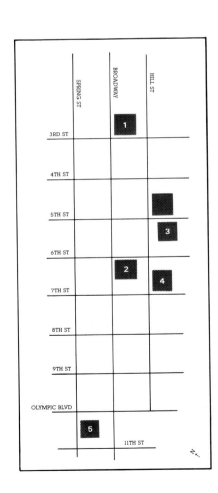

1   Bradbury Building, 1893
    George H. Wyman
    304 South Broadway

The exterior is unassuming, but the interior glass-canopied court expresses a vision of both futuristic architecture carried out in the forms and styles of the 1890s and European arcaded shopping streets built for the well-to-do. This interior, with its ironwork balustrades, open-caged elevators, and flights of open stairways, makes the Bradbury one of Los Angeles's greatest architectural monuments. A self-guided tour brochure is available at the door.

2   W.P. Story Building, 1908
    Morgan and Walls
    Southeast corner, Broadway and Sixth streets

Beaux Arts architecture was primarily a way of styling a building. Classical elements such as columns and cornices that once had a structural function were here applied to the surface of a steel-frame building to give the facade a proper look. During much of this century, this style was deprecated by Modern architects, and in the 1930s many Beaux Arts buildings were remodeled without concern for their original design. Thus in 1934 the same firm (now Morgan, Walls and Clements) redesigned the ground floor to cover up the old Beaux Arts facade. In the entrance to the parking garage on Sixth Street, however, they did create an exemplary Art Deco metal gate.

3   Security Building, 1906
    Parkinson and Bergstrom
    Southeast corner, Spring and Fifth streets

The Beaux Arts building was modeled after the Italian Renaissance *palazzo*, with a lower portion different in design from the central shank of the building. At the top was the "attic," usually an ornately styled section below the cornice. The Security Building epitomizes this three-tiered Beaux Arts design, and in this case the decorative motif is itself Florentine.

One of the flourishes of the Beaux Arts building was the cornice, which at least suggested that the roof extended outward beyond the wall. The Security Building presents its ornate cornice to the street and, along with that of the Rowan Building (1910; Parkinson and Bergstrom) to the north, provides a sense of visual closure to both the building and the street.

4   Lobby, Bank of America, 1924
    Schultze and Weaver
    Northeast corner, Spring and Seventh streets

This building was constructed in 1924 as the Hellman Bank. Of particular note is the lobby, one of the few that remains largely intact from the 1920s. Its spacious banking room has coffered ceilings, marble balustrades, and bronze writing desks. By comparison, the bank lobby of the Pacific Southwest Building at the northwest corner of Spring and Fifth streets was quite similar in appearance until its remodeling in 1961. Schultze and Weaver also designed the Los Angeles Biltmore Hotel.

3   Security Building

2   W.P. Story Building

STAIR   RAILING   DETAIL

1   Detail, Bradbury Building interior

4   Lobby, Bank of America

5   *Mayan Theater. On the right is the former Belasco Theatre, now the Metropolitan Community Church, 1060 South Hill Street, designed in 1926 by Morgan, Walls and Clements. It is in the Churrigueresque style.*

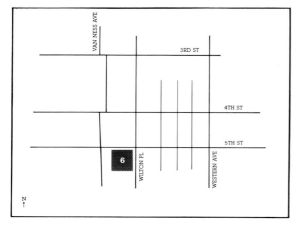

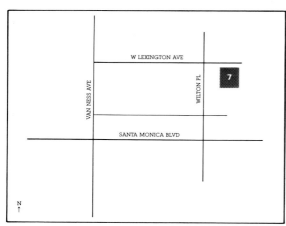

5   Mayan Theater, 1927
Morgan, Walls and Clements
1040 South Hill Street

Especially during the 1920s, architects began to look far beyond European antecedents for architectural imagery. The Mayan Theater looks to the Pre-Columbian architecture of the Mayans and faithfully reproduces Mayan architectural elements to create one of Los Angeles's most fanciful theaters. The facade was originally left in its grey concrete color, lending a greater degree of archaeological correctness to the facade.

6   Chateauesque Apartment
Wilton Place and Fifth Street

Many 1920s apartment buildings with elements taken from Chateaux of the Loire can be found in this part of Los Angeles, perhaps inspired by the European castles seen by young American architects in the First World War. Not only did Chateauesque buildings present a vision of a monied lifestyle, they allowed great flexibility in window arrangements and wall shapes that could make a complicated building visually pleasing.

7   Egyptian Revival Apartments, 1926
J.M. Close
747 North Wilcox Avenue

The Egyptian Revival of the 1920s probably had more to do with exotic movie sets than with King Tut. As architecture began to become strikingly visual, the Egyptian lent a color and grandeur that set an ordinary apartment building apart from its surroundings. A similar apartment by Close is at 5617 La Mirada Avenue, one block north.

8   Chinese Theatre, 1927
Meyer and Holler
6925 Hollywood Boulevard

This ultimate fantasy of the Chinese temple was originally so Chinese in details that even the water faucets in the lavatories had dragon-shaped handles. Actually most of the decor is Chinese Chippendale, or an English interpretation of the Orient. One enters the theater from a small forecourt through a stylized pagoda, under the protection of a great stone dragon.

9   Yamashiro, 1913
Franklin M. Small
1999 N. Sycamore Avenue

Designed for Adolph and Eugene Bernheimer, importers of Oriental art, this "Castle on the Hill" is a vision of sixteenth-century Japan. Everywhere you look are rich woods, carved ornament, and intricate embellishments that are as archaeologically correct as one could make them in 1913. Yamashiro is now a restaurant.

10   Spadena House, 1921
Henry Oliver
516 Walden Drive
Beverly Hills

Originally designed as the office of a movie production company in Culver City, this building was later moved to its present site and turned into a residence. It typifies the style of architecture called "Hansel and Gretel," which in the 1920s evoked brooding medieval forests and the Olde English village. The Spadena house, with its impossibly steep roof and windows that look crooked although they are not, even has an oversized broom sitting on the roof.

6 *Chateauesque apartment*

9 *Entrance gate to Yamashiro, 1913*

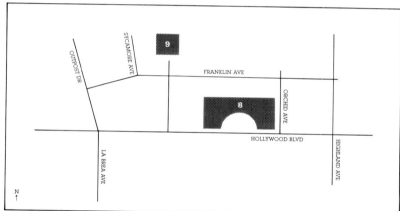
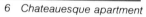

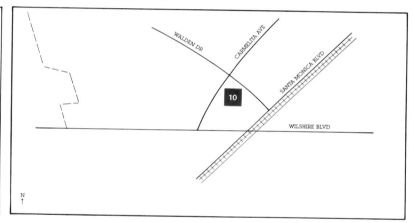

8 *Chinese Theatre*

7 *Egyptian Revival apartments*

TOUR 5

ART DECO AND STREAMLINE ARCHITECTURE

Today's Los Angeles streetscape is largely a product of the 1920s, when many of the city's major streets were constructed to accommodate the burgeoning automobile population. The optimism of the decade was picked up in architecture, as many of these streets were lined with Art Deco commercial buildings whose style reflected the new sense of movement and freedom. By the late 1930s, architectural imagery was more closely organized around the notion of speed, in applying streamlined designs not only to airplanes and trains, but to buildings as well.

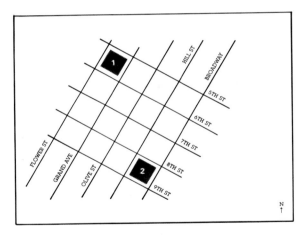

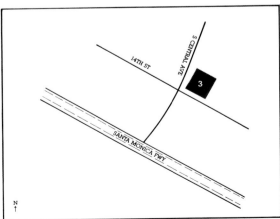

Los Angeles Central Library, 1926
Bertram G. Goodhue
630 West Fifth Street

The medieval cathedral was organized largely as a hall of allegorical art, to teach the lessons of Christianity through paintings, sculptures, and other visual media, as well as through the architecture itself. The Central Library is one of America's great allegorical buildings, though with a different theme: knowledge and learning. Inscriptions and sculptures throughout the library carry the message that the torch of knowledge is handed on from generation to generation through the illuminated book.

Reliefs jutting prominently from the exterior walls portray great historical figures and legends of wisdom, along with inscribed aphorisms extolling the joys of knowledge. Inside, the large spaces converge in a central rotunda painted in sunburst patterns. From the center hangs a zodiac chandelier circling an illuminated globe. Murals portray themes such as America's westward expansion, California history and, in the Children's Room, the Legend of Ivanhoe.

The architecture itself is the great precursor to Art Deco in Los Angeles. Goodhue incorporated monumental forms from several traditions: the mosaic-crowned pyramidal tower from the East, and the great interior vault from the West. The whole is accomplished in cubistic and geometric forms that, in a similar fashion to the architecture of the 1980s, announced the debt of architecture to tradition but boldly expressed the values of its own era.

2   Eastern Columbia Building, 1931
Claud Beelman
849 South Broadway

Many Art Deco buildings were decorated with geometrical designs, stylized plant motifs, and zigzags that expressed the ethic of machine design. Particularly in Los Angeles, color was applied to buildings as never before. The Eastern Columbia is faced with blue and gold terra cotta that rises in pulsating zigzags to the imposing clock tower. One originally entered the building under a huge golden sunburst to an interior arcade which separated the two stores on the ground floor.

3   Coca-Cola Bottling Plant, 1936
Robert V. Derrah
1334 South Central Avenue

In the 1930s, building owners discovered that they could remodel their buildings at a reasonable cost to give them a modern look. The Coca-Cola plant was an ordinary brick factory building until Derrah redesigned it into one of the great monuments of the Streamline Moderne. The building's owner was an avid boatman, and the white ocean-liner look expressed cleanliness in a period when bottled soft drinks were often suspected of being impure. In 1936, one observer wrote, "When the morning whistle blows—'All hands on deck!', the crew of the S.S. Coca Cola can lay to the oars and bottle before sundown 240,000 cases of pauses."

1   *Los Angeles Central Library.*

1   *Los Angeles Central Library, detail of south entrance.*

3   *Coca-Cola Bottling Plant, interior*

5   *Bullocks Wilshire*

7 *Pellissier Building and Wiltern Theater. Photo 1931.*

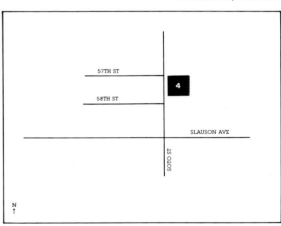

6 *Streamline apartments*

4 **Winnie and Sutch Building, ca. 1935**
5610 South Soto Street
Huntington Park

In some cases the Streamline Moderne expressed pure form rather than a programmatic motif, as in the Coca-Cola Building. In the Winnie and Sutch Building, continuous bands of horizontal windows are tied, as in a package, with pulsating horizontal piers. Together with the W. W. Henry Building to the north, this location provides a small Streamline ensemble.

5 **Bullocks Wilshire, 1929**
John and Donald Parkinson
3050 Wilshire Boulevard

An Art Deco masterpiece both in its architecture and interior design, Bullocks was one of the first major stores to cater to the automobile trade from the fashionable residential districts on the near west side. The principal entrance is to the rear, under a *porte-cochère* that faces the parking lot. Inside, each department expresses a different Art Deco motif, some in pastels and gold which were stylish colors of the late 1920s. The men's department has a Pre-Columbian motif that hearkens to the early work of Frank Lloyd Wright in Los Angeles.

6 **Streamline Apartments, 1938**
Milton J. Black
Northwest corner, Hobart Boulevard and Ninth Street

Streamlining was applied to apartment buildings as well as to commercial and industrial buildings during the 1930s. It was modern architecture, but as one writer noted, it made the machine for living in more livable and less like a machine than the stark forms of the International Style. In difficult economic times, money ordinarily spent for ornament could be used to increase glass area and provide amenities such as landscaping and roof gardens. Milton Black designed a number of Streamline apartments in Los Angeles; another not far away is at 462 South Cochran Avenue.

7 **Pellissier Building and Wiltern Theater, 1931**
Morgan, Walls and Clements
3790 Wilshire Boulevard

An Art Deco tower of turquoise terra cotta rises twelve stories to the building height limit imposed by the municipal charter at that time. One of the city's most exuberant Art Deco sunbursts is on the underside of the theater marquee. The theater, designed by G. Albert Lansburgh with interiors by Anthony B. Heinsbergen, was intended to evoke a "steaming jungle" of bright pinks, purples, and oranges, softened by low-level incandescent lighting.

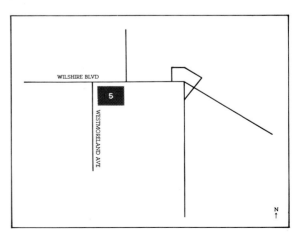

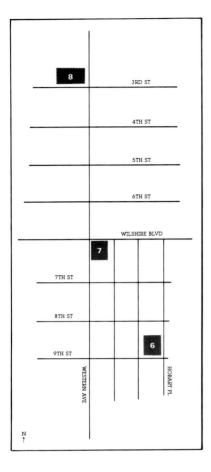

8   Crocker Bank

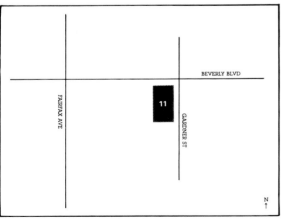

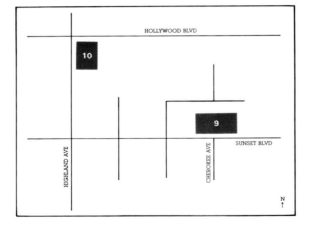

8   **Crocker Bank, ca. 1928**
    4300 West Third Street

In an era of unbounded building color combinations, glazed black terra cotta with bright gold trim was perhaps the ultimate eye-catcher. This small bank building is one of two in this color scheme left in the city; the other is at 5209 Wilshire Boulevard (1929; Morgan, Walls and Clements).

9   **Crossroads of the World, 1936**
    Robert V. Derrah
    6671 Sunset Boulevard

Derrah, who at the same time was designing the Coca-Cola Building Plant, here created the image of a ship sailing down a street lined with shops in quaint styles from ports around the world. The complex has recently been restored.

10 **Max Factor Make-Up Salon, 1931**
    S. Charles Lee
    1666 North Highland Avenue

Make-up was an integral part of the film industry, and in 1931 Max Factor commissioned S. Charles Lee, a theater architect noted for his elegant designs such as the Los Angeles Theatre downtown, to remodel an old furniture warehouse into this glamorous Art Deco office building and make-up salon. The facade is lavish with colored marble against a white, undulating wall articulated with glittering, mica-embedded piers. The ornamentation connotes cosmopolitan elegance: Classical Greek floral designs, American stars, and French swags. The interior is also largely intact.

11 **Pan Pacific Auditorium, 1935**
    Wurdeman and Becket
    7600 Beverly Boulevard

This building is exemplary both for the uninhibited architectural visions of the Streamline Moderne, and for its statement as a period piece of the Great Depression. The green and white facade beckons the visitor with four flagpole pylons shaped like streamlined cooling fins. Since funds for architectural design were limited in the 1930s, however, the auditorium itself is a huge unadorned enclosure.

11 Pan Pacific Auditorium

10 Max Factor Make-Up Salon

TOUR 6
THE MODERN MOVEMENT

The architecture of the Modern Movement is not a style as such, for it includes buildings constructed over the last half century that are products of intense individual visions, for example, that of Frank Lloyd Wright, and of certain conventions from the International Style of the 1930s that have evolved past mid-century. In common, however, is a statement of freedom from European architectural traditions, the structure of a building expressing its aesthetic, and a reflection of technological progress.

1   Barnsdall ("Hollyhock") house

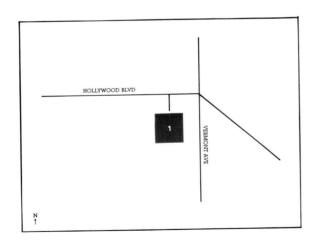

1 Barnsdall House, 1921
Frank Lloyd Wright
4800 Hollywood Boulevard

In 1918, oil heiress Aline Barnsdall purchased a thirty-six acre olive grove with the intention of building a residence for herself and a theater complex for the public. For her house, Wright designed a monolithic exterior that belies the open feeling of the interior; this creation of unfolding space was a hallmark of Wright's architecture. He lined the exterior with stylized hollyhocks, Mrs. Barnsdall's favorite flower. The home has been restored by the City of Los Angeles and is open a few days each month for public tours.

2 Lovell Health House, 1929
Richard J. Neutra
4616 Dundee Drive

Neutra's second commission in Los Angeles was this home for the naturopath P. M. Lovell. A classic of the International Style, the house has a steel frame and white concrete walls. The decorative elements of the exterior are the interplay of the cubic forms themselves rather than applied ornament; Neutra also designed a small parapet along the west end of the roof, giving the building the same sense of closure that the traditional cornice did.

3 CBS Building, 1938
William Lescaze
6121 Sunset Boulevard

Flat surfaces and the horizontal bands of windows characterized the early International Style. Radio was modern technology in the late 1930s, and the CBS Building—built before television—expressed that modernity both in its style and in the arcade of the main building, from which visitors could watch technicians route programs over the network from the glass-enclosed main control room.

4 Schindler House, 1922
Rudolph M. Schindler
833 North Kings Road

Schindler constructed his house with two living units joined by a common kitchen. The spaces were not for two traditional families, however, but for four adults, each of whom was given a separate studio space. A fifth studio space was built for guests. The home was the first building in Los Angeles fully to adopt the idiom of the International Style; its glass walls open onto a rear courtyard in a design that expressed the indoor-outdoor lifestyle popular in much Modern domestic architecture of later years. The Craftsman ethic is also present here—in the unpainted redwood beams that serve as the frame and the sliding doors of canvas.

3   CBS Building, photograph 1938.

2   Lovell "Health" house

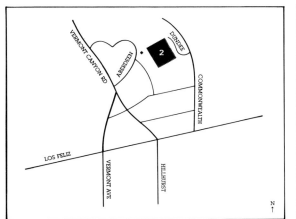

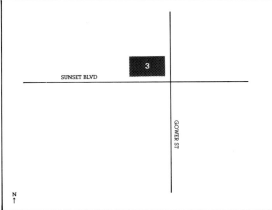

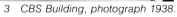

4

Schindler house, exterior and interior of Pauline Schindler studio, photographs ca. 1922.

6   *Carson-Roberts Building*

10   *Horatio West Court*

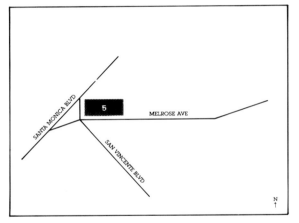

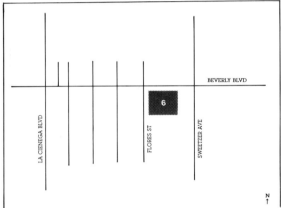

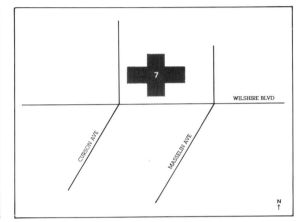

8   *Century Bank*

9   *Century Plaza Towers*

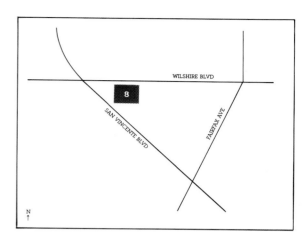

7   Prudential Building, photograph 1949

5   Pacific Design Center, 1975
Cesar Pelli for Victor Gruen Associates
8687 Melrose Avenue

Designed as a display hall for the whole-sale interior design trade, the Pacific Design Center is sheathed entirely in blue glass. The interior, which includes a fantastic escalator well, runs in diagonal spaces to lend a sense of the unexpected, and the galleria on the top floor is reminiscent of arcaded European shopping streets. The barrel vault above the galleria is the semicircular form one sees atop the building from afar.

6   Carson-Roberts Building, 1959
Craig Ellwood
8322 Beverly Boulevard

The Los Angeles master of the glass-and-steel building skeleton in the 1950s and 60s was undoubtedly Craig Ellwood, as expressed in several Case Study houses and his commercial buildings. Here the entire street facade is of thinly separated black glass panels which protect small balconies in front of the offices. The entire composition is raised on free-standing columns.

7   Prudential Building, 1948
Wurdeman and Becket
5757 Wilshire Boulevard

This early postwar building, which was built to the maximum height then allowed in Los Angeles, is a forerunner of the Corporate International Style highrise clad entirely in glass. The facades of the two wings flanking the central windowless core are largely glass, protected by horizontal sunscreens along each floor. The building also has hints of the late Moderne in the horizontal rows of bezeled windows on the east end.

8   Century Bank, 1972
Anthony Lumsden for DMJM
6420 Wilshire Boulevard

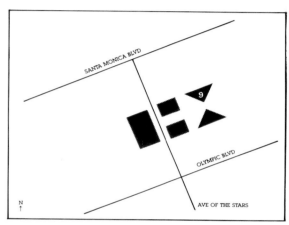

The look of the early 1970s in the Corporate International Style was that of electronic technology. The smoked-glass exteriors expressed the cool, quiet efficiency of solid-state electronics. Here, the building skin is elegantly carved, and a potted tree grows on each floor of the west side.

9   Century Plaza Towers, 1975
Minoru Yamasaki
2029–2049 Century Park East
Century City

The regional commercial and residential center of Century City was constructed beginning in the 1960s on a portion of the Twentieth Century-Fox film studios, the remainder of which can be seen along Pico Boulevard to the west. The focal point of Century City is the pair of triangular highrise buildings, whose silver corners glint in the sun and present a strikingly different aspect from each angle. Seen up close, however, the buildings rise from an impersonal and windswept plaza.

10   Horatio West Court, 1921
Irving Gill
140 Hollister Avenue
Santa Monica

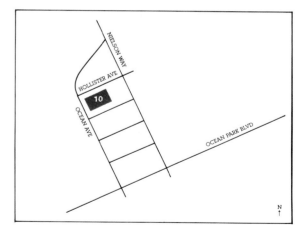

In the vanguard of the Modern Movement was Irving Gill, who began with Mission Revival forms and cleaned them of ornament to produce cubic forms articulated with arches. Much of his best work is now gone, but a remaining masterpiece, which has been restored, is this complex of four homes near the Santa Monica beach. The horizontal band of windows that give ocean sunlight to the upstairs rooms was an alteration, probably by Gill, later in the 1920s. The upper story was originally fronted by an open porch.

TOUR 7

LOS ANGELES TODAY

In the 1980s, innovative designers in Los Angeles are exploring realms far beyond the Modern Movement, in an emerging school of architecture characterized by strong individual visions and a new probing into the meaning of space and form. Alongside this innovation is a new interest in the city's heritage that has been given form in the burgeoning historic preservation movement. This tour includes examples of each; a more extensive tour of adaptively reused buildings, entitled "Buildings Reborn in Los Angeles," is available as a self-guided tour brochure from the Los Angeles Conservancy.

1 Oviatt Building, 1928
Walker and Eisen
617 South Olive Street

Alexander and Oviatt's was an elegant men's clothier that occupied the first three floors of this thirteen-story building. Largely Romanesque in style on the exterior, the building is a masterpiece of Art Deco design. After having fallen into disuse the building has recently been restored, with a restaurant in the former store on the ground floor which preserves the original clothing shop decor. The French marble, oak woodwork, and the original hand-carved oak elevators have been refurbished. The marquee and some interior glasswork was of Lalique glass, much of which has been lost and has been replaced with modern facsimiles. The upper floors of the building now serve as office space, and the penthouse residence of Mr. Oviatt has been restored to its Art Deco splendor.

2 Clifton's Silver Spoon
515 West Seventh Street

One of many successful examples of adaptive reuse of older buildings downtown, Clifton's is a cafeteria housed in the former Brock and Company Jewelry Store. Built in 1922, the building has ornate Mediterranean-inspired cast-plaster ceilings. The original period decor is supplemented with antique furnishings, including a display of local memorabilia in the second floor's original silver and crystal jewelry cabinets.

3 Morgenstern Warehouse, 1979
Eric Moss
1140–46 South Main Street

The developer of this warehouse in the garment district of Los Angeles believed that even pedestrian buildings should have some degree of excitement. The buildings are of concrete block, but the four warehouse entrances have been accented with vivid colors, signage, and exposed mechanical systems. Everything about the building was designed to elicit reaction, attempting to evoke a sense of enthusiasm for the city and the street.

3 Morgenstern Warehouse

1 Oviatt Building, entrance

2 Clifton's Silver Spoon

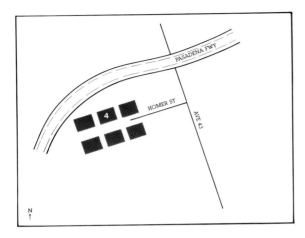

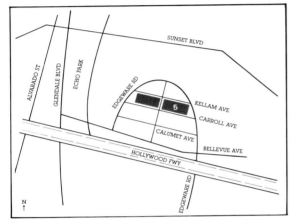

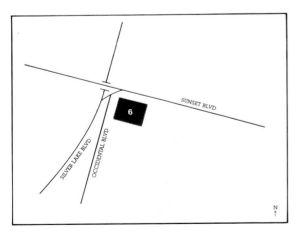

7   *Rodes house*

4   Heritage Square
3800 Homer Street

Prior to the turn of the century, Los Angeles developed a rich tradition of ornate Italianate, Queen Anne, and Eastlake homes, much of which has now been lost. In an attempt to save significant examples of this architecture, the Cultural Heritage Foundation has moved to this site several buildings threatened with demolition, has restored them, and has established an architectural museum. Heritage Square is being rebuilt as a replica of a nineteenth-century village, with historic residences, parks, and commercial buildings. The residential area will include a one-room schoolhouse, an early frame church with bell tower, and several outstanding residences such as the Hale house. The park will have open areas for public gatherings and for trolley cars to transport visitors between the residential and commercial area, which will include a bank, general store, ice cream parlor, firehouse, garden restaurant, and a trolley barn transportation museum.

5   Carroll Avenue
Off Edgeware Road, north of Temple Street

During the Boom of the 1880s, Angeleno Heights was developed as an exclusive residential suburb on a rise overlooking downtown Los Angeles. Today, eleven of the original Queen Anne homes still line Carroll Avenue, and two that had previously been demolished have been replaced. In 1975 a group of residents, concerned for the future of this remnant of Victoriana, established the Carroll Avenue Restoration Foundation to oversee the restoration of the homes. The result is a living legacy of early Los Angeles with beautifully restored Victorian homes. The Foundation has even provided vintage street lights of a type found in Los Angeles in the early years of this century. From Carroll Avenue there is a breathtaking view of downtown.

6   Jerde Partnership, 1908
2798 Sunset Boulevard

In 1908 the Los Angeles Pacific Railroad constructed the "Olive Substation," a power substation and car barn in the Mission Revival style, with ornately scalloped parapets and arched industrial windows and doors. In 1977 the Jerde Partnership purchased the buildings and refurbished them as architectural offices. A similar but unrestored substation, the Ivy Substation, may be seen at the intersection of Washington and Culver boulevards in Culver City.

7   Rodes House, 1979
Charles Moore and Robert Yudell
1406 Kenter Avenue

This small home in pink stucco evokes a Baroque garden pavilion and the work of the great Italian architect Palladio. The smooth, curved facade celebrates enclosure, and the symmetrical windows and doors are outlined in white to celebrate entry. Suggestions of wings at each side embrace the space in front of the house, which serves for plays and concerts given by the owner.

8   de Bretteville-Simon House, 1976
Peter de Bretteville
8067–71 Willow Glen Road

From the street one sees corrugated metal siding pierced by a few windows. Continuing uphill, however, one looks back to a glass curtain wall that continues around the rear of the house. The two homes, separated by a common entry court, are primarily two-story steel-frame cubes. Each interior is designed to suit the differing tastes of the two families—one largely in wood, the other celebrating the industrial origins of the structure.

6 *Olive Substation, now Jerde Partnership*

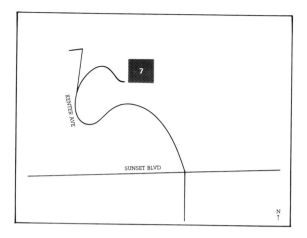

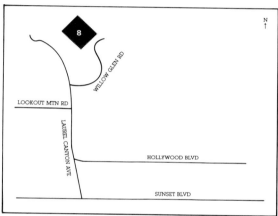

5 *Sessions house, 1330 Carroll Avenue,*
by Joseph Cather Newsom, 1888.

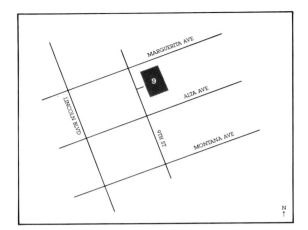

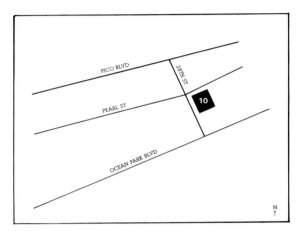

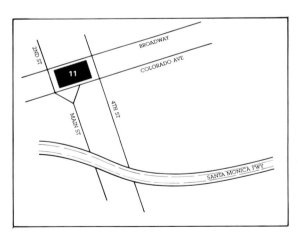

11   Santa Monica Place, interior

9   Freedman House, 1981
Kappe, Lotery, Boccato
533 Ninth Street, Santa Monica

A large F-shaped steel frame dominates the composition of this three-story (plus tower) home in grey stucco. It is a townhouse in the traditional sense, with enclosing walls on the exterior, but the interior is bathed with light from a central atrium, and in the middle of the ground floor grows a field of baby's breath that brings the outdoors to the inside.

10   Suntech Townhomes, 1980
Steve Wiseman
2433 28th Street
Santa Monica

This complex of eighteen solar townhouses has steel railings, stovepipe chimneys, silo-like stairwell hoods, and industrial lighting fixtures, all softened by the pastel colors of the walls. The trend in the early 1980s is to the two-story living space since it makes a small area seem larger.

11   Santa Monica Place
Bounded by Broadway, Second Street,
Colorado Boulevard and Fourth Street
Santa Monica

Santa Monica Place is one of a new breed of architecture—the regional shopping center in a downtown area. In the middle is a tall, skylit atrium with a pool and fountain, and interior shopping corridors radiate outward to meet the city. At the north entrance is a large greenhouse that looks out upon the older Santa Monica Mall, the pedestrianized former Third Street, and to the south the shopping center opens onto Sears, a fine Moderne department store building. Inside the center, the spaces are tight and therefore intimate, giving a sense of very special place, and the corridors run in unexpected diagonals to add a sense of complexity. It takes some time to find one's way, but the search is certainly not boring. Like much large-scale architecture, however, Santa Monica Place turns inward from the city except at the entrances. The surrounding streets are left as automobile alleys, destroying the sense of urban street that is characteristic of older downtowns.

11   *Santa Monica Place, south entrance*

10   *Suntech Townhomes*

ABOUT THE
LOS ANGELES CONSERVANCY

The Los Angeles Conservancy is a nonprofit, tax-exempt membership organization dedicated to the recognition, preservation, and revitalization of our urban environment. The conservancy directs its energies in the areas of *action, assistance,* and *awareness.* First, we actively promote policies and decisions in the private and public sectors that encourage the continued vitality of our landmarks, older buildings, and historic districts. Second, we provide a mutually supportive information network among the many urban conservation groups in the Los Angeles area. Third, we undertake activities designed to increase the public's awareness of and appreciation for the Los Angeles region's built environment and cultural heritage. We encourage your membership and support.

Major activities of the Los Angeles Conservancy include:

presenting quarterly membership meetings highlighting the urban heritage of Los Angeles

publishing an informative newsletter reporting on conservancy activities and items of interest to the historic preservation community

publishing tour guides to neighborhoods and other areas of architectural interest, including downtown Los Angeles, Hollywood, North University Park, and automobile-related architecture

presenting exhibitions on the cultural resources and historic preservation in Los Angeles, including the traveling exhibit "Buildings Reborn in Los Angeles"

providing a speakers' bureau on topics of interest in historic preservation and urban conservation

assisting neighborhood organizations with projects in urban conservation and historic preservation

consulting with government agencies, including review of and comment on public policies and programs affecting Los Angeles's cultural and historical resources.

supporting the designation of sites, structures, and districts as historical monuments

preparing feasibility studies for preservation and adaptive reuse projects

Most activities of the Los Angeles Conservancy are carried out by a number of active working committees organized by interested members.

*Beverly Hills City Hall, 450 North Cres-
cent Drive, Beverly Hills, by William J.
Gage, 1932.*

For membership information write

The Los Angeles Conservancy
Eastern Columbia Building, Suite 1225
849 South Broadway
Los Angeles, California 90014

or call (213) 623-CITY

NOTES

Left: detail, W. P. Story Building, by Morgan Walls and Morgan, 1916. Right: Newfield house, 250 South Burlingame Avenue, by Thornton M. Abell, 1961.

CHAPTER 1

1. Beck and Williams (1972, p. 30).

2. Bean (1968, p. 26).

3. Mexico had actually become independent from Spain in 1821, but the news did not reach California until the next year, when oaths of allegiance to Mexico were taken.
Prior to the founding of Misión San Francisco de Solano in what is now the city of Sonoma, the northernmost mission was at San Rafael; it was founded as an *asistencia*, or sub-mission in 1817 and elevated to full mission status in 1823. Thus, to be exact, there were only nineteen missions at the end of the Spanish period. Sonoma mission was actually founded in 1823, one year after the Spanish dominion over California ended.

4. A description of an early *presidio* is provided by Duflot de Mofras (1840).

5. The name "Gabrielino" is the Anglicized version of the Spanish "Gabrieleño," into which group the neighboring Fernandeño are usually subsumed for reference purposes. The Gabrielino called themselves *kumi-vit* (*kumi-* meaning "east"), and were so referred to by the Fernandeño, who were known to the Gabrielino as *pase-kwarum*, from the Gabrielino name for the San Fernando Valley (see Bean and Smith, 1978, p. 548).

6. Bean and Smith (1978, p. 542); Kroeber (1925).

7. For a recounting of the Chingichngich creation myth, see Bean and Smith (1978, p. 548).

8. The economy of the California missions is treated in Archibald (1976). For a horticultural history of southern California, see Padilla (1961).

9. The missions absorbed the best land between the Coast Range and the sea, leaving little arable land for other settlers, although several large land grants were awarded; for example, in the Los Angeles area, to Spanish soldiers Dominguez, Verdugo, and Nieto in 1784 (see Robinson, 1953; Webb, 1952, chapters 7 and 8).

10. Baer (1958, p. 11).

11. Ibid., p. 13.

12. Ibid., p. 13.

13. Ibid., p. 17.

14. Ibid., p. 95.

15. Ibid., p. 20. The lingering belief that the round roof tiles were formed on the Indians' thighs is certainly unfounded. Such roof tiles and their fabrication were known in Spain long before the colonization of California; at any rate, the tiles on the old missions ranged from eighteen to twenty-two inches in length, substantially longer than a normal thigh (see Shippey, 1948, p. 226). Baer has written (1958, p. 19) that the tiles were molded over a section of log that had been split endwise.

16. Baer (1958, p. 26); Newcomb (1914, p. 228).

17. Webb (1952) has suggested that the iron used in the missions was brought to California from Mexico.

18. In 1907, George Wharton James identified nine elements that served to define the Mission Revival style. Not all were present in every mission, however. The elements were:
Solid and massive walls, piers, and buttresses
Arched *corredores*
Espadañas
Terraced towers, surmounted by a lantern
Pierced campanile, either in tower or wall
Broad, unbroken mural masses
Wide, overhanging eaves
Long, sloping roofs covered with red clay tiles
Patio or inner court

19. Mission bells announced the hour for wakening, worship, labor, meals, and sleep. They are discussed in detail by Webb (1952, Chapter 5).

20. Baer (1958, p. 49).

21. Ibid., p. 44.

22. Ibid., pp. 20–22.

23. Geiger (1968, p. 340). A detailed history of San Gabriel Mission is offered by Engelhardt (1927).

24. Baer (1958, p. 20), Engelhardt (1927, p. 75).

25. Baer (1958, p. 46).

26. Weber (1968, p. 2).

27. Baer (1958, p. 43). A 350-foot-long arcade was constructed at San Gabriel in 1804 but is no longer extant.

28. Weber (1968, p. 20).

29. Weber (1975, p. 132).

30. Interview with William Mason, Los Angeles County Museum of Natural History, 1980.

31. Beilherz (1971, p. 97).

32. Winther (1935).

33. Guest (1962).

34. The exact title of the original pueblo is the subject of continuing controversy, despite the effort of Treutlein (1973) to establish the definitive name. "Porciúncula" was the name of a town and parish near Assisi.

35. Baugh (1942, p. 90).

36. Bowman (1896, p. 160); Baugh (1942, p. 90).

37. Smith (1955).

38. Mundigo and Crouch (1977, p. 248).

39. Beyond the settlement, each family received two *suertes* or farmlands distributed by lottery. From what remained were selected the *propios* (public lands), *dehesas* (pasture lands), *ejidos* (common lands), and the *realengas* (royal lands), to be used by later settlers (see Harlow, 1976, p. 5).

40. For a discussion of the early Plaza, see Mason and Duque (1981).

41. Crouch and Mundigo (1977, p. 414); Bowman (1896, p. 162).

42. Bancroft (1884, Vol. I, p. 345).

43. Crouch and Mundigo (1977, p. 414).

44. Bowman (1896, p. 162).

45. Mooney (1900, p. 44).

46. Owen (1960, p. 186, 199).

47. Crouch and Mundigo (1977, p. 414).

48. Guinn (1897–99, p. 248).

49. In New Mexico, the Spanish introduced the notion of an adobe brick that was poured in forms and allowed to dry, then stacked to build a wall, using adobe mortar in the interstices. The Indians had also used adobe, but they did not know bricks. They "puddled" the adobe in successively higher layers until the desired height of wall was reached.

50. Bowman (1896).

51. Mooney (1900, p. 45).

52. Parks (1928, p. 13).

53. Ibid., p. 13.

54. Ibid., p. 15.

55. Ibid., p. 15.

56. Guinn (1908, p. 123).

57. See Bean (1968, p. 63).

58. Ibid., p. 64.

59. See Robinson (1948, p. 30).

60. Webb (1952, Chapter 20); McWilliams (1946, p. 38).

CHAPTER 2

1. In 1800, Los Angeles had 315 residents. Nevertheless, it was the largest secular settlement in California; only the missions had larger populations (from a discussion with William Mason, 1980).

2. From the establishment of the California missions in 1769 until 1830, there had been no social intercourse whatever between California and the other Spanish colonial districts in Texas and New Mexico (including Arizona). See Warner (1908) and Lawrence (1931) for a discussion of early contacts.

3. Baugh (1942, p. 92).

4. Nelson (1959, p. 840).

5. Crouch and Mundigo (1977, p. 414).

6. Robinson (1966, p. 5).

7. Sonoratown was on the site of present-day Chinatown, to the north of Olvera Street. Chinatown moved here in the 1930s, when it was displaced from its former territory by the construction of Union Station.

8. Robinson (1966, p. 8).

9. Cleland (1951, pp. 161–2).

10. Ibid., p. 167.

11. Guinn (1895, pp. 63–68) has written of the paper town of Savana in the 1860s.

12. Barrows (1893, p. 55).

13. Quoted in Carr (1935, p. 119).

14. Parks (1928, p. 15).

15. Sanford (1950, p. 239).

16. Kirker (1973).

17. By 1830, public buildings, financial institutions, churches, and homes in the United States began to display Greek Classical facades. Americans who traveled west in the mid-nineteenth century carried this vision with them, building in its image as well as they could given the materials at hand. In New Mexico the Anglo immigrants placed red brick coping on the parapets of Spanish adobe structures and built simple white-faced *porticos* on their fronts, creating a high folk-architecture of the Greek Revival known locally as the Territorial Style. The Americans brought these forms to California as well, but the distance was much greater and the requisite materials scarcer, resulting in a uniquely Californian architectural development (see Pierson, 1976, pp. 417–420).

18. C. de Gante (1947).

19. Ricciute (1938).

20. Guinn (1897–99, p. 254).

21. Crouch and Mundigo (1977, p. 414); Guinn (1897–99, pp. 253–6).

22. Guinn (1897–99, pp. 253–6).

23. Quoted in Lawler (1953, p. 337).

24. *Los Angeles Herald*, March 17, 1875; *Los Angeles Commercial*, March 13, 1880; *Los Angeles Express*, February 8, 1888.

25. *Los Angeles Express*, July 24, 1883.

26. Quoted in Reinhardt (1973, p. 65).

27. Guinn (1897–99, pp. 49–50).

28. Centennial History (1876, p. 63).

29. *Los Angeles Semi-Weekly News*, May 1, 1866.

30. Ludwig Salvator (1878, p. 126); Barrows (1894).

31. According to Alan Gowans (1964, p. 316), the Italianate was not properly a revival style, but was more a manner of architecture. Advertised as a variant of the Gothic rather than as a new style, it was a useful means of decorating buildings in a fashion more acceptable to conservative clients, who could never accept what seemed to be the eccentric and foreign character of medieval Gothic forms. Loosely based on Italian Renaissance models, its use was free and informal. The Italianate served as the vital link between the Carpenter Gothic of the early nineteenth century and the High Victorian forms of the Queen Anne and Eastlake of the later nineteenth century.

32. Hitchcock (1958, p. 90).

33. The touted advantages of the castiron facades were resistance to strain and fire ("Practically, castiron is crushing-proof, for a column must be ten miles in height before it will crush itself by its own weight.") They were also easily prefabricated. They were usually made to resemble stone fronts, but the requirements of working with iron created an aesthetic of its own that was later copied by masonry facades.

Castiron buildings failed, however. They were more expensive than masonry buildings and had to be painted frequently to prevent rust. It was also discovered in Chicago and Boston that they melted in a fire. The great fires in those two cities in the 1870s killed the castiron building industry, but it had served as a precursor to the development of the steel frame that was to follow a decade later. The steel frame, however, was *inside* the building, not on its surface (see Maass, 1957, p. 101).

34. This discussion of the Bella Union has been taken primarily from Krythe (1951). Also see "Passing Away," *Los Angeles Daily Star*, June 26, 1870; "Closing of the Bella Union," *Los Angeles Daily Star*, July 1, 1870.

35. The cornice of the Bella Union is a few feet above the roof itself and serves merely as part of the false front, rather than actually supporting the roof overhang. Nevertheless, the cornice was aesthetically important. The building to the right of the Bella Union in the photographs has similar arched windows but no cornice, and it looks much less grand.

36. See also "Removal of Old Landmarks," *Los Angeles Star*, September 11, 1869.

37. Our knowledge of the original design and construction of the Pico House is limited and stems primarily from three sources; *Los Angeles Star*, April 23, 1870; *Los Angeles Daily News*, May 25, 1870; *Los Angeles Herald*, November 22, 1873.

38. Today nothing remains of the original interior, and little is known about its original design. From early newspaper descriptions we know the following: Off the Main St. entrance was a high-ceilinged lobby with a double grand staircase joining midway at a landing with a great mirror. The lobby opened into a patio, where caged birds and plants hung down over the galleries. On the second floor, looking out over the patio on one side and the Plaza on the other were two dining rooms, one reserved for families and children, both accommodating 130 guests. The second-floor rooms were usually arranged in suites, and there was a "public parlor richly furnished with two large chandeliers, where music was furnished nightly." The third floor was devoted entirely to sleeping rooms.

The architect, Ezra F. Kysor (1835–1907) was born in New York and left for Virginia City, Nevada, shortly after the Civil War. In 1868 he arrived in Los Angeles and practiced with another architect in the Temple Market Block. Kysor's first major commission was the Pico House, in 1869.

In 1876 he formed a partnership with his draftsman, Octavius Morgan (1850–1922). Morgan was born and educated in England, migrated to Denver in 1870, and in 1873 moved to Los Angeles. Kysor and Morgan designed, among other buildings, St. Vibiana's Cathedral.

After Kysor's retirement in 1888, Morgan joined John A. Walls (1858–1922) in organizing the firm of Morgan and Walls, with his son joining them in 1910 to form Morgan, Walls and Morgan. Their commissions included the Hollenbeck Home for the Aged, Farmers and Merchants Bank, and the W. P. Story Building. In 1920 Stiles Clements joined the partnership and the firm became Morgan, Walls and Clements until 1937, after which date Clements practiced alone until his death in 1955. Morgan, Walls and Clements created several masterpieces of Los Angeles architecture: the Richfield, Pellissier, Samson Tire, and Hollywood Turf Club buildings, and the Mayan Theater.

39. Ludwig Salvator (1878, p. 126).

40. Quoted in Reinhardt (1973, p. 77).

CHAPTER 3

1. The Southern Pacific Railroad completed a line from Los Angeles to San Francisco in 1876 and began building a second line from Los Angeles eastward. By 1883, direct trackage extended from Los Angeles via Tucson to New Orleans. Meanwhile the Atchison, Topeka, and Santa Fe was building a line over the Cajon Pass from Chicago via Flagstaff, running its own trains into Los Angeles by 1885.

2. Dumke (1944, p. 29).

3. Ibid., p. 25.

4. Brook (1896).

5. Ibid.

6. Dumke (1944, p. 175).

7. Netz (1915–17, p. 67).

8. Dumke (1944, p. 259).

9. Brook (1895).

10. Lummis (1895, p. 49).

11. Dumke (1944, p. 264).

12. Lummis (1895, p. 49).

13. James Early has traced the notion of "picturesque" to the great vogue of landscape painting which accompanied the developing Romantic sensibility in the early nineteenth century. Its roots lay with seventeenth-century landscape painters, whose visions inspired English garden designers and, later, architects, who became impatient with the formal symmetry of classical art. In the United States, Early attributes substantial influence to the chapter on buildings in Downing's *Treatise on the Theory and Practice of Landscape Gardening*. This and Downing's other work inspired a flood of writing on rural architecture that fit the landscape-painter image. It was not long before the values represented by the pastoral scene began to be translated into urban architectural forms (see Early, 1965, pp. 51–83).

14. See Oliver (1956, pp. 297–313).

15. Girouard (1977, p. 208).

16. Victoria Padilla (1961, p. 52) has written, "Many families during this period seemed to have a member wasting away with 'consumption' or a frail daughter suffering from the 'vapours,' and medical science seemed to be unable to offer alleviation of this melancholy state of affairs. Thus, when the news reached the East of a remarkable 'never-never-land' where the climate was so beneficent that all physical woes were put to rout, the number of sickly persons finding their way West was little short of staggering." For a treatise on California as a health paradise, see Remomdino (1892).

17. Even unpretentious homes in the 1880s were surrounded by profuse plantings of ornamentals in every hue, fragrance, and form; the estates of the wealthy became parks of great beauty. Only a few of the hundreds of species of ornamental plants that made each Los Angeles yard a mini-botanical garden were native to this region.

"In the eighties and nineties a man's status was symbolized by the sweep of the lawn that separated his house from the street and the number of specimen trees and palms that grew thereon," writes Victoria Padilla (1961, p. 59). "For such plantings conifers were often used, and the garden that did not have an araucaria, a deodar, a hedge of Monterey cypress, several oaks, and a pine or two was a poor place indeed. To lighten the preponderance of such dark foliaged material, palms were planted in abundance, and Southern California was never so rich in the variety of palm specimens enhancing private estates as during the last years of the century" (p. 236).

18. See Giedion (1967, pp. 351–355).

Left: detail, Valley Municipal Building, 14410 Sylvan Street, by Peter K. Schabarum, 1932. Right: Dann house, 1351 Londonderry Place, by J. R. Davidson, 1951.

19. Queen Anne architecture came to New England from Britain in the 1870s as the "Old English Style," which seemed to give the nostalgic frame of mind in America of that period an architectural expression. By 1876 the style was being featured in *Harper's Magazine* and, the following year, in *American Architect and Building News*.

20. In 1881, *California Architect and Building Review* went so far as to promulgate three advantages of bay windows in architecture. First was their contribution to the *exterior appearance* of a home. They furnished prominent features "upon which architects may display great taste and skilful treatment, as no special rule or law of architecture controls their delineation, except that of harmony and consistency."

The second advantage was their *interior conveniences*. Bay windows "increase facilities for sight-seeing and distant views, and afford cozy corners for loving hearts to discuss love matters and future prospects in life." The propriety of home life was of concern to the journal, although household roles taken for granted then would be unacceptable today by many (see, for example, "Ladies Make the Best Planners," *California Architect and Building Review*, September 1880, p. 82).

Third, of special interest to those who had come to California for their health, were the *sanitary advantages*:

It is a well-understood fact that women and children, and sometimes men, like to look out of windows; and if any special view is desired, in cases where there are no bay windows, the sash is raised and the head of the party desiring to see more than can be seen with the window closed,

21. See "Modern Aesthetic Houses," *California Architect and Building News*, April 1885, pp. 66–7.

22. Critics in the period seemed to be more sensitive than we are to the subtleties of Queen Anne designs. Also, the number of Queen Anne houses—or Eastlake, or Craftsman, or Mission Revival, for that matter—constructed in given districts and in given periods is not known. Thus, our knowledge of the actual fabric and streetscape of Los Angeles and its surrounding cities during most of their history is very limited.

23. See Gowans (1964, p. 336). In writing of the roots of the Arts and Crafts movement in America, Clark has suggested that during the 1870s the state of American decorative arts was appalling. Visitors to the great American Centennial Exposition of 1876 in Philadelphia, for example, "were generally awed by the mighty Corliss engine, while the more sensitive viewers and critics were often horrified by furniture exhibits that showed a taste for grandeur and no pride in craftsmanship" (Clark 1972, p. 9).

24. Advertisement in *Scientific American,* October 1881, p. 81.

25. The origins of Eastlake as an American architectural style divorced from its original intentions remains another challenging research topic in architectural history.

26. See "The Eastlake Style of Architecture," *California Architect and Building News*, October 1881, p. 97.

27. Ibid.

28. Samuel and Joseph Cather Newsom were trained as architects in the architectural office of their elder

37. Edwards (1907, p. 13).

38. Eyre (1911, p. 307).

39. Hopkins (1906, p. 35).

40. The quote that follows in the text is from Hopkins (1906, p. 36). Florence Fitch Kelly presented a series on "How to Furnish a Bungalow" in the journal *Indoors and Out* in 1907. Appropriate furnishings included:
   a) Draperies and upholstery: denims, canvases, and burlaps.
   b) Floor coverings: fiber mats or rag rugs.
   c) Tableware: "Select a number of pieces of some desired color and decoration and, using these as a basis, finish the complement of tableware with harmonizing or contrasting selections from here, there, and everywhere."
   d) Furniture: rough birch, reed and willow, wooden benches, white enamel, rustic hickory, or the standard Mission.

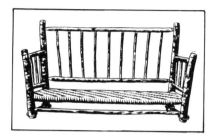

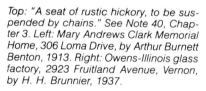

Top: "A seat of rustic hickory, to be suspended by chains." See Note 40, Chapter 3. Left: Mary Andrews Clark Memorial Home, 306 Loma Drive, by Arthur Burnett Benton, 1913. Right: Owens-Illinois glass factory, 2923 Fruitland Avenue, Vernon, by H. H. Brunnier, 1937.

is thrust out. Ordinarily this is injurious, since it subjects the party so acting to a strong current of air by the difference in the temperature of the external and internal atmospheres, if from no other cause; and if the system is heated by exercise or otherwise, or the party is enfeebled by ailments of any sort, and the pores of the skin open, the injurious effect is greatly increased. It is unquestionably a fact that hundreds of thousands have caught their death of cold by opening windows and extending their heads and shoulders through the open apertures . . .

One suspects, however, that these reasons may not be quite so straightforward. Bay windows may have been fine for sparking, but they certainly did not offer the only opportunity. They did serve to add more light to the room, but the notion of "light and airy room" was hardly compatible with the dark and cluttered interior decoration of the period (see Seale 1975). As for the dangers of leaning out, it is possible that this attitude reflected a reasoned social truth of the era, but an inspection of bay windows in San Francisco and Los Angeles reveals that most are double hung and may be opened as easily as any other window—one could lean even farther out a bay window than out a window flush with a wall.

For more substantial insight into the popularity of the bay window, therefore, one must return to its picturesqueness, its challenge to the architect. Each architectural creation was like a picture puzzle that could be put together in several ways, some beautiful, some grotesque, depending on the skill of the architect.

California Architect and Building News of May 1886, p. 66, stated that in San Francisco in the 1860s to 1880s, ninety-seven percent of all new dwellings were constructed with at least one bay window. The location and projection of bay windows built over the street line were regulated by city ordinance.

brothers, and from 1878 to 1886 they maintained their own offices in San Francisco and Oakland. During the Boom of the Eighties, Joseph Cather established a branch office in Los Angeles from 1903 to 1906 (Gebhard et al. 1979, pp. 19–24).

29. Gebhard et al. (1979).

30. For a discussion of the Arts and Crafts movement in the United States, see Clark (1972). The California Arts and Crafts is treated in Anderson et al. (1980).

31. The word "bungalow" is an Anglicized version of the Hindi "bangla," meaning "of Bengal," and was first applied to a thatched hut that was adopted by the British in India. It later became the term used for a popular English dwelling type that had similar characteristics. The California bungalow is so named probably because it looks somewhat like an Anglo-Indian bungalow, although there seems to be no architectural relationship (see Lancaster 1963, p. 104).

32. Robert Winter's book *The California Bungalow* (1980) treats the bungalow house form in its Craftsman manifestation as well as in other styles. There was, for example, the "Winter Bungalow" (Greenwood 1907), the "Gothic Bungalow" (Clous 1907), a Mission Revival bungalow out of concrete (Ripley 1907), and a portable bungalow that could be "shipped anywhere to the purchaser *flat*. May be set up ready for occupancy in a few hours" (advertisement for the Springfield Portable Construction Co., *Indoors and Out*, May 1907, p. 10).

33. Lazear (1907).

34. Lancaster (1963).

35. Wilson (1910, p. 3).

36. Edwards (1907, p. 13). The "perfect" bungalow was heated in winter by a small sheet-iron stove fueled with twisted-up newspapers that had been saved all summer and autumn (see Saunders, 1919, p. 242).

41. For further information on Greene and Greene, see Makinson (1977) and (1978).

42. The Swiss chalet imagery of the Craftsman bungalow was believed to be as suitable to hillsides in Southern California as it was to the Alps (see Byers, 1914).

43. Saunders (1919, p. 245).

44. Smith (1916).

45. Stoddart (1905, p. 295).

46. Ibid., as are the following quotations. In 1916, Bogardus published a study of Los Angeles house courts, in which he classified six types:
   a) Old Spanish adobe. Relics of earlier days taken over by tenement families.
   b) Shacks. "The worst type of dwelling, but are being eliminated as fast as possible."
   c) Barrack style. Courts constructed with three long rows of barrack-like structures on the three sides of an open lot. They were usually built of board and batten with the rough boards stained on the exterior and painted on the interior, and the long buildings were subdivided by partitions into living units. Toilet facilities were located in the open court that was sometimes entirely paved with asphalt. The court also served as the space for family washings, children's playground, woodyard, and garbage cans.
   d) Separate two-room houses. Similar to barrack courts but usually of more recent construction, they allowed more family privacy and more yard space per habitation.
   e) Concrete houses. Newer and more expensive house courts with free-standing dwelling units. The cottages usually had three rooms with indoor plumbing.
   f) Bungalow court. "It is of far higher type than the first four forms mentioned. Many are quite attractive. The open court is frequently covered by a lawn."

47. Matthews (1913, p. 461).

48. Ibid., and Bogardus (1916, p. 392). The source of the original statement by Riis is unknown.

49. Matthews (1913, p. 464).

50. Stoddart (1905, p. 296).

51. Matthews (1913, p. 464).

CHAPTER 4

1. Various founders of the Mission Revival movement have been proposed. George Wharton James, writing in 1903, suggested architect Lester S. Moore of Los Angeles (originally from Topeka, Kansas). Harold Kirker (1960, p. 122) asserted that the first architect to become seriously aware of the possibilities offered by the missions was Willis Polk, who had come to Los Angeles from Kentucky in 1889. The topic calls for further research.

2. For a discussion of this building, see Burg (1976, pp. 151–152).

3. See Pohlman (1974).

4. Jackson (1884, pp. 17–18).

5. Frank A. Pattee was a pharmacist who came to Los Angeles from Pennsylvania via Kansas in 1886. He opened a prescription drug store in Los Angeles, dropped the drug business in 1893, and became a solicitor for the Los Angeles Chamber of Commerce. Pattee jointly founded *Land of Sunshine* with the Englishman Harry Brook, who was working as an editorial writer for the *Los Angeles Times*, and the reporter Charles D. Willard, who had come from Michigan.

18. del Rio [Lummis] (1898), p. 175).

19. Late Mission Revival structures lost much of the naive simplicity that characterized the early years of the movement. Notre Dame High School of 1938, at Woodman and Riverside Drive in Sherman Oaks, for example, uses the motif of the *convento* at San Fernando. Its arcade, however, is carefully sited and designed to be strikingly handsome. Another late Mission Revival building, the Church of the Good Shepherd at Santa Monica Boulevard and Bedford Drive in Beverly Hills, makes no attempt at crudeness.

20. Benton (1911, p. 63).

21. Grey (1905, p. 3).

22. Benton (1911, p. 63).

23. Kirker (1960, p. 123). The Hayward Hotel at 206 West Sixth Street (Charles F. Whittlesey) is one of the few Mission Revival highrise buildings ever to have been designed. The evocation is thin, however, limited to window treatment and surface texture.

24. Gebhard (1967, p. 136).

25. Pomeroy (1957, p. 162).

26. Gebhard (1967, p. 134); Sanford (1950, p. 249). A Baltimore version of a large Mission Revival house is illustrated in *Indoors and Out*, vol. 4, no. 1, April 1907, p. 21. The reinforced concrete Mission Revival Episcopal Cathedral in Manila, Philippines, is illustrated in the *American Architect and Building News*, no. 1636, May 4, 1907.

27. The first Churrigueresque Revival building in Southern California may have been the First Congregational Church (1914; Myron Hunt) at Seventh and

39. See Gebhard and Winter (1977, p. 521) for a brief history of Santa Barbara architecture.

40. Morrow (1926, p. 51). The arcades may have turned Santa Barbara into a Spanish city, but certainly not into a Spanish Colonial California city. There were few if any arcades in California secular settlements during the Spanish period. The *corredores* were wooden canopies supported by wooden posts.
     Perhaps the most picturesque Spanish styled building in Southern California is the Santa Barbara County Courthouse (1929; William Mooser and Co.). For a description and encomium of this intensely self-conscious creation, see Finney (1929).

41. Requa (1927, p. 46).

42. Grey (1929, p. 36).

43. Sanford (1950, p. 249).

CHAPTER 5

1. Waldron (1959, p. 367).

2. "Los Angeles City Hall Tower to be Cut Down, *A&E*, October 1918, p. 114.

3. McCoy (1953).

4. Bellamy (1890, p. 157).

5. See, for example, the *Illustrated Los Angeles Herald*, March 1892, p. 9.

6. My appreciation to Tom Owen for this insight.

7. The Los Angeles Conservancy has prepared walking tours of buildings in this district.

8. The city's first building ordinance, no. 6108 n.s., became effective December 12, 1890.

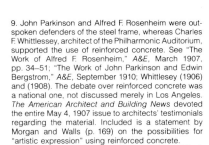

6. See Bingham (1955) for a biography of Lummis and the history of *Land of Sunshine*.

7. Lummis (1895, p. 49).

8. Ibid.

9. Lummis (1895, p. 65).

10. Ibid.

11. Hunt (1894). Sumner P. Hunt was born in Brooklyn in 1865. In 1889 he came to Los Angeles and entered the firm of Caulkin and Hans, where he worked until he formed a partnership with Theodore Eisen and A. W. Enger in 1895. In 1908 Hunt formed a partnership with Silas R. Burns, and they worked together for the next two decades. Their major works include the Southwest Museum, the Automobile Club of Southern California, and the Ebell Club on Wilshire Boulevard. Hunt served on the original Los Angeles Planning Commission (Withey and Withey 1956, pp. 311–2).

12. Benton (1911, p. 35). Arthur Burnett Benton was born in Peoria, Illinois, in 1859. He first worked as a clerk for the Santa Fe Railroad, and in 1891 moved to Los Angeles. He was the designer of the Glenwood Mission Inn in Riverside, which still stands, and the Arlington Hotel in Santa Barbara, built in 1910 and destroyed by an earthquake in 1925. Both were masterpieces of the Mission Revival. He also designed the Mary Andrews Clark Memorial Home and the first Friday Morning Club in Los Angeles.

13. Shinn (1895, p. 79).

14. Lummis (1898, p. 253).

15. Pohlman (1974, p. 5).

16. Shinn (1895, p. 79).

17. Bingham (1955, p. 104). This material is taken primarily from Bingham's history of the Landmarks Club, in (1955), pp. 103–111.

Lemon streets in Riverside. Its ornament is somewhat dry, however, and it was certainly not as influential as Goodhue's work (see Patterson 1964, p. 52).

28. Price (1915, p. 234).

29. The Panama-California Exposition was much smaller than its San Francisco competitor and attracted fewer visitors. Almost two million people attended the San Diego fair compared to nearly nineteen million who attended the Panama-Pacific Exposition in San Francisco. The architectural influence of the San Diego fair far outweighed its importance as a fair per se. (See Noffsinger 1955, p. 62).

30. See "The Panama-California Exposition in San Diego," *A&E*, December 1910, pp. 58–59.

31. Baxter (1901).

32. Price. (1915, p. 240).

33. Ibid., p. 234.

34. See Sanford (1947), Chapter 11: "Ultra-Baroque; the Mexican Churrigueresque, 1750–1800" for a discussion of the style.

35. The California State Building is in the form of a Greek cross with shallow transepts; a large tiled rotunda rises in the center. The frontispiece forms a veritable historical hall of fame for persons associated with the early history of San Diego. The glazed tile of the dome was designed by Goodhue and fired by Walter Nordhoff at his potteries in National City. For further description see Winslow (1916, pp. 30–38).

36. Hayworth Avenue is one block west of Fairfax Avenue. Of particular note are the blocks between Olympic and Pico.

37. Marsden (1919, p. 7).

38. Morrow (1921, p. 49). The bank was the County National Bank and Trust, designed by Myron Hunt.

9. John Parkinson and Alfred F. Rosenheim were outspoken defenders of the steel frame, whereas Charles F. Whittlessey, architect of the Philharmonic Auditorium, supported the use of reinforced concrete. See "The Work of Alfred F. Rosenheim," *A&E*, March 1907, pp. 34–51; "The Work of John Parkinson and Edwin Bergstrom," *A&E*, September 1910; Whittlesey (1906) and (1908). The debate over reinforced concrete was a national one, not discussed merely in Los Angeles. *The American Architect and Building News* devoted the entire May 4, 1907 issue to architects' testimonials regarding the material. Included is a statement by Morgan and Walls (p. 169) on the possibilities for "artistic expression" using reinforced concrete.
     Theater construction posed a particularly difficult problem because the building had to have a gaping hole in the center, and perhaps a balcony. Not only did great distances have to be spanned so that people under the balcony could see, but the spans had to support considerable weight. The Philharmonic Auditorium was the first all-reinforced concrete theater building in Los Angeles, followed in 1909 by the Majestic Theater on Broadway between Eighth and Ninth streets (Edelman and Barnett, architects). See "A California Theater of Reinforced Concrete" (1909).
     A similar debate had actually been carried out two decades earlier with respect to the balloon frame. See "Durability of Frame Buildings," *CA&BN*, November 1880, p. 105; "Balloon-Built Buildings; How False Statements Gather Strength," *CA&BN*, February 1881, p. 15.

10. At the Los Angeles City Council meeting of January 26, 1903, the committee on legislation recommended "that the President of the Council be authorized to appoint a Commission consisting of two architects who are members of the Los Angeles Chapter of the American Institute of Architects, the Superintendent of Buildings, one member of the Pacific Board of Fire

Left: Le Parc, Empyrean Way, Century City, by Caspar Ehmke, 1980. Right: Westwood Ambassador Apartments, 10427 Wilshire Boulevard, by Milton J. Black, 1940. Photograph 1940.

Above: entrance detail, Wiltern Theatre, Wilshire Boulevard and Western Avenue, 1931. Top left: Hollywood Pantages Theatre, 6233 Hollywood Boulevard, by B. Marcus Priteca, 1929. Top right: Women's powder room, Hollywood Pantages Theatre. Photograph 1929.

Underwriters, the Chief of the Fire Department, the City Electrician, and the City Plumbing Inspector, for the purpose of working in conjunction with the Committee on Legislation in revising the existing building laws and ordinances of the city, said Commission to serve without remuneration" (Minutes Books of the City of Los Angeles, vol. 66, p. 225).

This report was adapted by the city council, and at the meeting of February 2, 1903, Council President Bowen submitted the names of John Parkinson and John C. Austin, architects, and John S. Morrow, president of the Pacific Board of Fire Underwriters. All three nominees were approved by the council (Minutes Books, vol. 66, p. 387).

In the next two years the Committee held over 160 meetings that resulted in the revised building ordinance containing the height limitations. The ordinance was unanimously adopted by the city council at their meeting of December 27, 1904, and is entered as ordinance no. 10, 415, in Ordinance Book 11, page 319. It became effective February 9, 1905.

For their services, the city council awarded a sum of $500 each to Parkinson, Austin, and Morrow (Minutes Books, vol. 69, p. 755).

11. The *Los Angeles Times* report on the passage of the ordinance also fails to mention why the height limits were imposed (December 28, 1904, Pt. II, p. 2).

12. For example, the Spring Street Company submitted Petition no. 1824 "for change of Ordinance so as to permit a structure greater than the heights allowed by the present Ordinance." Petitions nos. 1875 (Central Fireproof Building Co.), 1876 (Municipal League of Los Angeles), 1877 (Builders' Exchange), all protested against the application for variance. These petitions are filed by number in the Los Angeles City Archives (1910).

13. Los Angeles City Council Minutes Books, vol. 83, December 20, 1910, p. 198.

14. Ibid., p. 224.

15. Many Los Angeles suburbs had height restrictions in the 1950s that were much more stringent than those of Los Angeles itself, for examples:
Torrance, Culver City, and Hawthorne: 35 feet
San Fernando: 45 feet
Beverly Hills: 60 feet, with some variances granted
Lynwood, Gardena, El Segundo, South Gate, and South Pasadena: 75 feet
Huntington Park: seven stories
Inglewood: 100 feet
Alhambra: 110 feet
Santa Monica: 120 feet
Pasadena: 130 feet
Long Beach: 180 feet

Burbank, Glendale, and Vernon: unlimited height
In succeeding years, many of these height restrictions have been eased. In Los Angeles, the first building to be approved under the post-1957 regulations was the nineteen-story California Bank Building at Sixth and Spring streets (Los Angeles. Department of City Planning. Report on Proposed Charter Amendment Relative to Height of Buildings, 1956, and *Engineering News-Record*, May 28, 1959, pp. 40–42).

16. About five hundred American architects studied at *L'Ecole des Beaux Arts* between 1846 and 1920, and a few after that date (see Noffsinger, 1955). Lansburgh's first commission in Los Angeles was the Orpheum (now Palace) Theater on Broadway in 1910; he maintained his office in San Francisco. See Chafee (1977) for a study of the architectural teaching of L'Ecole des Beaux Arts.

17. John Parkinson was born in England in 1861 and in 1885 migrated to Napa, California, where he practiced architecture for five years; he then worked in Seattle until 1894. In that year he settled in Los Angeles. His first important commission was the Currier Block on Third Street, between Spring Street and Broadway, and in that building he maintained his office for several years. His second major commission was the Homer Laughlin Building (today the site of the Grand Central Market) on Broadway, notable as the first Class "A" building in the city. His major commissions are listed in Withey and Withey (1956, pp. 456–7).

18. Thanks to Norton Stern for this information.

19. For an early description, see "The Work of Alfred F. Rosenheim, Architect," (1907) and Rosenheim (1906). Rosenheim also designed the Second Church of Christ, Scientist, at 947 West Adams Boulevard, completed in 1910. It is Los Angeles Historic-Cultural Monument No. 57. In that year he designed the Britt residence, 2141 West Adams, which has since been demolished. It was Historic-Cultural Monument No. 197. In the same year he designed the Cameo Theater, 588 South Broadway, which stands today as the best remaining example of a nickelodeon (a silent movie theater with an admission of five cents) in Los Angeles. The interior remains completely intact. For a history of the nickelodeon, see Merritt (1976). Rosenheim describes his career in a 1939 article in *A&E*, April, pp. 39–43.

20. In 1928, Edgell (p. 88) wrote from a revisionist perspective that "the proud client came to boast of his dwelling in terms of its being 'true Colonial' instead of objectively beautiful. Effects themselves desirable were often condemned on the ground that they were not 'truly Colonial,' and the cult of Colonial furniture stimulated the purchase . . . of pieces of dubious beauty merely because of their genuineness as Colonial work."

21. See McWilliams (1946), Chapter 7, "Years of the Boom," for a discussion of Los Angeles boosterism.

22. See Bartlett (1907).

23. See Hunter (1933, p. 108). In 1909 the Municipal Arts Commission included prominent Los Angeles citizens John Parkinson and Mrs. Sumner P. Hunt.

24. This discussion of the Los Angeles Civic Center is taken primarily from Wade (1966). Charles Mulford Robinson was known for his authorship of such works as "The Width and Arrangement of Streets; A Study in Town Planning," (New York: Engineering News Publishing Co., 1911).

25. This plan for Los Angeles is on file in the Municipal Reference Library in Los Angeles City Hall (see Robinson, 1909).

26. The San Francisco Civic Center stands as a reminder of what this plan and its architecture would have become. Part of the ethic of the civic center held that it had to be separate from the business and commercial functions of the city. Cook and Hall wrote that "Experience in city planning and a study of land valuations leads to the general conclusion that when Administrative Centers, or City Halls, are placed in the active business districts they tend to arrest the upward trend of property values in their neighborhood, whereas if Administrative Centers are located in an adjunct to the recognized business district they at once tend to stabilize, and frequently to increase, the property values (Cook and Hall 1923, p. 11). Unfortunately, the subsequent experience with the Los Angeles Civic Center and many others suggests that the opposite is in fact true. A self-contained civic center does little for the property surrounding it, since it isolates itself from the city rather than drawing the city toward it.

27. The Allied Architects Association of Los Angeles was a cooperative society of thirty-three architects formed in 1921 to design public buildings. Octavius Morgan was the president and Edwin Bergstrom the vice president (see *Southwest Builder and Contractor*, July 8, 1921, p. 10).

28. Jennings (1928, p. 37).

29. Los Angeles City Hall was exempt from the height limitation because the California Supreme Court had declared in the case of C. J. Kubach Company versus Hugh J. McGuire, President of the Board of Public Works, 199 Cal 215, that the City Charter height limitations did not apply to the construction of public buildings in the city. However, the city council in 1926 submitted the matter to a vote of the electorate, who approved the 452-foot city hall tower by a seventy percent majority (see Los Angeles. Department of City Planning. Report on Proposed Charter Amendment Relative to Height of Buildings, 1956, p. 5–6).

Left: lobby, Hollywood Pantages Theatre. Photograph 1929. Right: detail, Million Dollar Theatre; sculpture by Joe Morra, 1918.

30. Austin (1928, p. 25).

31. The early Main Street theater district is now almost entirely extinct. The Adolphus Theater still has its terra cotta facade, but the building now serves as the entrance to a parking lot, and a driveway goes through the lobby. Two later theaters still remain: the Linda Lea at Fourth and Main streets is a nickelodeon from 1910. Its front has been orientalized. The California Theater (1918; A. B. Rosenthal) has a neo-Baroque facade and an intact marquee. It was the first Spanish-language house in Los Angeles.

32. Sexton (1927, pp. 14–16).

33. Also see "Modern Tendencies in Theater Design," *A&E*, July 1928, pp. 55–56. For further references on theater architecture, see Stoddard (1978), and in particular Pawley (1913) and Flagg (1919). Early marquee designs are discussed by Fallon (1915).

34. The United Artists Theater is not presently within the Broadway historic district.

35. Jennings (1923, p. 77) said, "Like all other sections of the temple of art, the doors, vestibules and lobby of the film palace are painted or carved with hieroglyphics. Even the shades of the chandeliers bloom with picture paintings of the ancient race that struggled to compile an alphabet. Vases, large and small, made like those of mystic Egypt, are a part of the decorative scheme, while from every side gleams the birdlike countenance of Isis, acclaimed by the Egyptians as the supreme of all goddesses."

36. Yama Shiro was designed as a residence for Adolph and Eugene Bernheimer, importers of Oriental art. It still stands at 1999 North Sycamore Avenue, and is today a restaurant. See O'Dodd (1923), Lancaster (1963, p. 121).

37. See Arnold C. Breakman (1976), *The Search for the Gold of Tutankhamun*, New York: Mason/Charter.

38. For a discussion and illustrations of *Intolerance*, see Mast (1976, pp. 82–84), and *This Fabulous Century*, vol. 2, 1910–1920; New York: Time-Life Books, 1969, pp. 72–77.

39. "Chinese Theater at Hollywood, California," *American Architect*, August 20, 1927, p. 251.

40. Woollett (1928).

41. Note, for example, the Kiefer house at 1204 West 27th Street (1895; Sumner P. Hunt and Theodore Eisen).

42. Lippiatt (1928, p. 24).

43. Other notable examples are at Fifth Street and Wilton Place, 1164 South High Point Drive, and 8324 Fountain Avenue in Los Angeles.

44. Other examples of the Hansel and Gretel are the Bryce house, 2327 Hill Drive in Eagle Rock (1923; Egasse and Brauch), a bungalow court (ca. 1926) at Glendale Boulevard and Loma Vista Place, and a group of dwellings at Ridgewood and Fernwood streets (ca. 1925).

45. For a discussion of these styles in the San Francisco area and the sources of their imagery, see Gebhard (1976).

46. Stacy-Judd (1926, p. 59). The hotel was named the "Aztec" because the name sounded better than "Mayan."

47. At Santa Clara and Laurel streets in Ventura.

48. For further details see Robinson (1931).

49. Heinly (1912, p. 729).

50. Fogelson (1967, p. 148).

51. Los Angeles *Examiner*, Nov. 17, 1911.

52. Kelker (1925, p. 37). Automobile registration in the county rose 150 percent from 1920 to 1924—from 200,000 to 500,00—and over half of these vehicles traveled daily to downtown (Fogelson 1967, p. 152). According to Clarence Snethen of the Los Angeles Traffic Commission, congestion in Los Angeles was worse than anywhere else in the United States in 1924 (Snethen 1924, p. 196).

53. Fogelson (1967, p. 148).

54. For a brief treatment of the petroleum industry in Los Angeles, see McWilliams (1946, pp. 135–7). For a discussion of the film industry see Mast (1976, pp. 82–85).

55. See McWilliams (1946, pp. 136–7) for a discussion of the All-Year Club of Southern California.

56. McWilliams (1946, p. 135). The population of the city of Los Angeles increased from 577,000 in 1920 to 1,238,000 in 1930.

CHAPTER 6

1. McWilliams (1946, p. 135).

2. For a discussion see Lofland (1973, p. 64).

3. See McShane (1979) for a social history of street paving. Not only was the ease of travel increasing as never before, but the speed as well. Western Air Express inaugurated the first regularly scheduled air passenger service in the United States on its air mail run from Los Angeles to Salt Lake City in 1926, and in 1930 direct, coast-to-coast air travel was scheduled for the first time, taking twenty-eight hours in contrast to the more than seventy-two hours by train (see Davies, 1964, pp. 50–52).

4. Woehlke (1911).

5. Hancock (1949, pp. 171–2).

6. Schindler (1930). See also Hancock (1949, pp. 267–270).

7. See McGroarty (1930, pp. 29–41) and Seares (1930, pp. 40–43). The shopping center was planned by Harland Bartholemew and Associates.

Today, Westwood has far outgrown its original plans, but vestiges of its Mediterranean streetscape still remain. The turreted corner of Ralphs Grocery Store (now a theater and restaurant) at 1150 Westwood Boulevard (1929; Russell Collins) may still be seen from Wilshire Boulevard. "The Dome," (now a bank) at Westwood Boulevard and Broxton Avenue (1929; Allison and Allison), originally housed the offices of the Janss Investment Company, developer of the tract. Holmby Hall, an ensemble of stores on Westwood Boulevard between Weyburn and LeConte avenues (1929; Gordon B. Kaufmann and John and Donald Parkinson) still exists, including the tower at the corner of Weyburn.

8. *A&E*, September 1930, pp. 111-12. The building did not have a rear parking lot, but it did have a rear automobile entrance where patrons could leave their cars to be parked in the garage.

9. "Bullocks Wilshire Boulevard Store," *A&E*, December 1929, pp. 45-52.

10. Two of these towers from the 1930s still standing are that of the Fox Westwood Village Theater (1931; P. O. Lewis) at 961 Broxton Avenue and the Owl Drug Store (now Julian Medical) at 6380 Hollywood Boulevard (1934; Morgan, Walls and Clements). For a discussion of 1930s gas station styles see White (1935).

11. In 1949, Ralph Hancock noted that "The May Company figures 85 percent of its business comes in through its back door and that is why the entire side of the building facing its parking lot has a much more attractive appearance than its more conventional front. A protective canopy and loading ramp is flanked by show windows as pretentious as those facing Wilshire" (p. 163).

12. The honor of first automobile-oriented shopping center is usually given to J. C. Nichols' Country Club Plaza in Kansas City, built in 1923. For a discussion see Ehrlich (1979, pp. 72–74).

13. The world's first drive-in bank was apparently in Los Angeles. Actually it was located in a converted garage in Vernon. For a discussion and illustrations, see "Banking by Automobile," *Scientific American*, September 1937, p. 151.

14. Fogelson (1967, p. 153).

15. Shaw (1927).

Above: Los Angeles County Medical Center, 1200 North State Street, by the Allied Architects of Los Angeles, 1933. Top left: Walker house, 2100 Kenilworth Avenue, by R. M. Schindler, 1936. Top right: interior, Walker house, Photograph 1936.

16. For an account of Autobahn development, see Schreiber (1961, pop. 231–233).

17. "First Parkway for Los Angeles," *Engineering News-Record,* July 21, 1938, pp. 79–82.

18. There is some disagreement as to what this style should actually be called. Whiffen (1969) and Dwyer (1974) call it "Modernistic" because that is the name used by some of its practitioners. Gebhard, in his many writings, calls it "Zigzag Moderne." Vlack (1974) and Robinson and Bletter (1975), writing about New York City, refer to "Art Deco."

19. Architectural training was not the great watershed between designers remaining in traditional styles and those who embraced the new Art Deco. Stiles O. Clements, the greatest creator of Art Deco and Streamline buildings in Los Angeles—and perhaps the city's most gifted visual thinker—had attended *L'Ecole des Beaux Arts.* It was not even a matter of rejecting traditional styles by individual firms. Morgan, Walls and Clements were designing Spanish buildings such as the Chapman Market at the same time that some of their Art Deco masterpieces such as the Richfield Building were on the boards. John and Donald Parkinson were designing Spanish buildings in Westwood Village concurrently with Art Deco buildings such as the Title Guarantee Building at Fifth and Hill streets. Rather, Art Deco took its place as one style among many from which one might choose.

20. Gebhard (1969). Vlack (1974) also presents a chapter on symbolism in Art Deco architecture. See also Dwyer (1974) and Robinson and Bletter (1975), pp. 41–68.

21. For a comment by Robert Field to this effect, see Schippers (1964, p. 387).

22. Regarding the Los Angeles Stock Exchange, Jones (1931), p. 27, wrote that "the ornament throughout the building is based principally on plant life, expressing only the essentials, life and growth. All traces of actual plant forms which can be recognized by leaf or flower have been suppressed."

23. For a discussion of concrete in Art Deco architecture, see Hanson (1930).

24. David Gebhard prepared a privately published eulogy to the building, with photographs, on the occasion of its demolition in 1969. The respondents who provided mental maps of downtown Los Angeles for Kevin Lynch's book *The Image of the City* usually could describe only two buildings in any detail from memory: the City Hall and, in Lynch's terms, the "ugly, black and gold Richfield Building" (Lynch, 1960, p. 35).

25. See "Modern Design for Los Angeles Commercial Building," *A&E,* June 1931, pp. 27–29.

26. An illustrated discussion of how architectural terra cotta was designed and made in the 1920s may be found in W. A. Starrett (1928), *Skyscrapers and the Men who Build Them;* New York: Scribner's. See Chapter 17: "Brick, Terra Cotta, and the Ceramics—the Technique of Ceramic Masonry," pp. 213–237.

27. *A&E,* April 1931, p. 47.

28. The night photograph of the Title Guarantee Building is in *A&A,* September 1931, p. 40. A similar photograph of the Pellissier Building is in *A&A,* December 1931, p. 36.

29. Harris (1928, p. 58).

30. Van Wyck (1929).

31. One of the most dramatic transformations of the sign resulting from the use of neon was in the theater marquee. During the 1930s, marquees grew in size, their sides slanted toward approaching automobiles rather than standing straight to be read by pedestrians, and they were adorned with brightly flashing neon. Marquees remaining from the 1930s are on the Orpheum Theater, 842 South Broadway (1936), the Hollywood Theater, 6764 Hollywood Boulevard (ca. 1937), and the Hollywood Pantages (1930). There are large roof signs from this period on several downtown buildings as well, including the Orpheum.

32. Garren (1930, p. 43).

33. See Jones (1931, p. 29).

34. See "Bullocks Wilshire Boulevard Store—Los Angeles," *A&E,* December 1929, p. 45. Etched and sandblasted glass was also commonly used decoratively. For a discussion see Avery (1934).

35. PWA-supported buildings were not intended to express principles of modernity, but were "designed with great simplicity and a very sparing use of ornament, emphasis being placed on line, good composition, scale, and proportion" (United States. Public Works Administration, 1939; p. xiv).

36. In 1964, the architect Robert Field said that "our buildings in the twenties tended to be on the garish side. We loaded them with ornament, but then that was the way we were living then. It was a kind of false-front era. . . . There wasn't much behind it. We discovered that in the crash" (quoted in Schippers, 1964).

37. For a history of industrial design and streamline styling see Bush (1975) and Heskett (1980).

38. "A Steel Arrow," *A&A,* June 1937, p. 9; see Repp (1980, p. 83).

39. For a brief history of Southern California supermarkets, see Shindler (1980).

40. Wright (1938, p. 28). The preceding quotations are from the same source.

41. In his 1930 pathbreaking book on the Modern Movement called *The New World Architecture,* Sheldon Cheney illustrates an ocean liner with the caption "The builders of machines are teaching the architects" (p. 79).

42. "The Coca-Cola Plant," *A&A,* November 1936, p. 43. Derrah was born in Salt Lake City in 1895 and came to Los Angeles in 1924. He also designed the Southern California Gas Company building at 820 South Flower Street. Derrah died in 1946.

43. *A&A,* January 1937, p. 25.

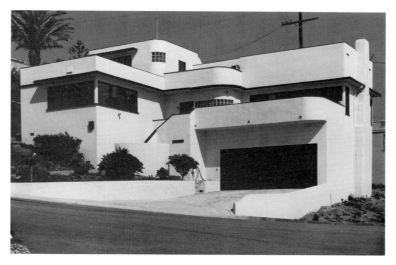

44. Advertisement in *A&E*, July 1935, pp. 2–3.

45. See *A&E*, August 1936, p. 18.

46. See *A&A*, December 1934, p. 24.

47. For before and after photographs see *A&E*, June 1937, p. 38.

48. See Foulkes (1934); "Good Architecture made this Building Rentable," *A&E*, February 1930, pp. 74–76; "Modernizing Boosts Rental Values," *A&E*, August 1936, pp. 15–21.

CHAPTER 7

1. Gill (1916, pp. 141–2).

2. This influence can be seen in his A. D. German warehouse of 1915 in Wright's home town of Richland Center, Wisconsin.

3. Scully (1960, p. 25).

4. The discussion of Schindler is taken from the pioneering work of Esther McCoy (1960), plus Gebhard (1967a) and (1971).

5. Oliver house, 2236 Micheltorena Street; Buck house, 805 South Genessee Avenue; Walker house, 2100 Kenilworth Avenue; Rodakiewica house, 9121 Alto Cedro Drive.

6. Quoted in Spade (1971, p. 11).

7. Neutra's first commission in Los Angeles was the Jardinette Apartments (1927), 5128 West Marathon Street, Hollywood.

8. See Space (1971, p. 13).

9. Stein (1966, p. 189).

10. Spade (1971, p. 16). This tendency had already been anticipated in his Beckstrom house (1941), 1400 Via Monte Mar, where full sliding glass doors separate the interior spaces from the gardens.

11. Ain's work is discussed in Gebhard (1980).

12. Raphael Soriano was born in 1907 on the Isle of Rhodes, and came to the United States in 1924. He received his B. Arch. from USC in 1934 and worked with Neutra until establishing his own practice in 1936.

13. Voilich (1945, p. 25).

14. Los Angeles County. Regional Planning Commission. (1943).

15. See McCoy (1962).

16. The eight architects were J. R. Davidson, Richard J. Neutra, Spaulding and Rex, Wurster and Bernardi, Ralph Rapson, Whitney Smith, Thornton Abell, Charles Eames, and Eero Saarinen (see McCoy, 1962, p. 9; also Entenza, 1945, p. 37).

17. In 1938, the Southern California honor awards for architecture were given primarily to homes in the American Colonial and English Georgian styles (see *A&E*, October 1938, p. 21).

18. McCoy (1962, p. 10).

19. Nadeau (1960, p. 276).

20. *A&A*, July 1938, pp. 28–9.

21. Hunt (1972, p. 13); *A&E*, June 1949, pp. 16–21. The General Petroleum Building was designed prior to the Prudential Building but completed later.

22. See *AR*, October 1948, p. 116.

23. See *A&E*, October 1950, pp. 10.

24. See *PA*, November 1951, pp. 83–85. At the same time, experimentation with building compositions led to the horizontal "groundscraper" industrial buildings of the 1960s. In 1947 the Rexall Drug Company turned a skyscraper on its side for its headquarters at Beverly and La Cienega boulevards. This long, two-story building is constructed around four large, landscaped interior courts that serve as employee dining and recreation areas and also provide light to the interior offices. The form of the building remains, although its exterior has been extensively remodeled (see Roller, 1947).

25. *AR*, March 1962, pp. 167–70.

26. Craig Ellwood was born in Texas in 1922, and began work as a draftsman for a contractor who did work for Neutra, Soriano, and other Modern architects, before beginning architectural design himself (see McCoy, 1962, p. 209).

CHAPTER 8

1. "Schulitz," *L.A. Architect,* June 1977.

2. For a fuller treatment, see Stern (1975).

3. Bloomer and Moore discuss Wright's Winslow House in *Body, Memory and Architecture* (1977), pp. 119–124.

4. My appreciation to David Cooper, Frederick Fisher, Michael Folonis, Joseph Giovannini, Craig Hodgetts, Coy Howard, Ray Kappe, Anthony Lumsden, Esther McCoy, Thom Mayne, Eric Moss, Frances Offenhauser and Steve Wiseman for their helpful discussions on contemporary architecture in Los Angeles.

5. "Tudor Style at Top of Popularity List," Los Angeles *Times*, June 1, 1980, Sec. 10, p. 1.

6. The rehabilitation of the Biltmore is discussed by Ross (1978). In 1981 the hotel received an honor award from the National Trust for Historic Preservation.

LOS ANGELES' BUNKER HILL

1. For more information on the Beaudry water works development in the city, see Fogelson (1967, pp. 37–39).

2. The principal source for this discussion is the excellent study by Patricia Adler, *The Bunker Hill Story* (Glendale: La Siesta Press, 1964). Other accounts include Hylen (1976), a personal narration with excellent photographs; and Pugsley (1977), an anecdotal treatment.

3. Wheelock (1961).

Above: Streamline house, 7540 Whitlock Avenue; ca. 1938. Top right: Eames house, 203 Chautauqua Boulevard; by Charles Eames, 1949. Top left: interior, Eames house. Photograph 1949.

BIBLIOGRAPHY

The bibliography lists the sources cited in this book, plus other important writings on Los Angeles architecture. It is by no means a complete bibliography. For more detailed information on specific buildings, the card catalog in the California Room of the Los Angeles Central Library has a complete list of references to Los Angeles area buildings found in the holdings of the Los Angeles Public Library. The catalog is updated continuously by Tom Owen.

Two books should be cited in particular as seminal works: David Gebhard and Robert Winter's *A Guide to Architecture in Los Angeles and Southern California* (Santa Barbara: Peregrine Smith, 1977); and Judson A. Grenier, Doyce B. Nunis, Jr., and Jean Bruce Poole's *A Guide to Historic Places in Los Angeles County* (Dubuque: Kendall/Hunt, 1978).

The following frequent entries are abbreviated:

A&A	(California) Arts and Architecture
A&E	(Western) Architect and Engineer
AF	Architectural Forum
AR	Architectural Record
CA&BN	California Architect and Building News
PA	Progressive Architecture
PHSSC	Publications, Historical Society of Southern California
QHSSC	Quarterly, Historical Society of Southern California
SCQ	Southern California Quarterly

Stone bungalows, Ninth and Olive streets, Burbank; 1923.

A

Adams, Edward F. (1888), "Soldiers' Home at Santa Monica," *Overland Monthly*, September, p. 225.

Alden, Charles H. (1912), "The Historic Precedent in Coast Architecture," *A&E*, July, pp. 80–83.

Adler, Patricia (1964), *The Bunker Hill Story*. Glendale, California: La Siesta Press.

"Aliso Village, Los Angeles," *A&E*, January 1943, pp. 13–32.

Allen, Harris (1922), "Recent Theaters Designed by G. Albert Lansburgh, Architect," *A&E*, November, pp. 47–69.

——————— (1927), "Architecture in Los Angeles," *Overland Monthly*, May, p. 138.

——————— (1930), "A Building Designed for Today," *A&A*, January, pp. 21-22.

Allison, David H. (1930), "Seven Years of Architectural Control in Palos Verdes," *A&E*, January, pp. 53–56.

"All-Marble Building for I. Magnin and Co.," *A&E*, June 1939, pp. 19–23.

Alpaugh, Norman W. (1926), "The Asbury Apartments, Los Angeles," *A&E*, May.

American Institute of Architects, Southern California Chapter, *Guidelines for Preservation, Restoration, and Alterations to the Central Library of Los Angeles*. Los Angeles, September 1978.

"An American Venice," *AR*, October 1906, pp. 347–50.

Anderson, Timothy J. et al., eds. (1980), *California Design 1910*. Santa Barbara: Peregrine Smith.

"Angelino Heights House and Walking Tour," Los Angeles: Carroll Avenue Restoration Foundation (1980).

Archibald, Robert (1976), "The Economy of the Alta California Missions," *SCQ*, Summer, pp. 227–40.

Arwas, Victor (1980), *The Glass of René Lalique*. New York: Rizzoli.

Austin, John C. (1926), "The Al Malaikah Temple, Los Angeles," *A&E*, June, p. 79.

——————— (1928), "The Los Angeles City Hall," *AF*, July, pp. 25–28.

Avery, C. Earl (1934), "Sandblasting," *A&E*, August, pp. 41–45.

B

Bach, Richard F. (1917), "The Southwest Museum," *AR*, July, pp. 18–26.

"Back to Elegance: Renovated Alexandria Hotel," *Newsweek*, June 29, 1970, p. 74.

Baer, Kurt (1958), *Architecture of the California Missions*. Berkeley: UC Press.

Bakewell, John (1928), "The Pasadena City Hall," *A&E*, June, pp. 35–39.

Balio, Tino, ed. (1976), *The American Film Industry*. Madison: University of Wisconsin Press.

Bancroft, Hubert Howe (1884–1890), *History of California*, 7 vols. San Francisco: A.L. Bancroft.

Banham, Reyner (1971), *Los Angeles: The Architecture of Four Ecologies*. Baltimore: Penguin Books, 1973.

"The Bank that Stayed" [Remodeling of bank building, Spring and Sixth], *AF*, February 1961, pp. 82–85.

"Banking by Automobile: First Drive-In Bank in the World," *Scientific American*, September 1937, p. 151.

Barrows, Henry D. (1893), "Reminiscences of Los Angeles in the Fifties and Early Sixties," *PHSSC*, vol. 3, pp. 55–62.

——————— (1894), "Recollections of the Old Court House and its Builder," *PHSSC*, vol. 3, pp. 40-46.

——————— (1894a), "Capt. Alexander Bell and the Bell Block," *PHSSC*, vol. 3, pp. 11–18.

Bartlett, Dana M. (1907), *The Better City*. Los Angeles: The Neuner Company Press.

——————— (1910), *Los Angeles, California: The City Beautiful*. Los Angeles: Municipal Reference Bureau.

Bartlett, Lanier and Virginia Stivers (1932), *Los Angeles in Seven Days*. New York: Tobert M. McBride.

Basten, Fred E. (1974), *Santa Monica Bay: the First 100 Years*. Los Angeles: Douglas-West.

Baugh, Ruth E. (1942), "Site of Early Los Angeles," *Economic Geography*, January, pp. 87–96.

Baxter, Sylvester (1901), *Spanish Colonial Architecture in Mexico*. Boston: J.B. Millet.

"Bay Windows," *CA&BN*, March 1881, pp. 21–22.

Bean, Lowell J. and Charles R. Smith (1978), "Gabrielino," in Robert F. Heizer, ed., *Handbook of North American Indians*, vol. 8: California, pp. 538–49, Washington, D.C.: Smithsonian Institution.

Bean, Walton Ebbert (1968), *California, an Interpretive History*. New York: McGraw-Hill.

Beck, Warren A. and David A. Williams (1972), *California: A History of the Golden State*. Garden City: Doubleday.

Beilharz, Edwin F. (1971), *Felipe de Neve, First Governor of California*. San Francisco: California Historical Society.

Bellamy, Edward (1890), *Looking Backward, 2000–1887*. Boston: Houghton.

Benton, Arthur Burnett (1911), "The California Mission and its Influence upon Pacific Coast Architecture," *A&E*, February, pp. 35–75.

Bingham, Edwin R. (1955), *Charles F. Lummis, Editor of the Southwest*. San Marino: Huntington Library.

"A Bit of Prague in Los Angeles," *A&A*, November 1935, p. 25.

Bloomer, Kent C. and Charles W. Moore (1977), *Body, Memory and Architecture*. New Haven: Yale University Press.

Bogardus, Emory S. (1916), "House Court Problem," *American Journal of Sociology*, November, pp. 391–99.

Boltz, Howard O. (1969), "Guide to Landscape Architecture in Los Angeles," *Landscape Architecture*, January, pp. 117–21.

Bowman, Mary M. (1896), "Old Los Angeles and the Plaza," *Land of Sunshine*, March, pp. 160–62.

Braden, Arthur (1927), "Impressions of the Wilshire Boulevard Christian Church," *A&E*, November, p. 98.

Bradley, Bill (1979), *Last of the Great Stations*. Glendale, California: Interurbans.

Breindel, Matthew (1980), *Los Angeles: Hollywood, Venice, Santa Monica*. Köln: DuMont. (in German).

Brino, G. (1975), "Learning from Walt Disney: Urbanisme et Bande Dessinnée," *Werk*, no. 8, pp. 741–46.

"A British Criticism of the New Los Angeles City Hall," *A&E*, November 1927, p. 63.

Brook, Harry E. (1894), "Old and New Los Angeles," *Land of Sunshine*, August, pp. 56–57.

——— (1895), "Reminiscences of the Boom," *Land of Sunshine*, January–February, pp. 25-26, 46-47.

Bruner, E.L. (1926), "California Type of Architecture," *A&E*, October, pp. 97–99.

"Bullocks Wilshire Boulevard Store," *A&E*, December 1929, pp. 45–52.

"Burbank City Hall," *A&E*, August 1943, pp. 18–23.

Burg, David F. (1976), *Chicago's White City of 1893*. Lexington: University Press of Kentucky.

Bush, Donald J. (1975), *The Streamlined Decade*. New York: George Braziller.

Byers, Charles A. (1914), "A Hillside Home in Los Angeles," *AR*, October, pp. 369–71.

——— (1919), "The Popular Bungalow-Court Idea," *A&E*, October, pp. 80–85.

C

C. de Gante, Pablo (1947), *La Arquitectura de Mexico en el Siglo XVI*. Mexico: Cooperative Talleres Graficos de la Nacion.

"A California Theater of Reinforced Concrete," *A&E*, May 1909, pp. 67–73.

Campbell, Don G. (1979), "Old Subway Terminal to be Renovated," *Los Angeles Times*, Aug. 19, pt. 9, p. 1.

Carr, Harry (1935), *Los Angeles: City of Dreams*. New York: Grossett and Dunlap.

"Centennial History," Actual title is *Historical Sketch of Los Angeles County, California*. Los Angeles: Lewis Lewin, 1876.

"Century Plaza Hotel," *A&A*, December 1964, pp. 24–25.

Above: Streamline apartment, 462 South Cochran Avenue, by Milton J. Black, 1938. Photograph 1938. Top: interior, Sultan house, 744 Brooktree Road, by Ray Kappe, 1976. Photograph 1976.

Chafee, Richard (1977), "The Teaching of Architecture at the Ecole des Beaux Arts," in Drexler, ed., (1977).

Cheney, Charles H. (1930), "Palos Verdes; Eight Years of Development," *A&E*, January, pp. 35–40.

Cheney, Sheldon (1930), *The New World Architecture.* New York: Tudor.

"Chinese Theater at Hollywood, California," *American Architect*, August 20, 1927, pp. 251–68.

"Church of Our Lady of Lourdes," *AF*, July 1932, pp. 13–16.

Cini, Zelda and Bob Crane (1980), *Hollywood: Land and Legend.* Westport, Conn: Arlington House.

"City Hall by Victor Gruen and Associates" [Redondo Beach], *A&A*, October 1962, pp. 12–13.

Clark, Robert Judson, ed. (1972), *The Arts and Crafts Movement in America, 1876–1916.* Princeton: Princeton University Press.

Cleland, Robert G. (1951), *The Cattle on a Thousand Hills; Southern California, 1855–1880.* San Marino: Huntington Library.

————— (1951a), *El Molino Viejo.* Los Angeles: Ward Ritchie.

D

Davies, R.E.G. (1964), *A History of the World's Airlines.* London: Oxford University Press.

del Rio, Juan [Lummis] (1898), "So Far, So Good," [progress of the Landmarks Club], *Land of Sunshine* March, pp. 171–2.

"Development of the Moving-Picture Theatre," *A&E*, February 1915, pp. 51–60.

Drexler, Arthur, ed. (1977), *The Architecture of the Ecole des Beaux Arts.* New York: Museum of Modern Art.

Dreyfuss, John (1978), "Pan Pacific: Beleaguered Manifestation of an Era," *Los Angeles Times*, April 9, pt. 9, p. 1.

————— (1979), "Irving Gill, the Forgotten Architect," *Los Angeles Times*, April 13, p. IV–24.

————— (1980), "Architecture: Charles Moore," *Architectural Digest*, March, pp. 140–7.

Dudley, Miriam (1977), "The Powell Library Building," UCLA pamphlet.

Ehrlich, George (1979), *Kansas City, Missouri: An Architectural History.* Kansas City: Historic Kansas City Foundation.

Eisner, Simon (1945), "Future Cities: A Challenge," *A&A*, January.

"An Eleven Unit Apartment House," *A&A*, Feb. 1936, p. 23.

Engelhardt, Zephyrin (1927), *San Gabriel Mission and the Beginnings of Los Angeles.* San Gabriel: San Gabriel Mission.

Entenza, John (1945), "The Case Study House Program," *A&A*, January, pp. 37–9.

Evans, E.A. (1928), "United Artists Theater; Los Angeles," *A&E*, August, pp. 35–9.

Eyre, Wilson (1911), "The Origin of the Bungalow," *Country Life in America*, February 15.

F

Fallon, John T. (1915), "The Marquise and its Design," *AR*, vol. 38, pp. 555–63.

Ice Rink, now United States Post Office, 171 Arroyo Parkway, Pasadena, by Cyril Bennett, 1940. Photograph 1940.

Cline, William H. (1911), "The New Orpheum Theater Building, Los Angeles," *A&E*, September.

Clous, D.A. (1907), "A Bungalow in the Gothic Style," *Indoors and Out*, April, pp. 18–9.

"The Coca-Cola Plant," *A&A*, November 1936, p. 43.

"Colorado Street Bridge," *Engineering News*, July 24, 1913, pp. 146–50. Also see *Good Roads*, May 2, 1914, pp. 255–8 and *Municipal Engineering*, November 1914, pp. 378–80.

Cook, W.D. and George D. Hall (1923), "An Administrative Center for Los Angeles," *California Southland*, May, pp. 9–11.

Craig, Margaret (1925), "The Community Playhouse, Pasadena," *AF*, August, pp. 77–80.

Croly, Herbert D. (1913), "The Country House in California," *AR*, December, pp. 483–519.

"Cross Roads of the World," *A&A*, January 1937, pp. 24–5.

Crouch, Dora P. and Axel I. Mundigo (1977), "The City Planning Ordinaces of the Laws of the Indies Revisited; Part II: Three American Cities," *Town Planning Review*, October, pp. 397–418.

Crump, Spencer (1970), *Ride the Big Red Cars.* Corona del Mar: Trans-Anglo Books.

Current, Karen (1974), *Greene and Greene; Architects in the Residential Style.* Fort Worth: Amon Carter Museum of Western Art.

Duell, Prentice (1921), "A Note on California Architecture," *California Southland*, September.

Duflot de Mofras, M. Eugène (1840), "Exploration de territoire de l'Orégon, des Californies et de la Mer Vermeille," Paris: Librairie de la Societé de Géographie, 1844. Reprinted in Egenhoff (1952), p. 52.

Dumke, Glenn S. (1944), *The Boom of the Eighties in Southern California*, San Marino: Huntington Library.

Duncombe, Arthur (1924), "Beautiful Architecture a Magnet for Trade," *California Southland*, September.

Dwyer, Donald H. (1974), "Modernistic Architecture, America's Contribution to Art Deco," pp. 15–19 in *Art Deco and its Origins*, Huntington, New York: Hechscher Museum.

E

Early, James (1965), *Romanticism and American Architecture.* New York: A.S. Barnes.

Edgell, George H. (1928), *American Architecture of To-Day.* New York: Scribners.

Edwards, G.W. (1907), "The Word 'Bungalow,' " *Indoors and Out*, April, pp. 13–5.

Egenhoff, Elizabeth L. (1952), "Fabricas; A collection of Pictures and Statements on the Mineral Materials used in Building in California prior to 1850," *California Journal of Mines and Geology*, April 1952, supplement.

Feldman, Eddy (1972), *The Art of Street Lighting in Los Angeles.* Los Angeles: Dawson's Book Shop.

Ferguson, Jim (1938), "West Coast's First Large Housing Project" [San Gabriel Village], *A&E*, November, pp. 41–4.

Finney, M. Mac Leon (1929), "The Court House Beautiful," *A&E*, July, pp. 35–45.

"First Parkway for Los Angeles," *Engineering News-Record*, July 21, 1938, pp. 79–82.

Fiske, Turbesé L. and Keith Lummis (1975), *Charles F. Lummis: The Man and his West.* Norman: University of Oklahoma Press.

Flagg, Edwin H. (1919), "Evolution of Architectural and Other Features of Moving Picture Theaters," *A&E*, May.

Flodin, H.L. (1931), "Building Architectural Beauty into a Viaduct" [Fourth Street Viaduct], *Roads and Streets*, September, pp. 367–9.

Fogelson, Robert M. (1967), *The Fragmented Metropolis: Los Angeles, 1850–1930.* Cambridge: Harvard University Press.

Foulkes, Edward T. (1934), "Modernization," *A&E*, Sept., pp. 11–8.

G

Garren, William I. (1930), "Civilization: Metal and Architects," *A&E*, February, pp. 42–8.

Gebhard, David (1967), "The Spanish Colonial Revival in Southern California," *Society of Architectural Historians Journal*, May, pp. 31–47.

——————— (1967a), *R.M. Schindler.* An exhibition of the architecture of R.M. Schindler (1887–1953). Santa Barbara: University of California Art Galleries.

——————— (1969), *Richfield Building, 1928–1968.* (privately published).

——————— (1969a), *Kem Weber: The Moderne in Southern California, 1929–1941.* Santa Barbara: University of California Art Galleries.

——————— (1971), *Schindler.* New York: Viking.

——————— (1976), "Life in the Dollhouse," pp. 99–119 in Sally Woodbridge, ed., *Bay Area Houses.* New York: Oxford University Press.

——————— (1980), "Cathedral Has Spirit, but it's All Done with Mirrors" [Crystal Cathedral], *Los Angeles Herald Examiner,* May 21, 1980, p. B-1.

——————— (1981), "Reading the Central Library," *California Living,* May 17, pp. 8–13.

Girouard, Mark (1977), *Sweetness and Light: The Queen Anne Movement, 1860–1900.* Oxford: Clarendon.

Goldberger, Paul (1978), "Double Exposure for the Industrial Style; Home designed by Peter de Bretteville," *New York Times Magazine,* July 23, p. 46.

Goodnow, Mark N. (1928), "California Seeks the Architectural Truth," *A&E,* December, p. 63.

——————— (1929), "Architecture for the Merchant," *A&E,* June, pp. 35–40.

——————— (1930), "Architectural Aspects of Pacific Airports," *A&E,* November, pp. 29–42.

Goldstein, Barbara (1980), "Frank O. Gehry and Associates," *PA,* March, pp. 69–75.

——————— (1981), "Venetian Masque" [Gagosian Gallery], *PA,* February, pp. 87–90.

Goodwin, J.E. (1930), "New Library Building for UCLA," *Library Journal,* May 15, pp. 451–2.

——————— (1897–99) "The Story of a Plaza," *PHSSC,* vol. 4, pp. 247–56.

——————— (1897–99a), "Los Angeles in the Adobe Age," *PHSSC,* vol. 4, pp. 49–55.

——————— (1901), "The Passing of the Old Pueblo," *PHSSC,* vol. 5, pp. 113–20.

——————— (1908), "California under the Rule of Spain and Mexico," *PHSSC,* vol. 7, pp. 119–28.

——————— (1908a), "From Pueblo to Ciudad: the Municipal and Territorial Expansion of Los Angeles," *PHSSC,* vol. 7, pp. 216–21.

H

Hadley, Homer M. (1936), "New Home of the California Fruit Growers' Exchange," *A&E,* February, pp. 9–14.

Hall, George D. (1920), "The Estate of Mr. W.L. Dodge, Hollywood, California," *A&E,* April, p. 87.

Hamilton, Frederick (1926), "Recent Work of Albert C. Martin, Architect," *A&E,* June.

——————— (1980), *The Architecture of Gregory Ain.* An exhibition at the UCSB Art Museum; University of California at Santa Barbara.

——————— et al (1979), *Samuel and Joseph Cather Newsom: Victorian Architectural Imagery in California, 1878–1908.* Santa Barbara: University of California Art Galleries.

——————— and Harriett von Bretton (1975), *L.A. in the Thirties.* Salt Lake: Peregrine Smith.

Geiger, Maynard (1968), "The Building of Mission San Gabriel, 1771–1828," *SCQ,* March, pp. 33–42.

"General Petroleum Building," *A&E,* June 1949, pp. 16–20.

Giedion, Siegfried (1967), *Space, Time, and Architecture.* Cambridge: Harvard University Press.

Gill, Brendan (1980), "Reflections, the Horizontal City," *New Yorker,* September 15, p. 109.

Gill, Irving (1916), "The Home of the Future: The New Architecture of the West: Small Homes for a Great Country," *The Craftsman,* May, pp. 140–151.

Giovannini, Joseph (1979), "Wiltern Theatre Slated to be Razed," Los Angeles *Herald-Examiner,* Feb. 25, p. E-2.

——————— (1979a), "Eminent Victorians; the Vanishing Houses of Orange," *California Living* Sunday magazine of the *Los Angeles Herald Examiner,* July 15, pp. 12–15.

Gowans, Alan (1964), *Images of American Living: Four Centuries of Architecture and Furniture as Cultural Expression.* Philadelphia.

Grant, K.C. (1931), "A Modern Baking Plant" [Helms Bakeries], *A&E,* July, pp. 59–61.

Greenwood, William (1907), "A Design for a Summer and Winter Bungalow," *Indoors and Out,* April, pp. 16–7.

Grey, Elmer (1905), "Architecture in Southern California," *AR,* January, pp. 1–17.

——————— (1929), "The Work of Reginald Johnson," *A&E,* April, pp. 35–89.

——————— (1929a), "The Romance of the Pasadena Community Playhouse," *A&E,* June, pp. 61–5.

"Griffith Observatory and Hall of Science," *A&A,* March 1935, p. 12; also see *A&E,* January 1935, pp. 41–3.

"Griffith Planetarium," *AF,* February 1935, pp. 156–61.

Gruenbaum, Victor (1942), "Some Notes on Modern Store Design," *A&E,* February, pp. 15–22.

Guest, Florian (1962), "The Establishment of the Villa de Branciforte," *California Historical Society Quarterly,* March, pp. 29–50.

Guinn, James M. (1895), "Los Angeles in the late Sixties and Early Seventies," *PHSSC,* vol. 3, pp. 63–8.

——————— (1895a), "The Plan of Old Los Angeles," *PHSSC,* vol 3, pp. 40–50.

Hamlin, Talbot F. (1941), "What Makes it American: Architecture in the Southwest and West," *Pencil Points,* March, pp. 339–44.

Hancock, Ralph (1949), *Fabulous Boulevard.* New York: Funk and Wagnalls.

Hannaford, Donald R. (1931), *Spanish Colonial or Adobe Architecture in California, 1800–1850,* New York: Architectural Book Publishing Co.

Hanson, Frederick A. (1930), "The New Architectural Medium Concrete," *A&E,* January, pp. 89–98.

Harlow, Neal (1976), *Maps and Surveys of the Pueblo Lands of Los Angeles.* Los Angeles: Dawson's Book Shop.

Harris, Frank, ed. (1951), *A Guide to Contemporary Architecture in Southern California.* Los Angeles: Watling.

Harris, John W. (1928), "Neon Tube Lighting Adaptable to Architectural Detail," *A&E,* May, pp. 57–8.

Heinly, B.A. (1912), "The Remodeling of a City Square in Los Angeles," *American City,* May, pp. 728–30.

Helgeson, Terry (1973), "The Hollywood Pantages," Washington, D.C.: Theater Historical Society.

Henstell, Bruce (1980), *Los Angeles: An Illustrated History.* New York: Alfred A. Knopf.

Heskett, John (1980), *Industrial Design.* New York: Oxford University Press.

Hill, Laurence L. (1929), *La Reina: Los Angeles in Three Centuries.* Los Angeles: Security Trust and Savings Bank.

Hite Building, Seventh and Carondelet streets, by Morgan, Walls and Clements, ca. 1923.

Hitchcock, Henry-Russell (1958) *Architecture: 19th and 20th Centuries*. Baltimore: Penguin.

———————— and Philip Johnson (1932), *The International Style*. New York: Norton, 1966.

"Hollywood Turf Club," *AF*, October 1938, pp. 261–4.

Honnold, Douglas (1956), *Southern California Architecture: 1769–1956*. New York: Reinhold.

Hoover, Roy (1961), "The Adobe de Palomares," *QHSSC*, December, pp. 415–20.

Hopkins, Una Nixson (1906), "The California Bungalow," *A&E*, April, pp. 33–9

Howard, John Galen (1916), "Country House Architecture on the Pacific Coast," *AR*, October, pp. 323–56.

Hugo Ballin's Mural for Griffith Observatory," *Art Digest*, August 1935, p. 21.

Hunt, Sumner P. (1894), "The Adobe in Architecture," *Land of Sunshine*, July.

Hunt, William D. (1972), *Total Design; Architecture of Welton Becket and Associates*. New York: McGraw-Hill.

Hunter, Burton L. (1933), *The Evolution of Municipal Organization and Administrative Practice in the City of Los Angeles*. Los Angeles: Parker, Stone and Baird.

Hunter, Paul Robinson, ed. (1939), *Residential Architecture in Southern California*. Los Angeles: Southern California Chapter, American Institute of Architects.

Hutton, William Rich (1956), *Sketches of California, 1847–1852*. San Marino: Huntington Library.

Hyers, Faith Holmes (1926), "The New Public Library, Los Angeles," *A&E*, November, p. 77; also see *Libraries*, February 1926, pp. 74–7.

———————— (1926a), "Significance of Los Angeles' New Library," *Library Journal*, August, pp. 663–6.

Hylen, Arnold (1976), *Bunker Hill, a Los Angeles Landmark*. Los Angeles: Dawson's Book Shop.

I

"Imaginative Version of the Row House" [Landfair Apartments], *AR*, October 1944, p. 91.

J

Jackson, Helen Hunt (1884), *Ramona*. Boston: Roberts Bros.

James, George Wharton (1903), "The Influence of the Mission Style on the Civic and Domestic Architecture of Modern California," *The Craftsman*, vol. 5.

———————— (1907), "The Mission Style in Modern Architecture," *Indoors and Out*, vol. 4; in five parts, nos. 2–6.

Japenga, Ann (1981), "Reincarnation of Mission Inn," *Los Angeles Times*, May 14, pt. 5, p. 1.

Jennings, Frederick (1923), "A Theater Designed in the Egyptian Style," *A&E*, March, pp. 77–84.

———————— (1925), "Recent Hotel Architecture in California" [Los Angeles Biltmore], *A&E*, January.

———————— (1928), "The Los Angeles City Hall," *A&E*, May, pp. 33–9.

Johnson, Reginald D. (1926), "Development of Architectural Styles in California," *A&E*, October, pp. 108-9.

Jones, Frederick W. (1926), "Architecture—East and West," *A&E*, November, pp. 93–7.

———————— (1931), "The Los Angeles Stock Exchange," *A&E*, March, pp. 25–45.

———————— (1942), "Pueblo del Rio; Los Angeles' Most Recent Housing Project," *A&E*, September, pp. 11–20.

Judson, William L. (1908), "The Architecture of the Missions," *PHSSC*, vol. 7, pp. 114–8.

Above: Los Angeles Bonaventure Hotel, Fifth and Figueroa streets, by John Portman, 1976. Top: Pompeian Room, Doheny Mansion, Chester Place, interior by Alfred F. Rosenheim, 1906.

K

Keally, Francis (1903), "Architectural Treatment of the Airport," *A&E*, November, pp. 43–51.

Kelker, de Leuw and Co. (1925), *Report and Recommendations on a Comprehensive Rapid Transit Plan for the City and County of Los Angeles*. Chicago.

Kipling, Lockwood (1911), "The Origin of the Bungalow," *Country Life in America*, February 15.

Kirker, Harold (1960), *California's Architectural Frontier*. Santa Barbara: Peregrine Smith, 1973.

———————— (1972), "California Architecture and its Relation to Contemporary Trends in Europe and America," *California Historical Quarterly*, Winter, pp. 289–305.

Knight, Arthur (1969), *The Hollywood Style*. New York: Macmillan.

Kroeber, Alfred L. (1925), *Handbook of the Indians of California*. Bulletin no. 78, Bureau of American Ethnology. Washington, D.C.: Smithsonian Institution.

Krythe, Mamie R. (1951), "First Hotel of Old Los Angeles; the Romantic Bella Union," *QHSSC*, in four parts, nos. 1–3, March–December.

———————— (1955), "Pico House; the Finest Hotel South of San Francisco," *QHSSC*, June.

———————— (1956), "Round House George and his Garden of Paradise," *QHSSC*, September, pp. 247–54.

L

Lancaster, Clay (1958), "The American Bungalow," *Art Bulletin*, September.

———————— (1963), *The Japanese Influence in America*. New York: Walton H. Rawls.

Lansburgh, A. Albert (1927), "The El Capitan Theater and Department Store Building, Hollywood," *A&E*, February.

———————— (1928), "Warner Bros. New Theater, Hollywood," *A&E*, December, pp. 65–73.

Lawler, Oscar (1953), "The Pico House," *QHSSC*, December, pp. 335–42.

Lawrence, Eleanor (1931), "Mexican Trade between Santa Fe and Los Angeles, 1830–1848," *California Historical Society Quarterly*, vol. 10, pp. 27–39.

Lazear, M.H. (1907), "The Evolution of the Bungalow in California," *Indoors and Out*, April, pp. 7–12 and May, pp. 69–73.

Lee, S. Charles (1948), "The Influence of West Coast Designers on the Modern Theater," *Journal of the Society of Motion Picture Engineers*, April, pp. 329–36.

Leech, Ellen (1936), "Schools," *A&A*, November, pp. 29–36.

"Lever Brothers Company," *PA*, November 1951, p. 83.

Lippiatt, Leslie (1928), "A Bit of old Normandy in California," *California Southland*, May, p. 24.

Littler, Charles R. (1939), "A Dream Come True" [Los Angeles Union Passenger Terminal], *A&A*, June, p. 28.

Lofland, Lyn H. (1973), *A World of Strangers; Order and Action in Urban Public Space*. New York: Basic Books.

Longworth, R.W. (1975), "Julia Morgan; Some Introductory Notes," *Perspecta*, vol. 15, pp. 74–86.

Los Angeles. Department of City Planning (1956), *Report on Proposed Charter Amendment Relative to Height of Buildings*. Los Angeles.

"Los Angeles Biltmore Hotel," *AR*, November 1923.

"Los Angeles Branch, Federal Reserve Bank of San Francisco," *American Architect*, June 1932, pp. 71–6.

Los Angeles County. Regional Planning Commission (1943), *Freeways for the Region*, Los Angeles.

"Los Angeles Gives its Oil Wells a Facial," *Business Week*, February 24, 1968, pp. 104–6.

"Los Angeles Hotels," *Land of Sunshine*, April 1898, pp. 300–3.

"Los Angeles' New Skyline," *Time* Oct. 11, 1968, pp. 101–2.

"Los Angeles Stock Exchange," *AF*, May 1931, p. 523; also see *A&A*, February 1931, p. 49.

"Los Angeles Times Building," *A&A*, October 1935, p. 20, also see *A&E*, March 1935, pp. 46–9.

"Los Angeles Yesterday and Today; Contrasting Photographs," *Sunset*, January 1910, pp. 17–48.

Lucas, Charles (1980), "Penthouses Scaled for Luxury" [Oviatt Building], *Los Angeles Home and Garden*, July, p. 28.

Ludwig Salvator, archduke of Austria (1879), *Los Angeles in the Sunny Seventies*. Los Angeles: McAlister and Zeitlin, 1929.

Lummis, Charles F. (1895), "Something About the Adobe," *Land of Sunshine*, February, pp. 48–50.

———————— (1895a), "The Lesson of the Adobe," *Land of Sunshine*, March, pp. 65–7.

———————— (1898), "The Old Missions," *Land of Sunshine*, April, pp. 247–53.

Lynch, Kevin (1960), *The Image of the City*. Cambridge: MIT Press.

M

Maass, John (1957), *The Gingerbread Age*. New York: Rinehard and Winston.

McCoy, Esther (1953), "A Vast Hall Full of Light," *A&A*, April, pp. 20–1.

——————— (1960), *Five California Architects*. New York: Reinhold.

——————— (1962), *Case Study Houses 1945–1962*. Los Angeles: Hennessey and Ingalls, 1977; 2nd. ed.

——————— (1965), "West Coast Architects V: John Lautner," *A&A*, August, p. 22.

——————— (1968), *Craig Ellwood: Architecture*. New York: Walker.

——————— (1975), "Arts and Architecture Case Study Houses," *Perspecta*, no. 15, pp. 54–73.

——————— (1976), "The Blue Bombshell" [Pacific Design Center], *PA*, October, pp. 78–82.

McGroarty, John S. (1930), "Westwood Village; A Year and a Day to Build," *A&E*, August, pp. 29–41.

McKelvey, Kathleen (1976), "The Restoration of the Palomares Adobe," *Pomona Valley Historian*, Spring, pp. 47–78.

McMillan, Elizabeth with Leslie Heumann (1981), "New Venice," *Newsletter*, Society of Architectural Historians, Southern California Chapter, April.

McPherson, Melville (1911), "The Transplanted Italian Villa," *A&E*, November, pp. 45–50.

McShane, Clay (1979), "Transforming the Use of Urban Space. A Look at the Revolution in Street Pavements, 1880–1924," *Journal of Urban History*, May, pp. 279–307.

McWilliams, Carey (1946), *Southern California: An Island on the Land*. Santa Barbara: Peregrine Smith, 1973.

"A Mail Order Store Building in Los Angeles" [Sears], *AR*, July 1928, pp. 65–9.

Makinson, Randall L. (1977), *Greene and Greene: Architecture as Fine Art*. Salt Lake City: Peregrine Smith.

——————— (1978), *Greene and Greene: Furniture and Related Designs*. Salt Lake City: Peregrine Smith.

Marquis, D.E. (1929), "Spanish Stores of Morgan, Walls and Clements," *AF*, June, pp. 901–16.

——————— (1930), "Archaeological Aspects of the Mayan Theater," *Art and Archaeology*, March, pp. 98–111.

Marsden, R.A. (1919), "Choosing the Architecture for a Town [Fullerton]," *California Southland*, December 1919–January 1920, pp. 7–8.

Mason, William and Jeanne Duque (1981), "Los Angeles Plaza: Living Symbol of our Past," *Terra*, Winter, pp. 15–22.

Mast, Gerald (1976), *A Short History of the Movies*, Indianapolis: Bobbls-Merrill.

Matthews, William H. (1913), "House Courts of Los Angeles," *Survey*, July 5, pp. 461–7.

Merritt, Russell (1976), "Nickelodeon Theaters 1905–1914: Building an Audience for the Movies," in Tino Balio, ed., (1976), pp. 59–82.

Miller, Henry (1856), *Account of a Tour of the California Missions*. San Francisco, 1952.

Miller, John C. (1972), "Moderne Theatres of the West," *Marquee*, 1st qtr, pp. 3–11.

Miller, Leonard E. (1949), "Prudential Insurance Building," *A&E*, March, pp. 14–20.

Mills, Kay (1981), "Prefab Aesthetics; Making Beauty out of Junk is Frank Gehry's Mission," *Los Angeles Times*, January 18, sec. 5, p. 3.

"The Mirror Building," *A&E*, February 1949, pp. 14–25.

Mitchell, W. Garden (1909), "The Architecture of Mexico," *A&E*, March, pp. 72–5.

"Modern Design and Methods Feature Los Angeles Office Building" [E. Clem Wilson Bldg.], *A&E*, September 1930, pp. 111–2.

"Modern Design for Los Angeles Commercial Building" [Eastern Columbia], *A&E*, June 1931, pp. 27–9.

"Modern Tendencies in Theatre Design" [Tower Theater], *A&E*, July 1928, pp. 55–6, 75–79.

"Modernizing Boosts Rental Values," *A&E*, August 1936, pp. 15–21.

Mooney, Mary E. (1900), "Side-Lights on Old Los Angeles," *PHSSC*, vol. 5, pp. 43–8.

Moore, Charles W. (1965), "You Have to Pay for the Public Life," *Perspecta*, no. 9/10, pp. 57–106. [Examples of his work].

Morrow, Irving F. (1921), "A Step Toward California Architecture," *A&E*, August.

——————— (1926), "New Santa Barbara," *A&E*, July, pp. 43–83.

——————— (1938), "Recent Architecture of Allison and Allison," *A&E*, May, pp. 13–33.

Morton, David (1979), "Look Again; Morgenstern Warehouse," *PA*, June, pp. 66–70.

Mundigo, Axel I. and Dora P. Crouch (1977), "The City Planning Ordinances of the Laws of the Indies Revisited; Part I: Their Philosophy and Implications," *Town Planning Review*, July, pp. 247–68.

N

Nadeau, Remi (1960), *Los Angeles; from Mission to Modern City*. New York: Longmans, Green and Co.

Neely, Jo (1918), "A Dream Come True" [Million Dollar Theater], *A&E*, May.

Neff, Wallace (1964). *Architecture in Southern California*. Chicago: Rand McNally.

Nelson, Howard J. (1959), "The Spread of an Artificial Landscape over Southern California," Association of American Geographers, *Annals*, September.

Netz, Joseph (1915-17), "The Great Los Angeles Real Estate Boom of 1887," *PHSSC*, vol. 10, pp. 54-68.

Neuhaus, Eugen (1916), *The San Diego Garden Fair*, San Francisco: Paul Elder and Co.

Neutra, Richard (1935), "The New Building in California," *A&A*, January, p. 13.

"New Studio is Novelty" [Spadena House], Los Angeles *Express*, April 6, 1921, p. 19.

Newcomb, Rexford (1914), "Architecture of the California Missions," *PHSSC*, vol. 9, pp. 225–35.

Newmark, Marco R. (1953), "Early California Resorts," *QHSSC*, June, pp. 129–52.

——————— (1954), "The Life of Jonathan Temple," *QHSSC*, March, pp. 46–8.

Noffsinger, James P. (1955), *The Influence of the Ecole des Beaux Arts on the Architects of the United States*. Washington, D.C.: Catholic University Press.

O

O'Connor, Ben H. (1941), "Planning the Super Market," *A&E*, Sept. 1941, pp. 15–9.

O'Dodd, George V. (1923), "The Castle on the Hill (Yama Shiro)," *A&E*, June, pp. 87–94.

Oliver, John W. (1956), *History of American Technology*. New York: Ronald Press.

Orr, Robert H. (1928), "First National Bank Building, Azusa," *A&E*, October, p. 56.

Osman, M.E. (1976), "Julia Morgan of California: A Passion for Quality and Anonymity," *AIA Journal*, June, pp. 44–8.

Owen, J. Thomas (1960), "The Church by the Plaza; a History of the Pueblo Church of Los Angeles," *QHSSC*, March, pp. 5–28 and June, pp. 186–204.

P

Padilla, Victoria (1961), *Southern California Gardens*. Berkeley: University of California Press.

Papademetriou, Peter (1976), "Images from a Silver Screen," *PA*, October, pp. 70–7.

Parks, Marion (1928), "In Pursuit of Vanished Days," *PHSSC*, vol. 14, pp. 7–64, pp. 135–207.

"Pasadena's Beautiful Bridge," *Scientific American*, December 6, 1913, p. 423.

Pastier, John (1980), *Cesar Pelli*. New York: Whitney Library of Design.

Patterson, Tom (1964), *Landmarks of Riverside*. Riverside: Press-Enterprise Co.

Pawley, Frederick A. (1932), *Theatre Architecture: A Brief Bibliography*. New York: Theatre Arts.

"Pergolas," *A&E*, March 1910, pp. 1–9.

Perry, E.P. (1928), "Lee Lawrie Sculptures of the Los Angeles Public Library," *AIA Journal*, May, p. 164.

"Pershing Square Garage," *A&E*, March 1951, p. 12.

Pierson, William (1976), *American Buildings and their Architects: the Colonial and Neo-Classical Styles* New York: Anchor Books.

Pildas, Ave (1980), *Movie Palaces*. New York: Clarkson N. Potter.

Pitt, Leonard (1966), *The Decline of the Californios*. Berkeley: University of California Press.

Plummer, Kathleen Church (1974), "The Streamlined Moderne," *Art in America*, January–February, pp. 46–54.

Above: El Greco apartments, 1028 Tiverton Avenue, by Pierpont and Walter S. Davis, 1929. Top: Garred house, 7445 Woodrow Wilson Drive, by Milton Caughey, 1949.

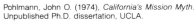

Left: Municipal Light, Water and Power Building, 2417 Daly Street, by S. Charles Lee, ca. 1935. Right: Elks Building, 607 South Parkview Street, by Curlett and Beelman, 1927.

Pohlmann, John O. (1974), *California's Mission Myth*. Unpublished Ph.D. dissertation, UCLA.

'ortfolio of the Friday Morning Club of Los Angeles," *A&E*, Oct. 1924, pp. 79-91.

Powell, Herbert J. (1938), "Trends in Present Day School Design," *A&E*, November 1938, p. 23.

"Power Personified in Stone and Concrete" [Edison Bldg.], *A&A*, April 1931, pp. 47-9.

Price C.E. (1902), "A Unique Railway" [Angels Flight], *Scientific American*, August 9, p. 86.

Price, C. Matlock (1915), "Panama-California Exposition; Bertram G. Goodhue and the Renaissance of Spanish Colonial Architecture," *AR*, March, pp. 229-51.

'rudential Insurance Building," *A&A*, May 1949, p. 42.

Pugsley, William (1977), *Bunker Hill: Last of the Lofty Mansions*. Corona del Mar: Trans-Anglo Books.

R

Raup, H.F. (1959), "Transformation of Southern California to a Cultivated Land," Association of American Geographers *Annals*, September, pp. 58-79.

Rebori, A.N. (1927), "Frank Lloyd Wright's Textile-Block Slab Construction," *AR*, Dec. 1927, p. 449.

Reinhardt, Richart (1973), "On the Brink of Doom: Southern California in 1877 as Witnessed by Mrs. Frank Leslie," *California Historical Quarterly*, Spring, pp. 64-79.

Reiter, Beth R. (1973), "The Old San Dimas Hotel," *Pomona Valley Historian*, Summer, pp. 93-109.

Remondino, P.C. (1892), *The Mediterranean Shores of America*. Philadelphia: Davis.

Repp, Stan (1980), *The Super Chief: Train of the Stars*. San Marino: Golden West Books.

Requa, Richard D. (1927), "An Architectural Style for Southern California," *A&E*, June, pp. 45-7.

Ricciuti, Italo W. (1938), *New Orleans and its Environs; the Domestic Architecture 1727-1870*. New York: Helburn.

"Richfield Building," *AR*, June 1930, pp. 505-10; also American Architect, May 1931, pp. 44-5.

Ripley, Hubert G. (1907), "How Bill Jones Built a Fireproof Bungalow for $2,500." *Indoors and Out*, August, pp. 299-31.

Robinson, Cervin and Rosemarie Haag Bletter (1975), *Skyscraper Style: Art Deco New York*. New York: Oxford University Press.

Robinson, Charles Mulford (1909), *Los Angeles, California: The City Beautiful*. Report to the Mayor, the City Council, and the Board of Municipal Art Commissioners. In Los Angeles Municipal Arts Commission Report, 1909.

Robinson, William W. (1931), *The Story of Pershing Square*. Los Angeles: Title Insurance and Trust Co.

_____ (1948), *Land in California*. Berkeley: University of California Press.

_____ (1953), "The Dominguez Rancho," *QHSSC*, December, pp. 343-6.

_____ (1966), *Maps of Los Angeles*. Los Angeles: Dawson's Book Shop.

Roehrig, Frederick L. (1929), "Los Angeles Power and Light Plants," *A&E*, November, pp. 75-6.

Roller, Albert F. (1947), "World Headquarters; Office Building Rexall Drug Company," *A&E*, October, p. 19.

Rosenheim, Alfred F. (1906), "A Mammoth Department Store" [Hamburber Co.], *A&E*, August, pp. 36-7.

_____ (1939), "A Half Century of Architectural Practice," *A&E*, April, pp. 39-43.

Ross, Michael F. (1978), "A Come-Back with Kudos" [Biltmore Hotel], *PA*, November, pp. 65-70.

Rothman, Walter E. (1950), "The Pico House," Los Angeles County Museum *Quarterly*, Summer, pp. 1-9.

S

Sanderson, George (1936), "An Architectural Californiac Looks at His Case," *A&A*, August, p. 16.

Sanford, Trent E. (1947), *Architecture in Mexico*. New York: Norton.

_____ (1950), *The Architecture of the Southwest: Indian, Spanish, American*. New York: Norton.

Saunders, Charles F. (1919), *Under the Sky in California*. New York: McBride.

Schindler, Pauline G. (1930), "A Significant Contribution to Culture [Bullocks Wilshire]," *A&A*, January.

Schippers, Donald J. (1964) "Walker and Eisen: Twenty Years of Los Angeles Architecture, 1920-1940" *SCQ*, December, pp. 371-94.

Schreiber, Hermann (1961), *The History of Roads*. London: Barrie and Rockliff.

Schultze, Leonard (1923), "The Architecture of the Modern Hotel" *AR*, November, pp. 199-204.

Scully, Vincent, Jr. (1960), *Frank Lloyd Wright*, New York: Braziller.

Seale, William (1975), *Tasteful Interlude: American Interiors Through the Camera's Eye, 1860-1917*. New York: Praeger.

Seares, Mabel Urmy (1919), "The Use of Mission Architecture," *California Southland*, in 2 parts, October 1919-January 1920.

_____ (1930), "Westwood Village: the Amazing Birth and Growth of a New College Community," *A&A*, July, pp. 41-3.

Sexton, Randolph W. and B.F. Betts (1927), *American Theaters of Today*. New York: Architectural Book Publishing Co.

"Shangri-La Hotel," *A&A*, May 1940, pp. 29-30.

Shaw, John C. (1927), "Los Angeles Builds Superhighway to Ocean Beach" [Pico Boulevard], *Engineering News-Record*, April 14, pp. 603-5.

Shindler, Merrill (1980), "Supermarket," *New West*, May 19, 1980, pp. 49-53.

Shinn, Charles H. (1895), "San Fernando Mission by Moonlight," *Land of Sunshine*, March, pp. 79-80.

Shippey, Lee (1948), *It's an Old California Custom*. New York: Vanguard.

Shochat, George (1950), "The Casa Adobe de San Rafael," *QHSSC*, December, pp. 269-92.

Sillo, Terry (1976). *Around Pasadena: An Architectural Study*. Pasadena: Gallery Productions.

Smith, Bertha H. (1916), "Dollar Down can Build a Town" [Watts], *Sunset*, March, pp. 37-8.

Smith, Robert C. (1955), "Colonial Towns of Spanish and Portugese America," Society of Architectural Historians *Journal*, December, pp. 3-12.

Snethen, Clarence R. (1924), "Los Angeles Making Scientific Study to Relieve Traffic Congestion," *American City*, September, pp. 196-7.

Spade, Rupert (1971), *Richard Neutra*. New York: Simon and Schuster.

Spaulding, Sumner M. (1929), "The Pleasant Isle of Catalina" *A&A*, November, pp. 18-23.

Splitter, Henry W. (1955), "Los Angeles as Described by Contemporaries, 1850-1890," *QHSSC*, June, and September.

"Spring Street," *Newsletter*, Society of Architectural Historians, Southern California Chapter, December 1980.

Sproul, Robert G. (1930), "The Architect and the University" [UCLA], *A&E*, October, pp. 31-90.

Left: Lobby, Title Insurance Building, 433 South Spring Street, by John and Donald Parkinson, 1928. Right: Lobby door, Title Insurance Building, 1928.

Stacy-Judd, Robert (1926), "Maya or Aztec Architecture," *A&E*, May, pp. 55–64.

——————— (1933–34), "An All-American Architecture," *A&E*, September 1933–February 1934.

Steilberg, Walter (1918), "Some Examples of the Work of Julia Morgan," *A&E*, vol. 55, pp. 34–101.

Stein, Clarence S. (1961), "A Triumph of the Spanish Colonial Style," in Winslow (1916).

——————— (1966), *Toward New Towns for America*. 3rd. ed; Cambridge: MIT Press.

Stephens, Harrison (1943), "Los Angeles Completes 5 Lanham Act Projects," *A&E*, September, pp. 13–25.

Stephens, Suzanne (1979), "Within the Walls of Modernism" [Nilsson House], *PA*, December pp. 60–5.

Stern, R.A.M. (1975), "Toward an Architecture of Symbolic Assemblages," *PA*, April, pp. 72–7.

Stoddard, Richard (1978), *Theatre and Cinema Architecture; a Guide to Information Sources*, Detroit: Gale Research Co.

Stoddart, Bessie B. (1905), "Courts of Sonoratown," *Charities and the Commons*, December 2, pp. 295–9.

Strand, Janaan (1974), *A Greene and Greene Guide*. Los Angeles, privately published.

Strand, Janann (1974), *A Greene and Greene Guide*. Pasadena: G. Dahlstrom.

Streatfield, David (1976), "The Evolution of the Southern California Landscape," *Landscape Architecture*, March, p. 39.

Sutherland, Henry A. (1965), "Requiem for the Los Angeles Philharmonic Auditorium," *SCQ*, Sept. pp. 303–46.

T

Treutlein, Theodore E. (1973), "Los Angeles, California: The Question of the City's Original Spanish Name," *SCQ*, Spring, pp. 1–8.

U

United States. Public Works Administration (1939), *Public Buildings: A Survey of Architecture of Projects Constructed by Federal and Other Governmental Bodies between the years 1933 and 1939 with the Assistance of the Public Works Administration*. Washington, D.C.

V

Van Wyck, Cecil (1929), "Neon Tube Lighting of Swimming Pools," *A&A*, April, p. 24.

"View of the Pacific: Mormon Temple," *Time*, December 21, 1953, p. 41.

Vlack, Don (1974), *Art Deco Architecture in New York, 1920–1940*. New York: Harper and Row.

Voilich, Francis (1945), "The Esthetics of City and Region," *A&A*, June 1945, p. 25.

W

Wade, Roni (1966), *A History of the Los Angeles Civic Center*. Mimeo. in the Los Angeles Municipal Reference Library.

Wagner, Anton (1935), *Los Angeles: Werden, Leben und Gestalt der Zweimillionenstadt in Südkalifornien*. Leipzig: Bibliographisches Institut.

Waldron, Granville A. (1959), "Courthouse of Los Angeles County," *QHSSC*, Dec. pp. 345–74.

Warner, Col. J.J. (1908), "Reminiscences of Early California," *PHSSC*, vol. 7, pp. 185–9.

"Warner Bros. New Theater, Hollywood." *A&E*, December 1928, pp. 65–73.

Waterbury, L.A. (1918), "Market and Warehouse Form Large Building Group" [Los Angeles Produce Terminal], *Engineering News-Record*, January 24, pp. 167–8.

Webb, Edith B. (1952), *Indian Life at the Old Missions*. Los Angeles: Willam F. Lewis.

Weber, Francis J. (1962), "A Historical Sketch of St. Vibiana's Cathedral," *SCQ*, March, pp. 43–56.

——————— (1968), *San Fernando Mission: an Historical Perspective*. Los Angeles.

——————— (1975), *The Mission in the Valley: A Documentary History of San Fernando Rey de España*. Los Angeles.

Weil, Martin (1981), "Uniroyal Tire Factory Historical Analysis," in *Uniroyal Project*, draft E.I.R., prepared for the City of Commerce by Phillips Brandt Reddick.

"Western 'Broadway' and 'Fifth Avenue' Combined" [Pellissier Bldg.], *A&A*, December 1931, pp. 36–7.

Wheeler, William H. (1928), "Southern California's Changing Architecture," *A&E*, July, pp. 35–42.

Wheelock, Walt (1961), *Angels Flight*. Glendale: La Siesta Press.

Whiffen, Marcus (1969), *American Architecture since 1780*. Cambridge: MIT Press.

White, Raymond (1935), "Oil Stations," *A&E*, October, pp. 29–36.

Whittlesey, Charles F. (1906), "California's Largest Reinforced Concrete Building" [Philharmonic Auditorium], *A&E*, March.

——————— (1908), "Reinforced Concrete Construction—Why I Believe in It," *A&E*, March, pp. 34–57.

Willey, D.A. (1906), "American Venice," *AR*, October, pp. 347–50.

Wilson, Henry L. (1910), *The Bungalow Book*. Chicago.

[Wilson, John A.] (1880), *Reproduction of Thompson and West's History of Los Angeles County*. Berkeley: Howell-North, 1959.

Winslow, Carleton M. (1916), *The Architecture and Gardens of the San Diego Exposition*. San Francisco: Paul Elder.

Winter, Robert (1974), "The Arroyo Culture," in *California Design 1910*. Santa Barbara: Peregrine Smith, pp. 10–29.

——————— (1980), *The California Bungalow*. Los Angeles: Hennessey and Ingalls.

Winther, Oscar O. (1935), "The Story of San Jose, 1777–1869; California's First Pueblo," *California Historical Society Quarterly*, March–June.

Withey, Henry F. (1918), "A Revival of True Andalusian Architecture," *A&E*, October pp. 63–79.

——————— and Elsie R. Withey (1956). *Biographical Dictionary of American Architects (Deceased)*. Los Angeles: New Age Pub. Co.

Woehlke, W.V. (1911), "Los Angeles—Homeland," *Sunset*, January, pp. 2–16.

Woollett, William L. (1928), "Architecture of the Pacific Southwest Exposition," *A&E*, September, pp. 57–9.

——————— (1932), "The Engineer's Aesthetic," *A&E*, June, pp. 43–7, and July, pp. 33–5.

"The Work of Alfred F. Rosenheim," *Architect and Engineer*, March 1907, pp. 34–51.

"The Work of John Parkinson and Edwin Bergstrom," *A&E*, September 1910.

Wright, J. Gordon (1938), "Food and Functionalism," *A&E*, October, pp. 28–9.

Y

Yaari, Moshe (1955), "The Merced Theater," *QHSSC*, September, pp. 195–210.

LIST OF ILLUSTRATION CREDITS

Glen Allison: 240

Architectural Record: 87

Leilani Austria: 14, 45, 70-71, 85, 164, 169-70, 186, 189, 210-11

The Bancroft Library: 26

Bruce Boehner: 1-2, 8, 10, 35, 57, 59, 64-65, 69, 71, 73, 76, 78-79, 82-85, 88-90, 92, 99-100, 103-9, 111-15, 118-19, 121-31, 133, 135, 138, 141, 159, 161-62, 171-75, 178, 186, 190-91, 193-95, 197, 200-1, 204, 207, 209, 211-12, 214-21, 225-26, 228-30, 233, 236, 238

California Historical Society/Title Insurance and Trust Company: 22, 26-27, 32-33, 35, 37-41, 44, 54-55, 66-68, 72, 77, 80-81, 86, 98-99, 110-11, 119, 176-77

California State Library, Sacramento: 195

Chicago Historical Society: 76

Tom Cunningham: 170

Zephyrin Engelhardt (*San Gabriel Mission*): 13

Carlos von Frankenberg, Julius Shulman Associates: 12, 18, 24, 47-48, 54, 69, 103, 189, 207, 216

Paul Gleye: 94, 165, 235, 237

Michael Goodwin: 95

Terry Helgesen: 105, 107, 218-19

Marie Harrington Collection: 33

The Huntington Library: 19, 29-30, 43, 51, 87, 176

Illustrated Los Angeles Herald: 46

Jerde Partnership: 75

Los Angeles County Museum of Natural History: 25, 34, 51

Los Angeles Public Library: 25, 31, 34, 37, 39, 44-45, 47

H. Wendell Mounce, AIA & Associates: 203

Julius Shulman: 6, 10, 15, 19, 23, 28, 36, 38, 42-43, 55-56, 58, 60, 62-64, 67, 69, 71, 74, 79, 91, 101, 104, 120, 129, 132-34, 136, 138-55, 158, 160, 162-63, 177, 182-83, 185, 187, 191, 193, 197-99, 201, 203-5, 208-9, 214-15, 217-18, 220-21, 223-24, 226-27, 229-30, 234-36, 239

University of California, Los Angeles, Department of Special Collections: 16-17, 20-21, 23-24, 41-42, 45-47, 52-54, 68, 73, 79, 97, 99, 101-2, 116-17, 176, 181.

University of California, Santa Barbara, Architectural Drawing Collection: 203

Tim Street-Porter: 168

Helmut Schulitz: 163

Town Planning Review: 26

Thomas P. Vinetz: 32, 35, 61, 70

Marc Wanamaker/Bison Archives: 135, 199

Don Williams: 37

Dan Zimbaldi: 156, 164-67, 170, 207

Riverside Municipal Museum: 98

Santa Barbara Historical Society: 87

INDEX

Numerals in *italics* refer to photographs and captions.

Page 233: skylight, Herman W. Hellman Building, by Alfred F. Rosenheim, 1904; lobby, Pacific Mutual Building, by W. J. Dodd, 1922. Page 234: Department of Water and Power Building, 111 North Hope Street, by Albert C. Martin and Associates, 1964. Page 235: Case Study House No. 21, 9038 Wonderland Park Avenue, by Pierre Koenig, 1958; Moorish apartments, Sweetzer and Waring avenues, ca. 1925. Page 236: Craftsman bungalow court, 627 West 30th Street; Yamashiro, 1999 North Sycamore Avenue, by Franklin M. Small, 1913. Page 237: Voss Apartments, 947 Eleventh Street, Santa Monica, ca. 1935; Vista del Arroyo Hotel, Pasadena. Page 238: Beverly Theater (now Fiorucci), 206 North Beverly Drive, by L. A. Smith, 1925. Page 239: interior, Shelton house, by Charles Moore and Ron Filson, 1977. Page 240: Carroll Avenue at night.